Database Performance at Scale

A Practical Guide

Felipe Cardeneti Mendes
Piotr Sarna
Pavel Emelyanov
Cynthia Dunlop

apress open

Database Performance at Scale: A Practical Guide

Felipe Cardeneti Mendes
São Paulo, Brazil

Pavel Emelyanov
Moscow, Russia

Piotr Sarna
Pruszków, Poland

Cynthia Dunlop
Carpinteria, CA, USA

ISBN-13 (pbk): 978-1-4842-9710-0
https://doi.org/10.1007/978-1-4842-9711-7

ISBN-13 (electronic): 978-1-4842-9711-7

Managing Director, Apress Media LLC: Welmoed Spahr
Acquisitions Editor: Jonathan Gennick
Development Editor: Laura Berendson
Editorial Project Manager: Shaul Elson
Copy Editor: Kezia Endsley

Cover designed by eStudioCalamar

Distributed to the book trade worldwide by Springer Science+Business Media LLC, 1 New York Plaza, Suite 4600, New York, NY 10004. Phone 1-800-SPRINGER, fax (201) 348-4505, e-mail orders-ny@springer-sbm.com, or visit www.springeronline.com. Apress Media, LLC is a California LLC and the sole member (owner) is Springer Science + Business Media Finance Inc (SSBM Finance Inc). SSBM Finance Inc is a **Delaware** corporation.

For information on translations, please e-mail booktranslations@springernature.com; for reprint, paperback, or audio rights, please e-mail bookpermissions@springernature.com.

Apress titles may be purchased in bulk for academic, corporate, or promotional use. eBook versions and licenses are also available for most titles. For more information, reference our Print and eBook Bulk Sales web page at http://www.apress.com/bulk-sales.

Any source code or other supplementary material referenced by the author in this book is available to readers on GitHub (https://github.com/Apress). For more detailed information, please visit https://www.apress.com/gp/services/source-code.

Paper in this product is recyclable

To Cristina and Snow
—Felipe

To Wiktoria
—Piotr

To Svetlana and Mykhailo
—Pavel

To David
—Cynthia

Table of Contents

About the Authors

Felipe Cardeneti Mendes is an IT specialist with years of experience using distributed systems and open-source technologies. He has co-authored three Linux books and is a frequent speaker at public events and conferences to promote open-source technologies. Felipe works as a solution architect at ScyllaDB.

Piotr Sarna is a software engineer who is keen on open-source projects and the Rust and C++ languages. He previously developed an open-source distributed filesystem and had a brief adventure with the Linux kernel. He's also a long-time contributor and maintainer of ScyllaDB, as well as libSQL and Turso. Piotr graduated from University of Warsaw with an MSc in computer science.

Pavel "Xemul" Emelyanov is an ex-Linux kernel hacker now speeding up row cache, tweaking the IO scheduler, and helping to pay back a technical debt for component interdependencies. He is a principal engineer at ScyllaDB.

Cynthia Dunlop is a technology writer who specializes in application development. She has co-authored four books and hundreds of articles on everything from C/C++ memory error detection to continuous testing and DevOps. Cynthia holds a bachelor's degree from UCLA and a master's degree from Washington State University.

About the Technical Reviewers

Botond Dénes has been a principal software engineer at ScyllaDB since 2017. Botond has mostly worked on making queries perform better and making sure their concurrency and resource consumption (especially memory) are kept in check. In addition, he has worked extensively on disaster recovery and diagnostics tools.

Ľuboš Koščo is a software engineer at ScyllaDB who works on upcoming ScyllaDB features, bug fixes, and workflows in Jenkins, Ansible automation, and migration tools (in Spark). During his time in AdTech, Ľuboš worked for Sizmek/Rocket Fuel, overseeing seven datacenters running infrastructure that delivered real-time bids and impressions for marketing campaigns. He also worked on cloud monitoring, virtualization, and datacenter management at Oracle and Sun Microsystems, and is one of the leaders of the source code search engine, OpenGrok.

ABOUT THE TECHNICAL REVIEWERS

 **Raphael S. Carvalho**, a.k.a. Raph, is a computer programmer steeped in hacker culture and kernel programming and a wannabe musician. In November 2013, Carvalho joined the Israeli startup Cloudius Systems (now ScyllaDB) and worked first on the filesystem technology from OSv, a cloud-based operating system, and later on ScyllaDB, a NoSQL data store compatible with Apache Cassandra that runs on top of Seastar. In 2018, Raph became fascinated with the Meltdown security bug and worked directly with the researchers who disclosed it. His name is now listed in the official Meltdown paper for his contributions to showing the applicability of the vulnerability in practice.

Acknowledgments

The process of creating this book has been a wild ride across many countries, cultures, and time zones, as well as around many obstacles. There are many people to thank for their assistance, inspiration, and support along this journey.

To begin, ScyllaDB co-founders Dor Laor and Avi Kivity—for starting the company that brought us all together, for pushing the boundaries of database performance at scale in ways that inspired this book, and for trusting us to share the collective sea monster wisdom in this format. Thank you for this amazing opportunity.

We thank our respective teams, and especially our managers, for supporting this side project. We hope we kept the core workload disruption to a minimum and did not inflict any "stop the world" project pauses.

Our technical reviewers—Botond Dénes, Ľuboš Koščo, and Raphael S. Carvalho—painstakingly reviewed the first draft of every page in this book and offered insightful suggestions throughout. Thank you for your thoughtful comments and for being so generous with your time.

Additionally, our unofficial technical reviewer and toughest critic, Kostja Osipov, provided early and (brutally) honest feedback that led us to substantially alter the book's focus for the better.

The Brazilian Ninja team (Guilherme Nogueira, Lucas Martins Guimarães, and Noelly Medina) rescued us in our darkest hour, allowing us to scale out and get the first draft across the finish line. Muito Obrigado!

Ben Gaisne is the graphic design mastermind behind the images in this book. Merci for transforming our scribbles into beautiful diagrams and putting up with about ten rounds of "just one more round of book images."

We are also indebted to many for their unintentional contributions on the content front. Glauber Costa left us with a treasure trove of materials we consulted when composing chapters, especially Chapter 9 on benchmarking. He also inspired the addition of Chapter 6 on getting data closer. Additionally, we also looked back to ScyllaDB blogs as we were writing—specifically, blogs by Avi Kivity (for Chapter 3), Eyal Gutkind (for Chapter 7), Vlad Zolotarov and Moreno Garcia (also for Chapter 7), Dor Laor (for Chapter 8), Eliran Sinvani (also for Chapter 8), and Ivan Prisyazhnyy (for Chapter 9).

ACKNOWLEDGMENTS

Last, but certainly not least, we thank Jonathan Gennick for bringing us to Apress. We thank Shaul Elson and Susan McDermott for guiding us through the publishing process. It has been a pleasure working with you. And we thank everyone involved in editing and production; having previously tried this on our own, we know it's an excruciating task and we are truly grateful to you for relieving us of this burden!

Introduction

Sisyphean challenge. Gordian knot. Rabbit hole. Many metaphors have been used to describe the daunting challenge of achieving database performance at scale. That isn't surprising. Consider just a handful of the many factors that contribute to satisfying database latency and throughput expectations for a single application:

- How well you know your workload access patterns and whether they are a good fit for your current or target database.

- How your database interacts with its underlying hardware, and whether your infrastructure is correctly sized for the present as well as the future.

- How well your database driver understands your database—and how well *you* understand the internal workings of both.

It's complex. And that's just the tip of the iceberg.

Then, once you feel like you're finally in a good spot, something changes. Your business experiences "catastrophic success," exposing the limitations of your initial approach right when you're entering the spotlight. Maybe market shifts mean that your team is suddenly expected to reduce latency—and reduce costs at the same time, too. Or perhaps you venture on to tackle a new application and find that the lessons learned from the original project don't translate to the new one.

Why Read/Write a Book on Database Performance?

The most common approaches to optimizing database performance are conducting performance tuning and scaling out. They are important—but in many cases, they aren't enough to satisfy strict latency expectations at medium to high throughput. To break past that plateau, other factors need to be addressed.

As with any engineering challenge, there's no one-size-fits-all solution. But there are a lot of commonly overlooked considerations and opportunities with the potential to help teams meet their database performance objectives faster, and with fewer headaches.

As a group of people with experience across a variety of performance-oriented database projects, we (the authors) have a unique perspective into what works well for different performance-sensitive use cases—from low-level engineering optimizations, to infrastructure components, to topology considerations and the KPIs to focus on for monitoring. Frequently, we engage with teams when they're facing a performance challenge so excruciating that they're considering changing their production database (which can seem like the application development equivalent of open heart surgery). And in many cases, we develop a long-term relationship with a team, watching their projects and objectives evolve over time and helping them maintain or improve performance across the shifting sands.

Based on our experience with performance-focused database engineering as well as performance-focused database users, this book represents what we think teams striving for extreme database performance—low latency, high throughput, or both—should be thinking about. We have experience working with multi-petabyte distributed systems requiring millions of interactions per second. We've engineered systems supporting business critical real-time applications with sustained latencies below one millisecond. Finally, we're well aware of commonly-experienced "gotchas" that no one has dared to tell you about, until now.

What We Mean by Database Performance at Scale

Database performance at scale means different things to different teams. For some, it might mean achieving extremely low read latencies; for others, it might mean ingesting very large datasets as quickly as possible. For example:

- **Messaging:** Keeping latency consistently low for thousands to millions of operations per second, because users expect to interact in real-time on popular social media platforms, especially when there's a big event or major news.

- **Fraud detection:** Analyzing a massive dataset as rapidly as possible (millions of operations per second), because faster processing helps stop fraud in its tracks.

- **AdTech:** Providing lightning fast (sub-millisecond P9999 latency) responses with zero tolerance for latency spikes, because an ad bid that's sent even a millisecond past the cutoff is worthless to the ad company and the clients who rely on it.

We specifically tagged on the "at scale" modifier to emphasize that we're catering to teams who are outside of the honeymoon zone, where everything is just blissfully fast no matter what you do with respect to setup, usage, and management. Different teams will reach that inflection point for different reasons, and at different thresholds. But one thing is always the same: It's better to anticipate and prepare than to wait and scramble to react.

Who This Book Is For

This book was written for individuals and teams looking to optimize distributed database performance for an existing project or to begin a new performance-sensitive project with a solid and scalable foundation. You are most likely:

- Experiencing or anticipating some pain related to database latency and/or throughput

- Working primarily on a use case with terabytes to petabytes of raw (unreplicated) data, over 10K operations per second, and with P99 latencies measured in milliseconds

- At least somewhat familiar with scalable distributed databases such as Apache Cassandra, ScyllaDB, Amazon DynamoDB, Google Cloud Bigtable, CockroachDB, and so on

- A software architect, database architect, software engineer, VP of engineering, or technical CTO/founder working with a data-intensive application

You might also be looking to reduce costs without compromising performance, but unsure of all the considerations involved in doing so.

We assume that you want to get your database performance challenges resolved, fast. That's why we focus on providing very direct and opinionated recommendations based on what we have seen work (and fail) in real-world situations. There are, of course, exceptions to every rule and ways to debate the finer points of almost any tip in excruciating detail. We'll focus on presenting the battle-tested "best practices" and anti-patterns here, and encourage additional discussion in whatever public or private channels you prefer.

What This Book Is NOT

A few things that this book is *not* attempting to be:

- A reference for infrastructure engineers building databases. We focus on people working with a database.

- A "definitive guide" to distributed databases, NoSQL, or data-intensive applications. We focus on the top database considerations most critical to performance.

- A guide on how to configure, work with, optimize, or tune any specific database. We focus on broader strategies you can "port" across databases.

There are already many outstanding references that cover the topics we're deliberately not addressing, so we're not going to attempt to re-create or replace them. See Appendix A for a list of recommended resources.

Also, this is not a book about ScyllaDB, even though the authors and technical reviewers have experience with ScyllaDB. Our goal is to present strategies that are useful across the broader class of performance-oriented databases. We reference ScyllaDB, as well as other databases, as appropriate to provide concrete examples.

A Tour of What We Cover

Given that database performance is a multivariate challenge, we explore it from a number of different angles and perspectives. Not every angle will be relevant to every reader—at least not yet. We encourage you to browse around and focus on what seems most applicable to your current situation.

To start, we explore challenges. Chapter 1 kicks it off with two highly fictionalized tales that highlight the variety of database performance challenges that can arise and introduce some of the available strategies for addressing them. Next, we look at the database performance challenges and tradeoffs that you're likely to face depending on your project's specific workload characteristics and technical/business requirements.

The next set of chapters provides a window into many often-overlooked engineering details that could be constraining—or helping—your database performance. First, we look at ways databases can extract more performance from your CPU, memory, storage, and networking. Next, we shift the focus from hardware interactions to algorithmic optimizations—deep diving into the intricacies of a sample performance optimization from the perspective of the engineer behind it. Following that, we share everything a performance-obsessed developer really *should* know about database drivers but never thought to ask. Driver-level optimizations —both how they're engineered and how you work with them—are absolutely critical for performance, so we spend a good amount of time on topics like the interaction between clients and servers, contextual awareness, maximizing concurrency while keeping latencies under control, correct usage of paging, timeout control, retry strategies, and so on. Finally, we look at the performance possibilities in moving more logic into the database (via user-defined functions and user-defined aggregates) as well as moving the database servers closer to users.

Then, the final set of chapters shifts into field-tested recommendations for getting better performance out of your database deployment. It starts by looking at infrastructure and deployment model considerations that are important to understand, whether you're managing your own deployment or opting for a database-as-a-service (maybe serverless) deployment model. Then, we share our top strategies related to topology, benchmarking, monitoring, and admin—all through the not-always-rosy lens of performance.

After all that, we hope you end up with a new appreciation of the countless considerations that impact database performance at scale, discover some previously overlooked opportunities to optimize your database performance, and avoid the common traps and pitfalls that inflict unnecessary pain and distractions on all too many dev and database teams.

Tip Check out our GitHub repo for easy access to the sources we reference in footnotes, plus additional resources on database performance at scale: `https://github.com/Apress/db-performance-at-scale`.

Summary

Optimizing database performance at the scale required for today's data-intensive applications often requires more than performance tuning and scaling out. This book shares commonly overlooked considerations, pitfalls, and opportunities that have helped many teams break through database performance plateaus. It's neither a definitive guide to distributed databases nor a beginner's resource. Rather, it's a look at the many different factors that impact performance, and our top field-tested recommendations for navigating them. Chapter 1 provides two (fun and fanciful) tales that surface some of the many roadblocks you might face and highlight the range of strategies for navigating around them.

A Taste of What You're Up Against: Two Tales

What's more fun than wrestling with database performance? Well, a lot. But that doesn't mean you can't have a little fun here. To give you an idea of the complexities you'll likely face if you're serious about optimizing database performance, this chapter presents two rather fanciful stories. The technical topics covered here are expanded on throughout the book. But this is the one and only time you'll hear of poor Joan and Patrick. Let their struggles bring you some valuable lessons, solace in your own performance predicaments... and maybe a few chuckles as well.

Joan Dives Into Drivers and Debugging

Lured in by impressive buzzwords like "hybrid cloud," "serverless," and "edge first," Joan readily joined a new company and started catching up with their technology stack. Her first project recently started a transition from their in-house implementation of a database system, which turned out to not scale at the same pace as the number of customers, to one of the industry-standard database management solutions. Their new pick was a new distributed database, which, as opposed to NoSQL, strives to keep the original ACID[1] guarantees known in the SQL world.

Due to a few new data protection acts that tend to appear annually nowadays, the company's board decided that they were going to maintain their own datacenter, instead of using one of the popular cloud vendors for storing sensitive information.

---

[1] Atomicity, consistency, isolation, and durability

© Felipe Cardeneti Mendes, Piotr Sarna, Pavel Emelyanov, Cynthia Dunlop 2023
F. C. Mendes et al., *Database Performance at Scale*, https://doi.org/10.1007/978-1-4842-9711-7_1

On a very high level, the company's main product consisted of only two layers:

- The *frontend*, the entry point for users, which actually runs in their own browsers and communicates with the rest of the system to exchange and persist information.

- The everything-else, customarily known as the *backend*, but actually includes load balancers, authentication, authorization, multiple cache layers, databases, backups, and so on.

Joan's first task was to implement a very simple service for gathering and summing up various statistics from the database and integrate that service with the whole ecosystem, so that it fetched data from the database in real-time and allowed the DevOps teams to inspect the statistics live.

To impress the management and reassure them that hiring Joan was their absolutely best decision this quarter, Joan decided to deliver a proof-of-concept implementation on her first day! The company's unspoken policy was to write software in Rust, so she grabbed the first driver for their database from a brief `crates.io` search and sat down to her self-organized hackathon.

The day went by really smoothly, with Rust's ergonomic-focused ecosystem providing a superior developer experience. But then Joan ran her first smoke tests on a real system. Disbelief turned to disappointment and helplessness when she realized that every third request (on average) ended up in an error, even though the whole database cluster reported to be in a healthy, operable state. That meant a debugging session was in order!

Unfortunately, the driver Joan hastily picked for the foundation of her work, even though open-source on its own, was just a thin wrapper over precompiled, legacy C code, with no source to be found. Fueled by a strong desire to solve the mystery and a healthy dose of fury, Joan spent a few hours inspecting the network communication with Wireshark,[2] and she made an educated guess that the bug must be in the hashing key implementation.[3] In the database used by the company, keys are hashed to later route requests to appropriate nodes. If a hash value is computed incorrectly, a request may be forwarded to the wrong node, which can refuse it and return an error instead.

---

[2] Wireshark is a great tool for inspecting network packets and more (`www.wireshark.org`).

[3] Loosely based on a legit hashing quirk in Apache Cassandra (`https://github.com/apache/cassandra/blob/56ea39ec704a94b5d23cbe530548745ab2420cee/src/java/org/apache/cassandra/utils/MurmurHash.java#L31-L32`).

Unable to verify the claim due to the missing source code, Joan decided on a simpler path—ditching the originally chosen driver and reimplementing the solution on one of the officially supported, open-source drivers backed by the database vendor, with a solid user base and regularly updated release schedule.

Joan's Diary of Lessons Learned, Part I

The initial lessons include:

1. Choose a driver carefully. It's at the core of your code's performance, robustness, and reliability.

2. Drivers have bugs too, and it's impossible to avoid them. Still, there are good practices to follow:

    a. Unless there's a good reason, choose the officially supported driver (if it exists).

    b. Open-source drivers have advantages. They're not only verified by the community, but they also allow deep inspection of the code, and even modifying the driver code to get even more insights for debugging.

    c. It's better to rely on drivers with a well-established release schedule since they are more likely to receive bug fixes (including for security vulnerabilities) in a reasonable period of time.

3. Wireshark is a great open-source tool for interpreting network packets; give it a try if you want to peek under the hood of your program.

The introductory task was eventually completed successfully, which made Joan ready to receive her first real assignment.

The Tuning

Armed with the experience gained working on the introductory task, Joan started planning how to approach her new assignment: a misbehaving app. One of the applications notoriously caused stability issues for the whole system, disrupting other workloads each time it experienced any problems. The rogue app was already based on an officially supported driver, so Joan could cross that one off the list of potential root causes.

This particular service was responsible for injecting data backed up from the legacy system into the new database. Because the company was not in a great hurry, the application was written with low concurrency in mind to have low priority and not interfere with user workloads. Unfortunately, once every few days something kept triggering an anomaly. The normally peaceful application seemed to be trying to perform a denial-of-service attack on its own database, flooding it with requests until the backend got overloaded enough to cause issues for other parts of the ecosystem.

As Joan watched metrics presented in a Grafana dashboard, clearly suggesting that the rate of requests generated by this application started spiking around the time of the anomaly, she wondered how on Earth this workload could behave like that. It was, after all, explicitly implemented to send new requests only when fewer than 100 of them were currently in progress.

Since collaboration was heavily advertised as one of the company's "spirit and cultural foundations" during the onboarding sessions with an onsite coach, she decided it was best to discuss the matter with her colleague, Tony.

> "Look, Tony, I can't wrap my head around this," she explained. "This service doesn't send any new requests when 100 of them are already in flight. And look right here in the logs: 100 requests in-progress, one returned a timeout error, and...," she then stopped, startled at her own epiphany.
>
> "Alright, thanks Tony, you're a dear—best rubber duck[4] ever!," she concluded and returned to fixing the code.

The observation that led to discovering the root cause was rather simple: The request didn't actually *return* a timeout error because the database server never sent such a response. The request was simply qualified as timed out by the driver, and discarded. But the sole fact that the driver no longer waits for a response for a particular request does not mean that the database is done processing it! It's entirely possible that the request was instead just stalled, taking longer than expected, and the driver gave up waiting for its response.

With that knowledge, it's easy to imagine that once 100 requests time out on the client side, the app might erroneously think that they are not in progress anymore, and happily submit 100 more requests to the database, increasing the total number of

---

[4] For an overview of the "rubber duck debugging" concept, see https://rubberduckdebugging.com/.

in-flight requests (i.e., concurrency) to 200. Rinse, repeat, and you can achieve extreme levels of concurrency on your database cluster—even though the application was supposed to keep it limited to a small number!

Joan's Diary of Lessons Learned, Part II

The lessons continue:

1.   Client-side timeouts are convenient for programmers, but they can interact badly with server-side timeouts. Rule of thumb: Make the client-side timeouts around twice as long as server-side ones, unless you have an extremely good reason to do otherwise. Some drivers may be capable of issuing a warning if they detect that the client-side timeout is smaller than the server-side one, or even amend the server-side timeout to match, but in general it's best to double-check.

2.   Tasks with seemingly fixed concurrency can actually cause spikes under certain unexpected conditions. Inspecting logs and dashboards is helpful in investigating such cases, so make sure that observability tools are available, both in the database cluster and for all client applications. Bonus points for distributed tracing, like OpenTelemetry[5] integration.

With the client-side timeouts properly amended, the application choked much less frequently and to a smaller extent, but it still wasn't a perfect citizen in the distributed system. It occasionally picked a victim database node and kept bothering it with too many requests, while ignoring the fact that seven other nodes were considerably less loaded and could help handle the workload too. At other times, its concurrency was reported to be exactly 200 percent larger than expected by the configuration. Whenever the two anomalies converged in time, the poor node was unable to handle all the requests it was bombarded with, and it had to give up on a fair portion of them. A long

---

[5] OpenTelemetry "is a collection of tools, APIs, and SDKs. Use it to instrument, generate, collect, and export telemetry data (metrics, logs, and traces) to help you analyze your software's performance and behavior." For details, see https://opentelemetry.io/.

study of the driver's documentation, which was fortunately available in mdBook[6] format and kept reasonably up-to-date, helped Joan alleviate those pains too.

The first issue was simply a misconfiguration of the non-default load balancing policy, which tried too hard to pick "the least loaded" database node out of all the available ones, based on heuristics and statistics occasionally updated by the database itself. Unfortunately, this policy was also "best effort," and relied on the fact that statistics arriving from the database were always legit. But a stressed database node could become so overloaded that it wasn't sending updated statistics in time! That led the driver to falsely believe that this particular server was not actually busy at all. Joan decided that this setup was a premature optimization that turned out to be a footgun, so she just restored the original default policy, which worked as expected.

The second issue (temporary doubling of the concurrency) was caused by another misconfiguration: an overeager speculative retry policy. After waiting for a preconfigured period of time without getting an acknowledgement from the database, drivers would speculatively resend a request to maximize its chances to succeed. This mechanism is very useful to increase requests' success rate. However, if the original request also succeeds, it means that the speculative one was sent in vain. In order to balance the pros and cons, speculative retry should be configured to resend requests only when it's very likely that the original one failed. Otherwise, as in Joan's case, the speculative retry may act too soon, doubling the number of requests sent (and thus also doubling concurrency) without improving the success rate.

Whew, nothing gives a simultaneous endorphin rush and dopamine hit like a quality debugging session that ends in an astounding success (except writing a cheesy story in a deeply technical book, naturally). Great job, Joan!

The end.

Patrick's Unlucky Green Fedoras

After losing his job at a ~~FAANG~~ MAANG (MANGA?) company, Patrick decided to strike off on his own and founded a niche online store dedicated to trading his absolute favorite among headwear, green fedoras. Noticing that a certain NoSQL database was recently trending on the front page of *Hacker News*, Patrick picked it for his backend stack.

---

[6] mdBook "is a command line tool to create books with Markdown." For details, see `https://rust-lang.github.io/mdBook/`.

After some experimentation with the offering's free tier, Patrick decided to sign a one-year contract with a major cloud provider to get a significant discount on its NoSQL database-as-a-service offering. With provisioned throughput capable of serving up to 1,000 customers every second, the technology stack was ready and the store opened its virtual doors to the customers. To Patrick's disappointment, fewer than ten customers visited the site daily. At the same time, the shiny new database cluster kept running, fueled by a steady influx of money from his credit card and waiting for its potential to be harnessed.

Patrick's Diary of Lessons Learned, Part I

The lessons started right away:

1. Although some databases advertise themselves as universal, most of them perform best for certain kinds of workloads. The analysis before selecting a database for your own needs must include estimating the characteristics of your own workload:

    a. Is it likely to be a predictable, steady flow of requests (e.g., updates being fetched from other systems periodically)?

    b. Is the variance high and hard to predict, with the system being idle for potentially long periods of time, with occasional bumps of activity?

    Database-as-a-service offerings often let you pick between provisioned throughput and on-demand purchasing. Although the former is more cost-efficient, it incurs a certain cost regardless of how busy the database actually is. The latter costs more per request, but you only pay for what you use.

2. Give yourself time to evaluate your choice and avoid committing to long-term contracts (even if lured by a discount) before you see that the setup works for you in a sustainable way.

The First Spike

March 17th seemed like an extremely lucky day. Patrick was pleased to notice lots of new orders starting from the early morning. But as the number of active customers skyrocketed around noon, Patrick's mood started to deteriorate. This was strictly correlated with the rate of calls he received from angry customers reporting their inability to proceed with their orders.

After a short brainstorming session with himself and a web search engine, Patrick realized, to his dismay, that he lacked any observability tools on his precious (and quite expensive) database cluster. Shortly after frantically setting up Grafana and browsing the metrics, Patrick saw that although the number of incoming requests kept growing, their success rate was capped at a certain level, way below today's expected traffic.

"Provisioned throughput strikes again," Patrick groaned to himself, while scrolling through thousands of "throughput exceeded" error messages that started appearing around 11am.

Patrick's Diary of Lessons Learned, Part II

This is what Patrick learned:

1. If your workload is susceptible to spikes, be prepared for it and try to architect your cluster to be able to survive a temporarily elevated load. Database-as-a-service solutions tend to allow configuring the provisioned throughput in a dynamic way, which means that the threshold of accepted requests can occasionally be raised temporarily to a previously configured level. Or, respectively, they allow it to be temporarily decreased to make the solution slightly more cost-efficient.

2. *Always* expect spikes. Even if your workload is absolutely steady, a temporary hardware failure or a surprise DDoS attack can cause a sharp increase in incoming requests.

3. Observability is key in distributed systems. It allows the developers to retrospectively investigate a failure. It also provides real-time alerts when a likely failure scenario is detected, allowing people to react quickly and either prevent a larger failure from happening, or at least minimize the negative impact on the cluster.

The First Loss

Patrick didn't even manage to recover from the trauma of losing most of his potential income on the only day throughout the year during which green fedoras experienced any kind of demand, when the letter came. It included an angry rant from a would-be customer, who successfully proceeded with his order and paid for it (with a receipt from the payment processing operator as proof), but is now unable to either see any details of his order—and he's still waiting for the delivery!

Without further ado, Patrick browsed the database. To his astonishment, he didn't find any trace of the order either. For completeness, Patrick also put his wishful thinking into practice by browsing the backup snapshot directory. It remained empty, as one of Patrick's initial executive decisions was to save time and money by not scheduling any periodic backup procedures.

How did data loss happen to him, of all people? After studying the consistency model of his database of choice, Patrick realized that there's consensus to make between consistency guarantees, performance, and availability. By configuring the queries, one can either demand linearizability[7] at the cost of decreased throughput, or reduce the consistency guarantees and increase performance accordingly. Higher throughput capabilities were a no-brainer for Patrick a few days ago, but ultimately customer data landed on a single server without any replicas distributed in the system. Once this server failed—which happens to hardware surprisingly often, especially at large scale—the data was gone.

Patrick's Diary of Lessons Learned, Part III

Further lessons include:

1. Backups are vital in a distributed environment, and there's no such thing as setting backup routines "too soon." Systems fail, and backups are there to restore as much of the important data as possible.

---

[7] A very strong consistency guarantee; see the Jepsen page on Linearizability for details (`https://jepsen.io/consistency/models/linearizable`).

2. Every database system has a certain consistency model, and it's crucial to take that into account when designing your project. There might be compromises to make. In some use cases (think financial systems), consistency is the key. In other ones, eventual consistency is acceptable, as long as it keeps the system highly available and responsive.

The Spike Strikes Again

Months went by and Patrick's sleeping schedule was even beginning to show signs of stabilization. With regular backups, a redesigned consistency model, and a reminder set in his calendar for March 16th to scale up the cluster to manage elevated traffic, he felt moderately safe.

If only he knew that a ten-second video of a cat dressed as a leprechaun had just gone viral in Malaysia… which, taking time zone into account, happened around 2am Patrick's time, ruining the aforementioned sleep stabilization efforts.

On the one hand, the observability suite did its job and set off a warning early, allowing for a rapid response. On the other hand, even though Patrick reacted on time, databases are seldom able to scale instantaneously, and his system of choice was no exception in that regard. The spike in concurrency was very high and concentrated, as thousands of Malaysian teenagers rushed to bulk-buy green hats in pursuit of ever-changing Internet trends. Patrick was able to observe a real-life instantiation of Little's Law, which he vaguely remembered from his days at the university. With a beautifully concise formula, $L = \lambda W$, the law can be simplified to the fact that concurrency equals throughput times latency.

Tip   For those having trouble with remembering the formula, think units. Concurrency is just a number, latency can be measured in seconds, while throughput is usually expressed in 1/s. Then, it stands to reason that in order for units to match, concurrency should be obtained by multiplying latency (seconds) by throughput (1/s). You're welcome!

Throughput depends on the hardware and naturally has its limits (e.g., you can't expect a NVMe drive purchased in 2023 to serve the data for you in terabytes per second, although we are crossing our fingers for this assumption to be invalidated in near future!) Once the limit is hit, you can treat it as constant in the formula. It's then clear that as concurrency raises, so does latency. For the end-users—Malaysian teenagers in this scenario—it means that the latency is eventually going to cross the magic barrier for average human perception of a few seconds. Once that happens, users get too frustrated and simply give up on trying altogether, assuming that the system is broken beyond repair. It's easy to find online articles quoting that "Amazon found that 100ms of latency costs them 1 percent in sales"; although it sounds overly simplified, it is also true enough.

Patrick's Diary of Lessons Learned, Part IV

The lessons continue…:

1. Unexpected spikes are inevitable, and scaling out the cluster might not be swift enough to mitigate the negative effects of excessive concurrency. Expecting the database to handle it properly is not without merit, but not every database is capable of that. If possible, limit the concurrency in your system as early as possible. For instance, if the database is never touched directly by customers (which is a very good idea for multiple reasons) but instead is accessed through a set of microservices under your control, make sure that the microservices are also aware of the concurrency limits and adhere to them.

2. Keep in mind that Little's Law exists—it's fundamental knowledge for anyone interested in distributed systems. Quoting it often also makes you appear exceptionally smart among peers.

Backup Strikes Back

After redesigning his project yet again to take expected and unexpected concurrency fluctuations into account, Patrick happily waited for his fedora business to finally become ramen profitable.

Unfortunately, the next March 17th didn't go as smoothly as expected either. Patrick spent most of the day enjoying steady Grafana dashboards, which kept assuring him that the traffic was under control and capable of handling the load of customers, with a healthy safe margin. But then the dashboards stopped, kindly mentioning that the disks became severely overutilized. This seemed completely out of place given the observed concurrency. While looking for the possible source of this anomaly, Patrick noticed, to his horror, that the scheduled backup procedure coincided with the annual peak load...

Patrick's Diary of Lessons Learned, Part V

Concluding thoughts:

1. Database systems are hardly ever idle, even without incoming user requests. Maintenance operations often happen and you must take them into consideration because they're an internal source of concurrency and resource consumption.

2. Whenever possible, schedule maintenance options for times with expected low pressure on the system.

3. If your database management system supports any kind of quality of service configuration, it's a good idea to investigate such capabilities. For instance, it might be possible to set a strong priority for user requests over regular maintenance operations, especially during peak hours. Respectively, periods with low user-induced activity can be utilized to speed up background activities. In the database world, systems that use a variant of LSM trees for underlying storage need to perform quite a bit of *compactions* (a kind of maintenance operation on data) in order to keep the read/write performance predictable and steady.

The end.

Summary

Meeting database performance expectations can sometimes seem like a never-ending pain. As soon as you diagnose and address one problem, another is likely lurking right behind it. The next chapter helps you anticipate the challenges and opportunities you are most likely to face given your technical requirements and business expectations.

CHAPTER 2

Your Project, Through the Lens of Database Performance

The specific database performance constraints and optimization opportunities your team will face vary wildly based on your specific workload, application, and business expectations. This chapter is designed to get you and your team talking about how much you can feasibly optimize your performance, spotlight some specific lessons related to common situations, and also help you set realistic expectations if you're saddled with burdens like large payload sizes and strict consistency requirements. The chapter starts by looking at technical factors, such as the read/write ratio of your workload, item size/type, and so on. Then, it shifts over to business considerations like consistency requirements and high availability expectations. Throughout, the chapter talks about database attributes that have proven to be helpful—or limiting—in different contexts.

Note   Since this chapter covers a broad range of scenarios, not everything will be applicable to your specific project and workload. Feel free to skim this chapter and focus on the sections that seem most relevant.

Workload Mix (Read/Write Ratio)

Whether it's read-heavy, write-heavy, evenly-mixed, delete-heavy, and so on, understanding and accommodating your read/write ratio is a critical but commonly overlooked aspect of database performance. Some databases shine with read-heavy

© Felipe Cardeneti Mendes, Piotr Sarna, Pavel Emelyanov, Cynthia Dunlop 2023
F. C. Mendes et al., *Database Performance at Scale*, https://doi.org/10.1007/978-1-4842-9711-7_2

workloads, others are optimized for write-heavy situations, and some are built to accommodate both. Selecting, or sticking with, one that's a poor fit for your current and future situation will be a significant burden that will be difficult to overcome, no matter how strategically you optimize everything else.

There's also a significant impact to cost. That might not seem directly related to performance, but if you can't afford (or get approval for) the infrastructure that you truly need to support your workload, this will clearly limit your performance.[1]

Tip   Not sure what your workload looks like? This is one of many situations where observability is your friend. If your existing database doesn't help you profile your workload, consider if it's feasible to try your workloads on a compatible database that enables deeper visibility.

Write-Heavy Workloads

If you have a write-heavy workload, we strongly recommend a database that stores data in immutable files (e.g., Cassandra, ScyllaDB, and others that use LSM trees).[2] These databases optimize write speed because: 1) writes are sequential, which is faster in terms of disk I/O and 2) writes are performed immediately, without first worrying about reading or updating existing values (like databases that rely on B-trees do). As a result, you can typically write a lot of data with very low latencies.

However, if you opt for a write-optimized database, be prepared for higher storage requirements and the potential for slower reads. When you work with immutable files, you'll need sufficient storage to keep all the immutable files that build up until compaction runs.[3] You can mitigate the storage needs to some extent by choosing compaction strategies carefully. Plus, storage is relatively inexpensive these days.

---

[1] With write-heavy workloads, you can easily spend millions per month with Bigtable or DynamoDB. Read-heavy workloads are typically less costly in these pricing models.

[2] If you want a quick introduction to LSM trees and B-trees, see Appendix A. Chapter 4 also discusses B-trees in more detail.

[3] *Compaction* is a background process that databases with an LSM tree storage backend use to merge and optimize the shape of the data. Since files are immutable, the process essentially involves picking up two or more pre-existing files, merging their contents, and producing a sorted output file.

The potential for read amplification is generally a more significant concern with write-optimized databases (given all the files to search through, more disk reads are required per read request).

But read performance doesn't necessarily need to suffer. You can often minimize this tradeoff with a write-optimized database that implements its own caching subsystem (as opposed to those that rely on the operating system's built-in cache), enabling fast reads to coexist alongside extremely fast writes. Bypassing the underlying OS with a performance-focused built-in cache should speed up your reads nicely, to the point where the latencies are nearly comparable to read-optimized databases.

With a write-heavy workload, it's also essential to have extremely fast storage, such as NVMe drives, if your peak throughput is high. Having a database that can *theoretically* store values rapidly ultimately won't help if the disk itself can't keep pace.

Another consideration: beware that write-heavy workloads can result in surprisingly high costs as you scale. Writes cost around five times more than reads under some vendors' pricing models. Before you invest too much effort in performance optimizations, and so on, it's a good idea to price your solution at scale and make sure it's a good long-term fit.

Read-Heavy Workloads

With read-heavy workloads, things change a bit. B-tree databases (such as DynamoDB) are optimized for reads (that's the payoff for the extra time required to update values on the write path). However, the advantage that read-optimized databases offer for reads is generally not as significant as the advantage that write-optimized databases offer for writes, especially if the write-optimized database uses internal caching to make up the difference (as noted in the previous section).

Careful data modeling will pay off in spades for optimizing your reads. So will careful selection of read consistency (are eventually consistent reads acceptable as opposed to strongly consistent ones?), locating your database near your application, and performing a thorough analysis of your query access patterns. Thinking about your access patterns is especially crucial for success with a read-heavy workload. Consider aspects such as the following:

- What is the nature of the data that the application will be querying mostly frequently? Does it tolerate potentially stale reads or does it require immediate consistency?

- How frequently is it accessed (e.g., is it frequently-accessed "hot" data that is likely cached, or is it rarely-accessed "cold" data)?

- Does it require aggregations, JOINs, and/or querying flexibility on fields that are not part of your primary key component?

- Speaking of primary keys, what is the level of cardinality?

For example, assume that your use case requires dynamic querying capabilities (such as type-ahead use cases, report-building solutions, etc.) where you frequently need to query data from columns other than your primary/hash key component. In this case, you might find yourself performing full table scans all too frequently, or relying on too many indexes. Both of these, in one way or another, may eventually undermine your read performance.

On the infrastructure side, selecting servers with high memory footprints is key for enabling low read latencies if you will mostly serve data that is frequently accessed. On the other hand, if your reads mostly hit cold data, you will want a nice balance between your storage speeds and memory. In fact, many distributed databases typically reserve some memory space specifically for caching indexes; this way, reads that inevitably require going to disk won't waste I/O by scanning through irrelevant data.

What if the use case requires reading from both hot and cold data at the same time? And what if you have different latency requirements for each set of data? Or what if you want to mix a real-time workload on top of your analytics workload for the very same dataset? Situations like this are quite common. There's no one-size-fits-all answer, but here are a few important tips:

- Some databases will allow you to read data without polluting your cache (e.g., filling it up with data that is unlikely to be requested again). Using such a mechanism is especially important when you're running large scans while simultaneously serving real-time data. If the large scans were allowed to override the previously cached entries that the real-time workload required, those reads would have to go through disk and get repopulated into the cache again. This would effectively waste precious processing time and result in elevated latencies.

- For use cases requiring a distinction between hot/cold data storage (for cost savings, different latency requirements, or both), then solutions using *tiered storage* (a method of prioritizing data storage based on a range of requirements, such as performance and costs) are likely a good fit.

- Some databases will permit you to prioritize some workloads over others. If that's not sufficient, you can go one step further and completely isolate such workloads logically.[4]

Note   You might not need all your reads. At ScyllaDB, we've come across a number of cases where teams are performing reads that they don't really need. For example, by using a read-before-write approach to avoid race conditions where multiple clients are trying to update the same value with different updates at the same time. The details of the solution aren't relevant here, but it is important to note that, by rethinking their approach, they were able to shave latencies off their writes as well as speed up the overall response by eliminating the unnecessary read. The moral here: Getting new eyes on your existing approaches might surface a way to unlock unexpected performance optimizations.

Mixed Workloads

More evenly mixed access patterns are generally even more complex to analyze and accommodate. In general, the reason that mixed workloads are so complex in nature is due to the fact that there are two competing workloads from the database perspective. Databases are essentially made for just two things: reading and writing. The way that different databases handle a variety of competing workloads is what truly differentiates one solution from another. As you test and compare databases, experiment with different read/write ratios so you can adequately prepare yourself for scenarios when your access patterns may change.

Be sure to consider nuances like whether your reads are from cold data (data not often accessed) or hot data (data that's accessed often and likely cached). Analytics use cases tend to read cold data frequently because they need to process large amounts of data. In this case, disk speeds are very important for overall performance. Plus, you'll want a comfortably large amount of memory so that the database's cache can hold the

---

[4] The "Competing Workloads" section later in this chapter, as well as the "Workload Isolation" section in Chapter 8, cover a few options for prioritizing and separating workloads.

data that you need to process. On the other hand, if you frequently access hot data, most of your data will be served from the cache, in such a way that the disk speeds become less important (although not negligible).

Tip   Not sure if your reads are from cold or hot data? Take a look at the ratio of cache misses in your monitoring dashboards. For more on monitoring, see Chapter 10.

If your ratio of cache misses is higher than hits, this means that reads need to frequently hit the disks in order to look up your data. This may happen because your database is underprovisioned in memory space, or simply because the application access patterns often read infrequently accessed data. It is important to understand the performance implications here. If you're frequently reading from cold data, there's a risk that I/O will become the bottleneck—for writes as well as reads. In that case, if you need to improve performance, adding more nodes or switching your storage medium to a faster solution could be helpful.

As noted earlier, write-optimized databases can improve read latency via internal caching, so it's not uncommon for a team with, say, 60 percent reads and 40 percent writes to opt for a write-optimized database. Another option is to boost the latency of reads with a write-optimized database: If your database supports it, dedicate extra "shares" of resources to the reads so that your read workload is prioritized when there is resource contention.

Delete-Heavy Workloads

What about delete-heavy workloads, such as using your database as a durable queue (saving data from a producer until the consumer accesses it, deleting it, then starting the cycle over and over again)? Here, you generally want to avoid databases that store data in immutable files and use tombstones to mark rows and columns that are slated for deletion. The most notable examples are Cassandra and other Cassandra-compatible databases.

Tombstones consume cache space and disk resources, and the database needs to search through all these tombstones to reach the live data. For many workloads, this is not a problem. But for delete-heavy workloads, generating an excessive amount of tombstones will, over time, significantly degrade your read latencies. There are ways and mechanisms to mitigate the impact of tombstones.[5] However, in general, if you have a delete-heavy workload, it may be best to use a different database.

It is important to note that occasional deletes are generally fine on Cassandra and Cassandra-compatible databases. Just be aware of the fact that deletes on append-only databases result in tombstone writes. As a result, these may incur read amplification, elevating your read latencies. Tombstones and data eviction in these types of databases are potentially long and complex subjects that perhaps could have their own dedicated chapter. However, the high-level recommendation is to exercise caution if you have a potentially delete-heavy pattern that you might later read from, and be sure to combine it with a compaction strategy tailored for efficient data eviction.

All that being said, it is interesting to note that some teams have successfully implemented delete-heavy workloads on top of Cassandra and Cassandra-like databases. The performance overhead carried by tombstones is generally circumvented by a combination of data modeling, a careful study of how deletes are performed, avoiding reads that potentially scan through a large set of deleted data, and careful tuning over the underlying table's compaction strategy to ensure that tombstones get evicted in a timely manner. For example, Tencent Games used the Time Window Compaction Strategy to aggressively expire tombstones and use it as the foundation for a time series distributed queue.[6]

Competing Workloads (Real-Time vs Batch)

If you're working with two different types of workloads—one more latency-sensitive than the other—the ideal solution is to have the database dedicate more resources to the more latency-sensitive workloads to keep them from faltering due to insufficient resources. This is commonly the case when you are attempting to balance OLTP (real-time) workloads, which are user-facing and require low latency responses, with

---

[5] For some specific recommendations, see the DataStax blog, "Cassandra Anti-Patterns: Queues and Queue-like Datasets" (`www.datastax.com/blog/cassandra-anti-patterns-queues-and-queue-datasets`)

[6] See the article, "Tencent Games' Real-Time Event-Driven Analytics System Built with ScyllaDB + Pulsar" (`https://www.scylladb.com/2023/05/15/tencent-games-real-time-event-driven-analytics-systembuilt-with-scylladb-pulsar/`)

OLAP (analytical) workloads, which can be run in batch mode and are more focused on throughput (see Figure 2-1). Or, you can prioritize analytics. Both are technically feasible; it just boils down to what's most important for your use case.

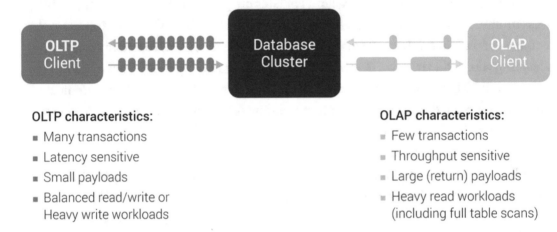

OLTP characteristics:

- Many transactions
- Latency sensitive
- Small payloads
- Balanced read/write or Heavy write workloads

OLAP characteristics:

- Few transactions
- Throughput sensitive
- Large (return) payloads
- Heavy read workloads (including full table scans)

Figure 2-1. *OLTP vs OLAP workloads*

For example, assume you have a web server database with analytics. It must support two workloads:

- The main workload consists of queries triggered by a user clicking or navigating on some areas of the web page. Here, users expect high responsiveness, which usually translates to requirements for low latency. You need low timeouts with load shedding as your overload response, and you would like to have a lot of dedicated resources available whenever this workload needs them.

- A second workload drives analytics being run periodically to collect some statistics or to aggregate some information that should be presented to users. This involves a series of computations. It's a lot less sensitive to latency than the main workload; it's more throughput oriented. You can have fairly large timeouts to accommodate for always full queues. You would like to throttle requests under load so the computation is stable and controllable. And finally, you would like the workload to have very few dedicated resources and use mostly unused resources to achieve better cluster utilization.

Running on the same cluster, such workloads would be competing for resources. As system utilization rises, the database must strictly prioritize which activities get what specific share of resources under contention. There are a few different ways you can handle this. Physical isolation, logical isolation, and scheduled isolation can all be acceptable choices under the right circumstances. Chapter 8 covers these options.

Item Size

The size of the items you are storing in the database (average payload size) will dictate whether your workload is CPU bound or storage bound. For example, running 100K OPS with an average payload size of 90KB is much different than achieving the same throughput with a 1KB payload. Higher payloads require more processing, I/O, and network traffic than smaller payloads.

Without getting too deep into database internals here, one notable impact is on the page cache. Assuming a default page cache size of 4KB, the database would have to serve several pages for the largest payload—that's much more I/O to issue, process, merge, and serve back to the application clients. With the 1KB example, you could serve it from a single-page cache entry, which is less taxing from a compute resource perspective. Conversely, having a large number of smaller-sized items may introduce CPU overhead compared to having a smaller number of larger items because the database must process each arriving item individually.

In general, the larger the payload gets, the more cache activity you will have. Most write-optimized databases will store your writes in memory before persisting that information to the disk (in fact, that's one of the reasons why they are write-optimized). Larger payloads deplete the available cache space more frequently, and this incurs a higher flushing activity to persist the information on disk in order to release space for more incoming writes. Therefore, more disk I/O is needed to persist that information. If you don't size this properly, it can become a bottleneck throughout this repetitive process.

When you're working with extremely large payloads, it's important to set realistic latency and throughput expectations. If you need to serve 200KB payloads, it's unlikely that any database will enable you to achieve single-digit millisecond latencies. Even if the entire dataset is served from cache, there's a physical barrier between your client and the database: networking. The network between them will eventually throttle your transfer speeds, even with an insanely fast client and database. Eventually, this will impact throughput as well as latency. As your latency increases, your client will eventually throttle down and you won't be able to achieve the same throughput that you could with smaller payload sizes. The requests would be stalled, queuing in the network.[7]

Generally speaking, databases should not be used to store large blobs. We've seen people trying to store gigabytes of data within a single-key in a database—and this isn't a great idea. If your item size is reaching this scale, consider alternative solutions. One solution is to use CDNs. Another is to store the largest chunk of your payload size in cold storage like Amazon S3 buckets, Google Cloud storage, or Azure blob storage. Then, use the database as a metadata lookup: It can read the data and fetch an identifier that will help find the data in that cold storage. For example, this is the strategy used by a game developer converting extremely large (often in the gigabyte range) content to popular gaming platforms. They store structured objects with blobs that are referenced by a content hash. The largest payload is stored within a cloud vendor Object Storage solution, whereas the content hash is stored in a distributed NoSQL database.[8]

Note that some databases impose hard limits on item size. For example, DynamoDB currently has a maximum item size of 400KB. This might not suit your needs. On top of that, if you're using an in-memory solution such as Redis, larger keys will quickly deplete your memory. In this case, it might make sense to hash/compress such large objects prior to storing them.

No matter which database you choose, the smaller your payload, the greater your chances of introducing memory fragmentation. This might reduce your memory efficiency, which might in turn elevate costs because the database won't be able to fully utilize its available memory.

Item Type

The item type has a large impact on compression, which in turn impacts your storage utilization. If you're frequently storing text, expect to take advantage of a high compression ratio. But, that's not the case for random and uncommon blob sequences.

---

[7] There are alternatives to this; for example, RDMA, DPDK and other solutions. However, most use cases do not require such solutions, so they are not covered in detail here.

[8] For details, see the Epic Games talk, "Using ScyllaDB for Distribution of Game Assets in Unreal Engine" (www.youtube.com/watch?v=aEgP9YhAbo8).

Here, compression is unlikely to make a measurable reduction in your storage footprint. If you're concerned about your use case's storage utilization, using a compression-friendly item type can make a big difference.

If your use case dictates a certain item type, consider databases that are optimized for that type. For example, if you need to frequently process JSON data that you can't easily transform, a document database like MongoDB might be a better option than a Cassandra-compatible database. If you have JSON with some common fields and others that vary based on user input, it might be complicated—though possible—to model them in Cassandra. However, you'd incur a penalty from serialization/deserialization overhead required on the application side.

As a general rule of thumb, choose the data type that's the minimum needed to store the type of data you need. For example, you don't need to store a year as a `bigint`. If you define a field as a `bigint`, most databases allocate relevant memory address spaces for holding it. If you can get by with a smaller type of `int`, do it—you'll save bytes of memory, which could add up at scale. Even if the database you use doesn't pre-allocate memory address spaces according to data types, choosing the correct one is still a nice way to have an organized data model—and also to avoid future questions around why a particular data type was chosen as opposed to another.

Many databases support additional item types which suit a variety of use cases. Collections, for example, allow you to store sets, lists, and maps (key-value pairs) under a single column in wide column databases. Such data types are often misused, and lead to severe performance problems. In fact, most of the data modeling problems we've come across involve misuse of collections. Collections are meant to store a small amount of information (such as phone numbers of an individual or different home/business addresses). However, collections with hundreds of thousands of entries are unfortunately not as rare as you might expect. They end up introducing a severe de-serialization overhead on the database. At best, this translates to higher latencies. At worst, this makes the data entirely unreadable due to the latency involved when scanning through the high number of items under such columns.

Some databases also support user created fields, such as User-Defined Types (UDTs) in Cassandra. UDTs can be a great ally for reducing the de-serialization overhead when you combine several columns into one. Think about it: Would you rather de-serialize four Boolean columns individually or a single column with four Boolean values? UDTs will typically shine on deserializing several values as a single column, which may give you a nice performance boost.[9] Just like collections, however, UDTs should not be misused—and misusing UDTs can lead to the same severe impacts that are incurred by collections.

Note   UDTs are quite extensively covered in Chapter 6.

Dataset Size

Knowing your dataset size is important for selecting appropriate infrastructure options. For example, AWS cloud instances have a broad array of NVMe storage offerings. Having a good grasp of how much storage you need can help you avoid selecting an instance that causes performance to suffer (if you end up with insufficient storage) or that's wasteful from a cost perspective (if you overprovision).

It's important to note that your selected storage size should not be equal to your total dataset size. You also need to factor in replication and growth—plus steer clear of 100 percent storage utilization.

For example, let's assume you have 3TB of already compressed data. The bare minimum to support a workload is your current dataset size multiplied by your anticipated replication. If you have 3TB of data with the common replication factor of three, that gives you 9TB. If you naively deployed this on three nodes supporting 3TB of data each, you'd hit near 100 percent disk utilization which, of course, is not optimal.

Instead, if you factor in some free space and minimal room for growth, you'd want to start with at least six nodes of that size—each storing only 1.5TB of data. This gives you around 50 percent utilization. On the other hand, if your database cannot support that much data per node (every database has a limit) or if you do not foresee much future data growth, you could have six nodes supporting 2TB each, which would store approximately 1.5TB per replica under a 75 percent utilization. Remember: Factoring in your growth is critical for avoiding unpleasant surprises in production, from an operational as well as a budget perspective.

---

[9] For some specific examples of how UDTs impact performance, see the performance benchmark that ScyllaDB performed with different UDT sizes against individual columns: "If You Care About Performance, Employ User Defined Types" (`https://www.scylladb.com/2017/12/07/performance-udt/`)

Note   We very intentionally discussed the dataset size from a *compressed* data standpoint. Be aware that some database vendors measure your storage utilization with respect to *uncompressed* data. This often leads to confusion. If you're moving data from one database solution to another and your data is uncompressed (or you're not certain it's compressed), consider loading a small fraction of your total dataset beforehand in order to determine its compression ratio. Effective compression can dramatically reduce your storage footprint.

If you're working on a very fluid project and can't define or predict your dataset size, a serverless database deployment model might be a good option to provide easy flexibility and scaling. But, be aware that rapid increases in overall dataset size and/or IOPS (depending on the pricing model) could cause the price to skyrocket exponentially. Even if you don't explicitly pay a penalty for storing a large dataset, you might be charged a premium for the many operations that are likely associated with that large dataset. Serverless is discussed more in Chapter 7.

Throughput Expectations

Your expected throughput and latency should be your "north star" from database and infrastructure selection all the way to monitoring. Let's start with throughput.

If you're serious about database performance, it's essential to know what throughput you're trying to achieve—and "high throughput" is not an acceptable answer. Specifically, try to get all relevant stakeholders' agreement on your target number of *peak* read operations per second and *peak* write operations per second *for each workload*.

Let's unravel that a little. First, be sure to separate read throughput vs write throughput. A database's read path is usually quite distinct from its write path. It stresses different parts of the infrastructure and taps different database internals. And the client/user experience of reads is often quite different than that of writes. Lumping them together into a meaningless number won't help you much with respect to performance measurement or optimization. The main use for average throughput is in applying Little's Law (more on that in the "Concurrency" section a little later in this chapter).

Another caveat: The same database's past or current throughput with one use case is no guarantee of future results with another—even if it's the same database hosted on identical infrastructure. There are too many different factors at play (item size, access patterns, concurrency... all the things in this chapter, really). What's a great fit for one use case could be quite inappropriate for another.

Also, note the emphasis on *peak* operations per second. If you build and optimize with an average in mind, you likely won't be able to service beyond the upper ranges of that average. Focus on the peak throughput that you need to sustain to cover your core needs and business patterns—including surges. Realize that databases can often "boost" to sustain short bursts of exceptionally high load. However, to be safe, it's best to plan for your likely peaks and reserve boosting for atypical situations.

Also, be sure not to confuse concurrency with throughput. *Throughput* is the speed at which the database can perform read or write operations; it's measured in the number of read or write operations per second. *Concurrency* is the number of requests that the client sends to the database at the same time (which, in turn, will eventually translate to a given number of concurrent requests queuing at the database for execution). Concurrency is expressed as a hard number, not a rate over a period of time. Not every request that is born at the same time will be able to be processed by the database at the same time. Your client could send 150K requests to the database, all at once. The database might blaze through all these concurrent requests if it's running at 500K OPS. Or, it might take a while to process them if the database throughput tops out at 50K OPS.

It is generally possible to increase throughput by increasing your cluster size (and/ or power). But, you also want to pay special attention to concurrency, which will be discussed in more depth later in this chapter as well as in Chapter 5. For the most part, high concurrency is essential for achieving impressive performance. But if the clients end up overwhelming the database with a concurrency that it can't handle, throughput will suffer, then latency will rise as a side effect. A friendly reminder that transcends the database world: No system, distributed or not, supports unlimited concurrency. Period.

Note   Even though scaling a cluster boosts your database processing capacity, remember that the application access patterns directly contribute to how much impact that will ultimately make. One situation where scaling a cluster may not provide the desired throughput increase is during a *hot partition*[10] situation, which causes traffic to be primarily targeted to a specific set of replicas. In these cases, throttling the access to such hot keys is fundamental for preserving the system's overall performance.

Latency Expectations

Latency is a more complex challenge than throughput: You can increase throughput by adding more nodes, but there's no simple solution for reducing latency. The lower the latency you need to achieve, the more important it becomes to understand and explore database tradeoffs and internal database optimizations that can help you shave milliseconds or microseconds off latencies. Database internals, driver optimizations, efficient CPU utilization, sufficient RAM, efficient data modeling… everything matters.

As with throughput, aim for all relevant stakeholders' agreement on the acceptable latencies. This is usually expressed as latency for a certain percentile of requests. For performance-sensitive workloads, tracking at the 99th percentile (P99) is common. Some teams go even higher, such as the P9999, which refers to the 99.99th percentile.

As with throughput, avoid focusing on *average* (mean) or median (P50) latency measurements. Average latency is a theoretical measurement that is not directly correlated to anything systems or users experience in reality. Averages conceal outliers: Extreme deviations from the norm that may have a large and unexpected impact on overall system performance, and hence on user experience.

For example, look at the discrepancy between average latencies and P99 latencies in Figure 2-2 (different colors represent different database nodes). P99 latencies were often double the average for reads, and even worse for writes.

---

[10] A hot partition is a data access imbalance problem that causes specific partitions to receive more traffic compared to others, thus introducing higher load on a specific set of replica servers.

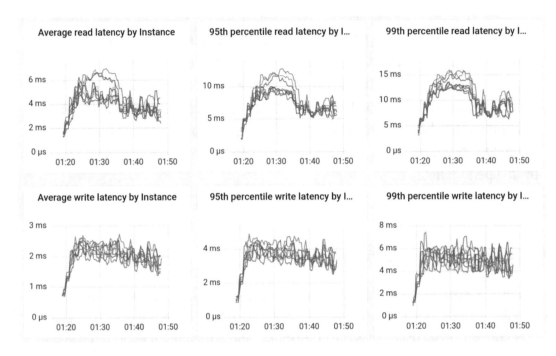

Figure 2-2. *A sample database monitoring dashboard. Note the difference between average and P99 latencies*

Note that monitoring systems are sometimes configured in ways that omit outliers. For example, if a monitoring system is calibrated to measure latency on a scale of 0 to 1000ms, it is going to overlook any larger measurements—thus failing to detect the serious issues of query timeouts and retries.

P99 and above percentiles are not perfect.[11] But for latency-sensitive use cases, they're the number you'll want to keep in mind as you are selecting your infrastructure, benchmarking, monitoring, and so on.

Also, be clear about what exactly is involved in the P99 you are looking to achieve. Database latency is the time that elapses between when the database receives a request, processes it, and sends back an appropriate response. Client-side latency is broader: Here, the measurement starts with the client sending the request and ends with the client receiving the database's response. It includes the network time and client-side

---

[11] For a detailed critique, see Gil Tene's famous "Oh Sh*t" talk (www.youtube.com/watch?v=1J8ydIuPFeU) as well as his recent P99 CONF talk on Misery Metrics and Consequences (https://www.p99conf.io/session/misery-metrics-consequences/).

processing. There can be quite a discrepancy between database latency and client-side latency; a ten times higher client-side latency isn't all that uncommon (although clearly not desirable). There could be many culprits to blame for a significantly higher client-side latency than database latency: excessive concurrency, inefficient application architecture, coding issues, and so on. But that's beyond the scope of this discussion—beyond the scope of this book, even.

The key point here is that your team and all the stakeholders need to be on the same page regarding what you're measuring. For example, say you're given a read latency requirement of 15ms. You work hard to get your database to achieve that and report that you met the expectation—then you learn that stakeholders actually expect 15ms for the full client-side latency. Back to the drawing board.

Ultimately, it's important to track both database latency and client-side latency. You can optimize the database all you want, but if the application is introducing latency issues from the client side, a fast database won't have much impact. Without visibility into both the database and the client-side latencies, you're essentially flying half blind.

Concurrency

What level of concurrency should your database be prepared to handle? Depending on the desired qualities of service from the database cluster, concurrency must be judiciously balanced to reach appropriate throughput and latency values. Otherwise, requests will pile up waiting to be processed—causing latencies to spike, timeouts to rise, and the overall user experience to degrade.

Little's Law establishes that:

$$L = \lambda W$$

where λ is the average throughput, W is the average latency, and L represents the total number of requests either being processed or on queue at any given moment when the cluster reaches steady state. Given that your throughput and latency targets are usually fixed, you can use Little's Law to estimate a realistic concurrency.

For example, if you want a system to serve 500,000 requests per second at 2.5ms average latency, the best concurrency is around 1,250 in-flight requests. As you approach the saturation limit of the system—around 600,000 requests per second for read requests—increases in concurrency will keep constant since this is the physical limit of the database. Every new in-flight request will only cause increased latency.

In fact, if you approximate 600,000 requests per second as the physical capacity of this database, you can calculate the expected average latency at a particular concurrency point. For example, at 6,120 in-flight requests, the average latency is expected to be 6120/600,000 = 10ms.

Past the maximum throughput, increasing concurrency will increase latency. Conversely, reducing concurrency will reduce latency, provided that this reduction does not result in a decrease in throughput.

In some use cases, it's fine for queries to pile up on the client side. But many times it's not. In those cases, you can scale out your cluster or increase the concurrency on the application side—at least to the point where the latency doesn't suffer. It's a delicate balancing act.[12]

Connected Technologies

A database can't rise above the slowest-performing link in your distributed data system. Even if your database is processing reads and writes at blazing speeds, it won't ultimately matter much if it interacts with an event-streaming platform that's not optimized for performance or involves transformations from a poorly-configured Apache Spark instance, for example.

This is just one of many reasons that taking a comprehensive and proactive approach to monitoring (more on this in Chapter 10) is so important. Given the complexity of databases and distributed data systems, it's hard to guess what component is to blame for a problem. Without a window into the state of the broader system, you could naively waste amazing amounts of time and resources trying to optimize something that won't make any difference.

If you're looking to optimize an existing data system, don't overlook the performance gains you can achieve by reviewing and tuning its connected components. Or, if your monitoring efforts indicate that a certain component is to blame for your client-side performance problems but you feel you've hit your limit with it, explore what's required to replace it with a more performant alternative. Use benchmarking to determine the severity of the impact from a performance perspective.

---

[12] For additional reading on concurrency, the Netflix blog "Performance Under Load" is a great resource (https://netflixtechblog.medium.com/performance-under-load-3e6fa9a60581).

Also, note that some database offerings may have ecosystem limitations. For example, if you're considering a serverless deployment model, be aware that some Change Data Capture (CDC) connectors, drivers, and so on, might not be supported.

Demand Fluctuations

Databases might experience a variety of different demand fluctuations, ranging from predictable moderate fluctuations to unpredictable and dramatic spikes. For instance, the world's most watched sporting event experiences different fluctuations than a food delivery service, which experiences different fluctuations than an ambulance-tracking service—and all require different strategies and infrastructure.

First, let's look at the predictable fluctuations. With predictability, it's much easier to get ahead of the issue. If you're expected to support periodic big events that are known in advance (Black Friday, sporting championships, ticket on sales, etc.), you should have adequate time to scale up your cluster for each anticipated spike. That means you can tailor your normal topology for the typical day-in, day-out demands without having to constantly incur the costs and admin burden of having that larger scale topology.

On the other side of the spikiness spectrum, there's applications with traffic with dramatic peaks and valleys across the course of each day. For example, consider food delivery businesses, which face a sudden increase around lunch, followed by a few hours of minimal traffic, then a second spike at dinner time (and sometimes breakfast the following morning). Expanding the cluster for each spike—even with "autoscaling" (more on autoscaling later in this chapter)—is unlikely to deliver the necessary performance gain fast enough. In these cases, you should provision an infrastructure that supports the peak traffic.

But not all spikes are predictable. Certain industries—such as emergency services, news, and social media—are susceptible to sudden massive spikes. In this case, a good preventative strategy is to control your concurrency on the client side, so it doesn't overwhelm your database. However, controlling concurrency might not be an option for use cases with strict end-to-end latency requirements. You can also scramble to scale out your clusters as fast as feasible when the spike occurs. This is going to be markedly simpler if you're on the cloud than if you're on-prem. If you can start adding nodes immediately, increase capacity incrementally—with a close eye on your monitoring results—and keep going until you're satisfied with the results, or until the peak has subsided. Unfortunately, there is a real risk that you won't be able to sufficiently scale out before the spike ends. Even if the ramp up begins immediately, you need to account for the time it takes to get data over to add new nodes, stream data to them, and rebalance the cluster.

If you're selecting a new database and anticipate frequent and sharp spikes, be sure to rigorously test how your top contenders respond under realistic conditions. Also, consider the costs of maintaining acceptable performance throughout these peaks.

Note   The word "autoscaling" insinuates that your database cluster auto-magically expands based on the traffic it is receiving. Not so. It's simply a robot enabling/disabling capacity that's pre-provisioned for you based on your target table settings. Even if you're not using this capacity, you might be paying for the convenience of having it set aside and ready to go. Also, it's important to realize that it's not instantaneous. It takes upwards of 2.5 hours to go from 0 rps to 40k.[13] This is not ideal for unexpected or extreme spikes.

Autoscaling is best when:

- Load changes have high amplitude

- The rate of change is in the magnitude of hours

- The load peak is narrow relative to the baseline[14]

ACID Transactions

Does your use case require you to process a logical unit of work with ACID (atomic, consistent, isolated, and durable) properties? These transactions, which are historically the domain of RDBMS, bring a severe performance hit.

---

[13] See The Burning Monk blog, "Understanding the Scaling Behaviour of DynamoDB OnDemand Tables" (https://theburningmonk.com/2019/03/understanding-the-scaling-behaviour-of-dynamodb-ondemand-tables/).

[14] For more on the best and worst uses of autoscaling, see Avishai Ish Shalom's blog, "DynamoDB Autoscaling Dissected: When a Calculator Beats a Robot" (www.scylladb.com/2021/07/08/dynamodb-autoscaling-dissected-when-a-calculator-beats-a-robot/).

It is true that distributed ACID compliant databases do exist—and that the past few years have brought some distinct progress in the effort to minimize the performance impact (e.g., through row-level locks or column-level locking and better conflict resolution algorithms). However, some level of penalty will still exist.

As a general guidance, if you have an ACID-compliant use case, pay special attention to your master nodes; these can easily become your bottlenecks since they will often be your primary query coordinators (more on this in Appendix A). In addition, if at all possible, try to ensure that the majority of your transactions are isolated to the minimum amount of resources. For example, a transaction spanning a single row may involve a specific set of replicas, whereas a transaction involving several keys may span your cluster as a whole—inevitably increasing your latency. It is therefore important to understand which types of transactions your target database supports. Some vendors may support a mix of approaches, while others excel at specific ones. For instance, MongoDB introduced multi-document transactions on sharded clusters in its version 4.2; prior to that, it supported only multi-document transactions on replica sets.

If it's critical to support transactions in a more performant manner, sometimes it's possible to rethink your data model and reimplement a use case in a way that makes it suitable for a database that's not ACID compliant. For example, one team who started out with Postgres for all their use cases faced skyrocketing business growth. This is a very common situation with startups that begin small and then suddenly find themselves in a spot where they are unable to handle a spike in growth in a cost-effective way. They were able to move their use cases to NoSQL by conducting a careful data-modeling analysis and rethinking their use cases, access patterns, and the real business need of what truly required ACID and what did not. This certainly isn't a quick fix, but in the right situation, it can pay off nicely.

Another option to consider: Performance-focused NoSQL databases like Cassandra aim to support isolated conditional updates with capabilities such as lightweight transactions that allow "atomic compare and set" operations. That is, the database checks if a condition is true, and if so, it conducts the transaction. If the condition is not met, the transaction is not completed. They are named "lightweight" since they do not truly lock the database for the transaction. Instead, they use a consensus protocol to ensure there is agreement between the nodes to commit the change. This capability was introduced by Cassandra and it's supported in several ways across different Cassandra-compatible databases. If this is something you expect to use, it's worth exploring the documentation to understand the differences.[15]

However, it's important to note that lightweight transactions have their limits. They can't support complex use cases like a retail transaction that updates the inventory only after a sale is completed with a successful payment. And just like ACID-compliant databases, lightweight transactions have their own performance implications. As a result, the choice of whether to use them will greatly depend on the amount of ACID compliance that your use case requires.

DynamoDB is a prime example of how the need for transactions will require more compute resources (read: money). As a result, use cases relying heavily on ACID will fairly often require much more infrastructure power to satisfy heavy usage requirements. In the DynamoDB documentation, AWS recommends that you ensure the database is configured for auto-scaling or that it has enough read/write capacity to account for the additional overhead of transactions.[16]

Consistency Expectations

Most NoSQL databases opt for eventual consistency to gain performance. This is in stark contrast to the RDBMS model, where ACID compliance is achieved in the form of transactions, and, because everything is in a single node, the effort on locking and avoiding concurrency clashes is often minimized. When deciding between a database with strong or eventual consistency, you have to make a hard choice. Do you want to sacrifice scalability and performance or can you accept the risk of sometimes serving stale data?

Can your use case tolerate eventual consistency, or is strong consistency truly required? Your choice really boils down to how much risk your application—and your business—can tolerate with respect to inconsistency. For example, a retailer who

---

[15] See Kostja Osipov's blog, "Getting the Most Out of Lightweight Transactions in ScyllaDB" (www.scylladb.com/2020/07/15/getting-the-most-out-of-lightweight-transactions-in-scylla/) for an example of how financial transactions can be implemented using Lightweight Transactions.

[16] See "Amazon DynamoDB Transactions: How it Works" (https://docs.aws.amazon.com/amazondynamodb/latest/developerguide/transaction-apis.html).

(understandably) requires consistent pricing might want to pay the price for consistent writes upfront during a weekly catalog update so that they can later serve millions of low-latency read requests under more relaxed consistency levels. In other cases, it's more important to ingest data quickly and pay the price for consistency later (for example, in the playback tracking use case that's common in streaming platforms—where the database needs to record the last viewing position for many users concurrently). Or maybe both are equally important. For example, consider a social media platform that offers live chat. Here, you want consistency on both writes and reads, but you likely don't need the highest consistency (the impact of an inconsistency here is likely much less than with a financial report).

In some cases, "tunable consistency" will help you achieve a balance between strong consistency and performance. This gives you the ability to tune the consistency at the query level to suit what you're trying to achieve. You can have some queries relying on a quorum of replicas, then have other queries that are much more relaxed.

Regardless of your consistency requirements, you need to be aware of the implications involved when selecting a given consistency level. Databases that offer tunable consistency may be a blessing or a curse if you don't know what you are doing. Consider a NoSQL deployment spanning three different regions, with three nodes each (nine nodes in total). A QUORUM read would essentially have to traverse two different regions in order to be acknowledged back to the client. In that sense, if your Network Round Trip Time (RTT)[17] is 50ms, then it will take *at least* this amount of time for the query to be considered successful by the database. Similarly, if you were to run operations with the highest possible consistency (involving all replicas), then the failure of a single node may bring your entire application down.

Note   NoSQL databases fairly often will provide you with ways to confine your queries to a specific region to prevent costly network round trips from impacting your latency. But again, it all boils down to you what your use case requires.

---

[17] *RTT* is the duration, typically measured in milliseconds, that a network request takes to reach a destination, plus the time it takes for the packet to be received back at the origin.

Geographic Distribution

Does your business need to support a regional or global customer base in the near-term future? Where are your users and your application located? The greater the distance between your users, your application, and your database, the more they're going to face high latencies that stem from the physical time it takes to move data across the network. Knowing this will influence where you locate your database and how you design your topology—more on this in Chapters 6 and 8.

The geographic distribution of your cluster might also be a requirement from a disaster recovery perspective. In that sense, the cluster would typically serve data primarily from a specific region, but failover to another in the event of a disaster (such as a full region outage). These kinds of setups are costly, as they will require doubling your infrastructure spend. However, depending on the nature of your use case, sometimes it's required.

Some organizations that invest in a multi-region deployment for the primary purpose of disaster recovery end up using them to host isolated use cases. As explained in the "Competing Workloads" section of this chapter, companies often prefer to physically isolate OLTP from OLAP workloads. Moving some isolated (less critical) workloads to remote regions prevents these servers from being "idle" most of the time.

Regardless of the magnitude of compelling reasons that may drive you toward a geographically dispersed deployment, here's some important high-level advice from a performance perspective (you'll learn some more technical tips in Chapter 8):

1. Consider the increased load that your target region or regions will receive in the event of a full region outage. For example, assume that you operate globally across three regions, and all these three regions serve your end-users. Are the two remaining regions able to sustain the load for a long period of time?

2. Recognize that simply having a geographically-dispersed database does *not* fully cover you in a disaster recovery situation. You also need to have your application, web servers, messaging queue systems, and so on, geographically replicated. If the only thing that's geo-replicated is your database, you won't be in a great position when your primary application goes down.

3. Consider the fact that geo-replicated databases typically require very good network links. Especially when crossing large distances, the time to replicate your data is crucial to minimize losses in the event of a disaster. If your workload has a heavy write throughput, a slow network link may bottleneck the local region nodes. This may cause a queue to build up and eventually throttle down your writes.

High-Availability Expectations

Inevitably, s#*& happens. To prepare for the worst, start by understanding what your use case and business can tolerate if a node goes down. Can you accept the data loss that could occur if a node storing unreplicated data goes down? Do you need to continue buzzing along without a noticeable performance impact even if an entire datacenter or availability zone goes down? Or is it okay if things slow down a bit from time to time? This will all impact how you architect your topology and configure things like replication factor and consistency levels (you'll learn about this more in Chapter 8).

It's important to note that replication and consistency both come at a cost to performance. Get a good feel for your business's risk tolerance and don't opt for more than your business really needs.

When considering your cluster topology, remember that quite a lot is at risk if you get it wrong (and you don't want to be caught off-guard in the middle of the night). For example, the failure of a single node in a three-node cluster could make you momentarily lose 33 percent of your processing power. Quite often, that's a significant blow, with discernable business impact. Similarly, the loss of a node in a six-node cluster would reduce the blast radius to only 16 percent. But there's always a tradeoff. A sprawling deployment spanning hundreds of nodes is not ideal either. The more nodes you have, the more likely you are to experience a node failure. Balance is key.

Summary

The specific database challenges you encounter, as well as your options for addressing them, are highly dependent on your situation. For example, an AdTech use case that demands single-digit millisecond P99 latencies for a large dataset with small item sizes requires a different treatment than a fraud detection use case that prioritizes the ingestion of massive amounts of data as rapidly as possible. One of the primary factors influencing how these workloads are handled is how your database is architected. That's the focus for the next two chapters, which dive into database internals.

CHAPTER 3

Database Internals: Hardware and Operating System Interactions

A database's internal architecture makes a tremendous impact on the latency it can achieve and the throughput it can handle. Being an extremely complex piece of software, a database doesn't exist in a vacuum, but rather interacts with the environment, which includes the operating system and the hardware.

While it's one thing to get massive terabyte-to-petabyte scale systems up and running, it's a whole other thing to make sure they are operating at peak efficiency. In fact, it's usually more than just "one other thing." Performance optimization of large distributed systems is usually a multivariate problem—combining aspects of the underlying hardware, networking, tuning operating systems, and finagling with layers of virtualization and application architectures.

Such a complex problem warrants exploration from multiple perspectives. This chapter begins the discussion of database internals by looking at ways that databases can optimize performance by taking advantage of modern hardware and operating systems. It covers how the database interacts with the operating system plus CPUs, memory, storage, and networking. Then, the next chapter shifts focus to algorithmic optimizations.[1]

---

[1] This chapter draws from material originally published on the Seastar site (`https://seastar.io/`) and the ScyllaDB blog (`https://www.scylladb.com/blog/`). It is used here with permission of ScyllaDB.

© Felipe Cardeneti Mendes, Piotr Sarna, Pavel Emelyanov, Cynthia Dunlop 2023
F. C. Mendes et al., *Database Performance at Scale*, https://doi.org/10.1007/978-1-4842-9711-7_3

CPU

Programming books tell programmers that they have this CPU that can run processes or threads, and what *runs* means is that there's some simple sequential instruction execution. Then there's a footnote explaining that with multiple threads you might need to consider doing some synchronization. In fact, how things are actually executed inside CPU cores is something completely different and much more complicated. It would be very difficult to program these machines if you didn't have those abstractions from books, but they are a lie to some degree. How you can efficiently take advantage of CPU capabilities is still very important.

Share Nothing Across Cores

Individual CPU cores aren't getting any faster. Their clock speeds reached a performance plateau long ago. Now, the ongoing increase of CPU performance continues horizontally: by increasing the number of processing units. In turn, the increase in the number of cores means that performance now depends on coordination across multiple cores (versus the throughput of a single core).

On modern hardware, the performance of standard workloads depends more on the locking and coordination across cores than on the performance of an individual core. Software architects face two unattractive alternatives:

- Coarse-grained locking, which will see application threads contend for control of the data and wait instead of producing useful work.

- Fine-grained locking, which, in addition to being hard to program and debug, sees significant overhead even when no contention occurs due to the locking primitives themselves.

Consider an SSD drive. The typical time needed to communicate with an SSD on a modern NVMe device is quite lengthy—it's about 20 μseconds. That's enough time for the CPU to execute tens of thousands of instructions. Developers should consider it as a networked device but generally do not program in that way. Instead, they often use an API that is synchronous (we'll return to this later), which produces a thread that can be blocked.

Looking at the image of the logical layout of an Intel Xeon Processor (see Figure 3-1), it's clear that this is also a networked device.

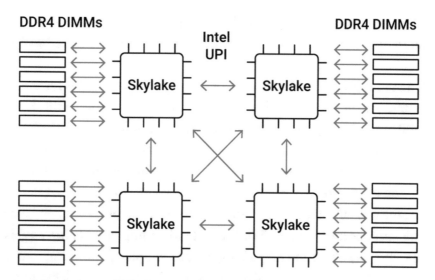

Figure 3-1. *The logical layout of an Intel Xeon Processor*

The cores are all connected by what is essentially a network—a dual ring interconnected architecture. There are two such rings and they are bidirectional. Why should developers use a synchronous API for that then? Since sharing information across cores requires costly locking, a shared-nothing model is perfectly worth considering. In such a model, all requests are sharded onto individual cores, one application thread is run per core, and communication depends on explicit message passing, not shared memory between threads. This design avoids slow, unscalable lock primitives and cache bounces.

Any sharing of resources across cores in modern processors must be handled explicitly. For example, when two requests are part of the same session and two CPUs each get a request that depends on the same session state, one CPU must explicitly forward the request to the other. Either CPU may handle either response. Ideally, your database provides facilities that limit the need for cross-core communication—but when communication is inevitable, it provides high-performance non-blocking communication primitives to ensure performance is not degraded.

Futures-Promises

There are many solutions for coordinating work across multiple cores. Some are highly programmer-friendly and enable the development of software that works exactly as if it were running on a single core. For example, the classic UNIX process model is designed to keep each process in total isolation and relies on kernel code to maintain a separate virtual memory space per process. Unfortunately, this increases the overhead at the OS level.

There's a model known as "futures and promises." A *future* is a data structure that represents some yet-undetermined result. A *promise* is the provider of this result. It can be helpful to think of a promise/future pair as a first-in first-out (FIFO) queue with a maximum length of one item, which may be used only once. The promise is the producing end of the queue, while the future is the consuming end. Like FIFOs, futures and promises decouple the data producer and the data consumer.

However, the optimized implementations of futures and promises need to take several considerations into account. While the standard implementation targets coarse-grained tasks that may block and take a long time to complete, optimized futures and promises are used to manage fine-grained, non-blocking tasks. In order to meet this requirement efficiently, they should:

- Require no locking

- Not allocate memory

- Support continuations

Future-promise design eliminates the costs associated with maintaining individual threads by the OS and allows close to complete utilization of the CPU. On the other hand, it calls for user-space CPU scheduling and very likely limits the developer with voluntary preemption scheduling. The latter, in turn, is prone to generating phantom jams in popular producer-consumer programming templates.[2]

Applying future-promise design to database internals has obvious benefits. First of all, database workloads can be naturally CPU-bound. For example, that's typically the case with in-memory database engines, and aggregates' evaluations also involve pretty intensive CPU work. Even for huge on-disk datasets, when the query time is typically dominated by the I/O, CPU should be considered. Parsing a query is a CPU-intensive task regardless of whether the workload is CPU-bound or storage-bound, and collecting, converting, and sending the data back to the user also calls for careful CPU utilization. And last but not least: Processing the data always involves *a lot* of high-level operations

---

[2] Watch the Linux Foundation video, "Exploring Phantom Traffic Jams in Your Data Flows," on YouTube (www.youtube.com/watch?v=IXS_Afb6Y4o) and/or read the corresponding article on the ScyllaDB blog (www.scylladb.com/2022/04/19/exploring-phantom-jams-in-your-data-flow/).

and low-level instructions. Maintaining them in an optimal manner requires a good low-level programming paradigm and future-promises is one of the best choices. However, large instruction sets need even more care; this leads to "execution stages."

Execution Stages

Let's dive deeper into CPU microarchitecture, because (as discussed previously) database engine CPUs typically need to deal with millions and billions of instructions, and it's essential to help the poor thing with that. In a very simplified way, the microarchitecture of a modern x86 CPU—from the point of view of top-down analysis—consists of four major components: frontend, backend, branch speculation, and retiring.

Frontend

The processor's frontend is responsible for fetching and decoding instructions that are going to be executed. It may become a bottleneck when there is either a latency problem or insufficient bandwidth. The former can be caused, for example, by instruction cache misses. The latter happens when the instruction decoders cannot keep up. In the latter case, the solution may be to attempt to make the hot path (or at least significant portions of it) fit in the decoded μop cache (DSB) or be recognizable by the loop detector (LSD).

Branch Speculation

Pipeline slots that the top-down analysis classifies as *bad speculation* are not stalled, but wasted. This happens when a branch is incorrectly predicted and the rest of the CPU executes a μop that eventually cannot be committed. The branch predictor is generally considered to be a part of the frontend. However, its problems can affect the whole pipeline in ways beyond just causing the backend to be undersupplied by the instruction fetch and decode. (Note: Branch mispredictions are covered in more detail a bit later in this chapter.)

Backend

The backend receives decoded μops and executes them. A stall may happen either because of an execution port being busy or a cache miss. At the lower level, a pipeline slot may be core bound either due to data dependency or an insufficient number of available execution units. Stalls caused by memory can be caused by cache misses at different levels of data cache, external memory latency, or bandwidth.

Retiring

Finally, there are pipeline slots that get classified as *retiring*. They are the lucky ones that were able to execute and commit their µop without any problems. When 100 percent of the pipeline slots are able to retire without a stall, the program has achieved the maximum number of instructions per cycle for that model of the CPU. Although this is very desirable, it doesn't mean that there's no opportunity for improvement. Rather, it means that the CPU is fully utilized and the only way to improve the performance is to reduce the number of instructions.

Implications for Databases

The way CPUs are architectured has direct implications on the database design. It may very well happen that individual requests involve a lot of logic and relatively little data, which is a scenario that stresses the CPU significantly. This kind of workload will be completely dominated by the frontend—instruction cache misses in particular. If you think about this for a moment, it shouldn't be very surprising. The pipeline that each request goes through is quite long. For example, write requests may need to go through transport protocol logic, query parsing code, look up in the caching layer, or be applied to the memtable, and so on.

The most obvious way to solve this is to attempt to reduce the amount of logic in the hot path. Unfortunately, this approach does not offer a huge potential for significant performance improvement. Reducing the number of instructions needed to perform a certain activity is a popular optimization practice, but a developer cannot make any code shorter infinitely. At some point, the code "freezes"—literally. There's some minimal amount of instructions needed even to compare two strings and return the result. It's impossible to perform that with a single instruction.

A higher-level way of dealing with instruction cache problems is called Staged Event-Driven Architecture (SEDA for short). It's an architecture that splits the request processing pipeline into a graph of stages—thereby decoupling the logic from the event and thread scheduling. This tends to yield greater performance improvements than the previous approach.

Memory

Memory management is the central design point in all aspects of programming. Even comparing programming languages to one another always involves discussions about the way programmers are supposed to handle memory allocation and freeing. No wonder memory management design affects the performance of a database so much.

Applied to database engineering, memory management typically falls into two related but independent subsystems: memory allocation and cache control. The former is in fact a very generic software engineering issue, so considerations about it are not extremely specific to databases (though they are crucial and are worth studying). As opposed to that, the latter topic is itself very broad, affected by the usage details and corner cases. Respectively, in the database world, cache control has its own flavor.

Allocation

The manner in which programs or subsystems allocate and free memory lies at the core of memory management. There are several approaches worth considering.

As illustrated by Figure 3-2, a so-called "log-structured allocation" is known from filesystems where it puts sequential writes to a circular log on the persisting storage and handles updates the very same way. At some point, this filesystem must reclaim blocks that became obsolete entries in the log area to make some more space available for future writes. In a naive implementation, unused entries are reclaimed by rereading and rewriting the log from scratch; obsolete blocks are then skipped in the process.

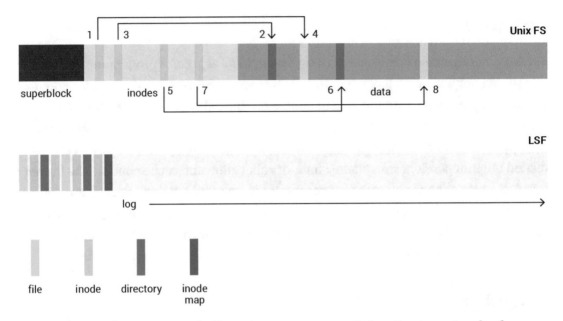

Figure 3-2. *A log-structured allocation puts sequential writes to a circular log on the persisting storage and handles updates the same way*

A memory allocator for naive code can do something similar. In its simplest form, it would allocate the next block of memory by simply advancing a next-free pointer. Deallocation would just need to mark the allocated area as freed. One advantage of this approach is the speed of allocation. Another is the simplicity and efficiency of deallocation if it happens in FIFO order or affects the whole allocation space. Stack memory allocations are later released in the order that's reverse to allocation, so this is the most prominent and the most efficient example of such an approach.

Using linear allocators as general-purpose allocators can be more problematic because of the difficulty of space reclamation. To reclaim space, it's not enough to just mark entries as free. This leads to memory fragmentation, which in turn outweighs the advantages of linear allocation. So, as with the filesystem, the memory must be reclaimed so that it only contains allocated entries and the free space can be used again. Reclamation requires moving allocated entries around—a process that changes and invalidates their previously known addresses. In naive code, the locations of references to allocated entries (addresses stored as pointers) are unknown to the allocator. Existing references would have to be patched to make the allocator action transparent to the caller; that's not feasible for a general-purpose allocator like malloc. Logging allocator use is tied to the programming language selection. Some RTTIs, like C++, can greatly facilitate this by providing move-constructors. However, passing pointers to libraries that are outside of your control (e.g., glibc) would still be an issue.

Another alternative is adopting a strategy of pool allocators, which provide allocation spaces for allocation of entries of a fixed size (see Figure 3-3). By limiting the allocation space that way, fragmentation can be reduced. A number of general-purpose allocators use pool allocators for small allocations. In some cases, those application spaces exist on a per-thread basis to eliminate the need for locking and improve CPU cache utilization.

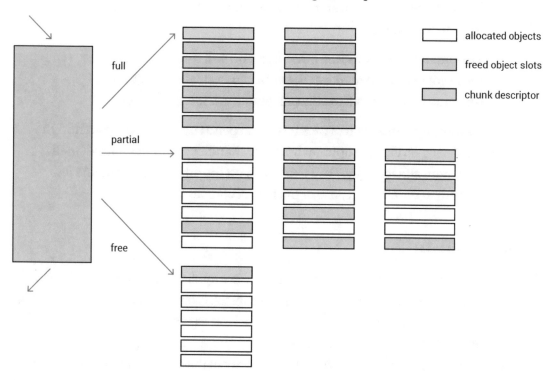

Figure 3-3. *Pool allocators provide allocation spaces for allocation of entries of a fixed size. Fragmentation is reduced by limiting the allocation space*

This pool allocation strategy provides two core benefits. First, it saves you from having to search for available memory space. Second, it alleviates memory fragmentation because it pre-allocates in memory a cache for use with a collection of object sizes. Here's how it works to achieve that:

1. The region for each of the sizes has fixed-size memory chunks that are suitable for the contained objects, and those chunks are all tracked by the allocator.

2. When it's time for the allocator to allocate memory for a certain type of data object, it's typically possible to use a free slot (chunk) in one of the existing memory slabs.[3]

3. When it's time for the allocator to free the object's memory, it can simply move that slot over to the containing slab's list of unused/free memory slots.

4. That memory slot (or some other free slot) will be removed from the list of free slots whenever there's a call to create an object of the same type (or a call to allocate memory of the same size).

The best allocation approach to pick heavily depends on the usage scenario. One great benefit of a log-structured approach is that it handles fragmentation of small sub-pools in a more efficient way. Pool allocators, on the other hand, generate less background load on the CPU because of the lack of compacting activity.

Cache Control

When it comes to memory management in a software application that stores lots of data on disk, you cannot overlook the topic of cache control. Caching is always a must in data processing, and it's crucial to decide what and where to cache.

If caching is done at the I/O level, for both read/write and mmap, caching can become the responsibility of the kernel. The majority of the system's memory is given over to the page cache. The kernel decides which pages should be evicted when memory runs low, decides when pages need to be written back to disk, and controls read-ahead. The application can provide some guidance to the kernel using the madvise(2) and fadvise(2) system calls.

The main advantage of letting the kernel control caching is that great effort has been invested by the kernel developers over many decades into tuning the algorithms used by the cache. Those algorithms are used by thousands of different applications and are

---

[3] We are using the term "slab" to mean one or more contiguous memory pages that contain pre-allocated chunks of memory.

generally effective. The disadvantage, however, is that these algorithms are general-purpose and not tuned to the application. The kernel must guess how the application will behave next. Even if the application knows differently, it usually has no way to help the kernel guess correctly. This results in the wrong pages being evicted, I/O scheduled in the wrong order, or read-ahead scheduled for data that will not be consumed in the near future.

Next, doing the caching at the I/O level interacts with the topic often referred to as IMR—*in memory representation*. No wonder that the format in which data is stored on disk differs from the form the same data is allocated in memory as objects. The simplest reason that it's not the same is byte-ordering. With that in mind, if the data is cached once it's read from the disk, it needs to be further converted or parsed into the object used in memory. This can be a waste of CPU cycles, so applications may choose to cache at the object level.

Choosing to cache at the object level affects a lot of other design points. With that, the cache management is all on the application side including cross-core synchronization, data coherence, invalidation, and so on. Next, since objects can be (and typically are) much smaller than the average I/O size, caching millions and billions of those objects requires a collection selection that can handle it (you'll learn about this quite soon). Finally, caching on the object level greatly affects the way I/O is done.

I/O

Unless the database engine is an in-memory one, it will have to keep the data on external storage. There can be many options to do that, including local disks, network-attached storage, distributed file- and object- storage systems, and so on. The term "I/O" typically refers to accessing data on local storage—disks or filesystems (that, in turn, are located on disks as well). And in general, there are four choices for accessing files on a Linux server: read/write, mmap, Direct I/O (DIO) read/write, and Asynchronous I/O (AIO/DIO, because this I/O is rarely used in cached mode).

Traditional Read/Write

The traditional method is to use the read(2) and write(2) system calls. In a modern implementation, the read system call (or one of its many variants—pread, readv, preadv, etc.) asks the kernel to read a section of a file and copy the data into the calling process address space. If all of the requested data is in the page cache, the kernel will copy it and return immediately; otherwise, it will arrange for the disk to read the requested data into the page cache, block the calling thread, and when the data is available, it will resume the thread and copy the data. A write, on the other hand, will usually[1] just copy the data into the page cache; the kernel will write back the page cache to disk some time afterward.

mmap

An alternative and more modern method is to memory-map the file into the application address space using the mmap(2) system call. This causes a section of the address space to refer directly to the page cache pages that contain the file's data. After this preparatory step, the application can access file data using the processor's memory read and memory write instructions. If the requested data happens to be in cache, the kernel is completely bypassed and the read (or write) is performed at memory speed. If a cache miss occurs, then a page-fault happens and the kernel puts the active thread to sleep while it goes off to read the data for that page. When the data is finally available, the memory-management unit is programmed so the newly read data is accessible to the thread, which is then awoken.

Direct I/O (DIO)

Both traditional read/write and mmap involve the kernel page cache and defer the scheduling of I/O to the kernel. When the application wants to schedule I/O itself (for reasons that we will explain later), it can use Direct I/O, as shown in Figure 3-4. This involves opening the file with the O_DIRECT flag; further activity will use the normal read and write family of system calls. However, their behavior is now altered: Instead of accessing the cache, the disk is accessed directly, which means that the calling thread will be put to sleep unconditionally. Furthermore, the disk controller will copy the data directly to userspace, bypassing the kernel.

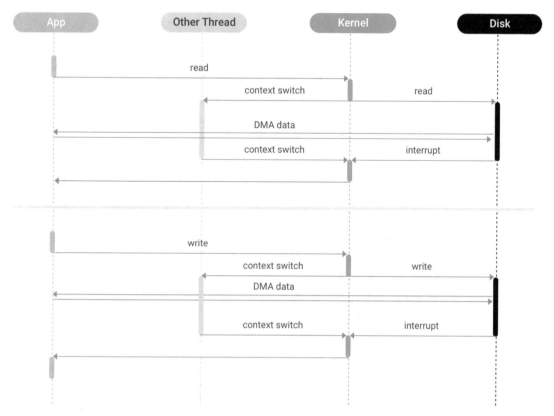

Figure 3-4. *Direct I/O involves opening the file with the O_DIRECT flag; further activity will use the normal read and write family of system calls, but their behavior is now altered*

Asynchronous I/O (AIO/DIO)

A refinement of Direct I/O, Asynchronous Direct I/O, behaves similarly but prevents the calling thread from blocking (see Figure 3-5). Instead, the application thread schedules Direct I/O operations using the io_submit(2) system call, but the thread is not blocked; the I/O operation runs in parallel with normal thread execution. A separate system call, io_getevents(2), waits for and collects the results of completed I/O operations. Like DIO, the kernel's page cache is bypassed, and the disk controller is responsible for copying the data directly to userspace.

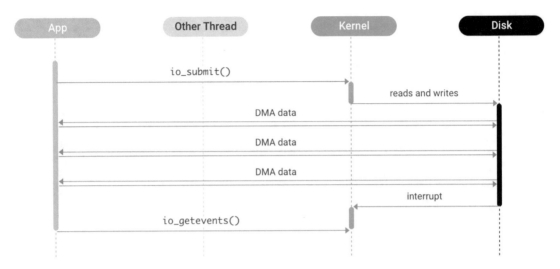

Figure 3-5. *A refinement of Direct I/O, Asynchronous Direct I/O behaves similarly but prevents the calling thread from blocking*

Note: io_uring   The API to perform asynchronous I/O appeared in Linux long ago, and it was warmly met by the community. However, as it often happens, real-world usage quickly revealed many inefficiencies, such as blocking under some circumstances (despite the name), the need to call the kernel too often, and poor support for canceling the submitted requests. Eventually, it became clear that the updated requirements were not compatible with the existing API and the need for a new one arose.

This is how the io_uring() API appeared. It provides the same facilities as AIO does, but in a much more convenient and performant way (it also has notably better documentation). Without diving into implementation details, let's just say that it exists and is preferred over the legacy AIO.

Understanding the Tradeoffs

The different access methods share some characteristics and differ in others. Table 3-1 summarizes these characteristics, which are discussed further in this section.

Table 3-1. *Comparing Different I/O Access Methods*

Characteristic	R/W	mmap	DIO	AIO/DIO
Cache control	Kernel	Kernel	User	User
Copying	Yes	No	No	No
MMU activity	Low	High	None	None
I/O scheduling	Kernel	Kernel	Mixed	User
Thread scheduling	Kernel	Kernel	Kernel	User
I/O alignment	Automatic	Automatic	Manual	Manual
Application complexity	Low	Low	Moderate	High

Copying and MMU Activity

One of the benefits of the mmap method is that if the data is in cache, then the kernel is bypassed completely. The kernel does not need to copy data from the kernel to userspace and back, so fewer processor cycles are spent on that activity. This benefits workloads that are mostly in cache (for example, if the ratio of storage size to RAM size is close to 1:1).

The downside of mmap, however, occurs when data is not in the cache. This usually happens when the ratio of storage size to RAM size is significantly higher than 1:1. Every page that is brought into the cache causes another page to be evicted. Those pages have to be inserted into and removed from the page tables; the kernel has to scan the page tables to isolate inactive pages, making them candidates for eviction, and so forth. In addition, mmap requires memory for the page tables. On x86 processors, this requires 0.2 percent of the size of the mapped files. This seems low, but if the application has a 100:1 ratio of storage to memory, the result is that 20 percent of memory (0.2% * 100) is devoted to page tables.

I/O Scheduling

One of the problems with letting the kernel control caching (with the mmap and read/write access methods) is that the application loses control of I/O scheduling. The kernel picks whichever block of data it deems appropriate and schedules it for write or read. This can result in the following problems:

- **A write storm.** When the kernel schedules large amounts of writes, the disk will be busy for a long while and impact read latency.

- **The kernel cannot distinguish between "important" and "unimportant" I/O.** I/O belonging to background tasks can overwhelm foreground tasks, impacting their latency[2]

By bypassing the kernel page cache, the application takes on the burden of scheduling I/O. This doesn't mean that the problems are solved, but it does mean that the problems *can* be solved—with sufficient attention and effort.

When using Direct I/O, each thread controls when to issue I/O. However, the kernel controls when the thread runs, so responsibility for issuing I/O is shared between the kernel and the application. With AIO/DIO, the application is in full control of when I/O is issued.

Thread Scheduling

An I/O intensive application using mmap or read/write cannot guess what its cache hit rate will be. Therefore, it has to run a large number of threads (significantly larger than the core count of the machine it is running on). Using too few threads, they may all be waiting for the disk leaving the processor underutilized. Since each thread usually has at most one disk I/O outstanding, the number of running threads must be around the concurrency of the storage subsystem multiplied by some small factor in order to keep the disk fully occupied. However, if the cache hit rate is sufficiently high, then these large numbers of threads will contend with each other for the limited number of cores.

When using Direct I/O, this problem is somewhat mitigated. The application knows exactly when a thread is blocked on I/O and when it can run, so the application can adjust the number of running threads according to runtime conditions.

With AIO/DIO, the application has full control over both running threads and waiting I/O (the two are completely divorced), so it can easily adjust to in-memory or disk-bound conditions or anything in between.

I/O Alignment

Storage devices have a block size; all I/O must be performed in multiples of this block size which is typically 512 or 4096 bytes. Using read/write or mmap, the kernel performs the alignment automatically; a small read or write is expanded to the correct block boundary by the kernel before it is issued.

With DIO, it is up to the application to perform block alignment. This incurs some complexity, but also provides an advantage: The kernel will usually over-align to a 4096 byte boundary even when a 512-byte boundary suffices. However, a user application using DIO can issue 512-byte aligned reads, which results in saving bandwidth on small items.

Application Complexity

While the previous discussions favored AIO/DIO for I/O intensive applications, that method comes with a significant cost: complexity. Placing the responsibility of cache management on the application means it can make better choices than the kernel and make those choices with less overhead. However, those algorithms need to be written and tested. Using asynchronous I/O requires that the application is written using callbacks, coroutines, or a similar method, and often reduces the reusability of many available libraries.

Choosing the Filesystem and/or Disk

Beyond performing the I/O itself, the database design must consider the medium against which this I/O is done. In many cases, the choice is often between a filesystem or a raw block device, which in turn can be a choice of a traditional spinning disk or an SSD drive. In cloud environments, however, there can be the third option because local drives are always ephemeral—which imposes strict requirements on the replication.

Filesystems vs Raw Disks

This decision can be approached from two angles: management costs and performance.

If you're accessing the storage as a raw block device, all the difficulties with block allocation and reclamation are on the application side. We touched on this topic slightly earlier when we talked about memory management. The same set of challenges apply to RAM as well as disks.

A connected, though very different, challenge is providing data integrity in case of crashes. Unless the database is purely in-memory, the I/O should be done in a way that avoids losing data or reading garbage from disk after a restart. Modern filesystems, however, provide both and are very mature to trust the efficiency of allocations and integrity of data. Accessing raw block devices unfortunately lacks those features (so they need to be implemented at the same quality on the application side).

From the performance point of view, the difference is not that drastic. On one hand, writing data to a file is always accompanied by associated metadata updates. This consumes both disk space and I/O bandwidth. However, some modern filesystems provide a very good balance of performance and efficiency, almost eliminating the I/O latency. (One of the most prominent examples is XFS. Another really good and mature piece of software is Ext4). The great ally in this camp is the `fallocate(2)` system call that makes the filesystem preallocate space on disk. When used, filesystems also have a chance to make full use of the extents mechanisms, thus bringing the QoS of using files to the same performance level as when using raw block devices.

Appending Writes

The database may have a heavy reliance on appends to files or require in-place updates of individual file blocks. Both approaches need special attention from the system architect because they call for different properties from the underlying system.

On one hand, appending writes requires careful interaction with the filesystem so that metadata updates (file size, in particular) do not dominate the regular I/O. On the other hand, appending writes (being sort of cache-oblivious algorithms) handle the disk overwriting difficulties in a natural manner. Contrary to this, in-place updates cannot happen at random offsets and sizes because disks may not tolerate this kind of workload, even if they're used in a raw block device manner (not via a filesystem).

That being said, let's dive even deeper into the stack and descend into the hardware level.

How Modern SSDs Work

Like other computational resources, disks are limited in the speed they can provide. This speed is typically measured as a two-dimensional value with *Input/Output Operations per Second* (IOPS) and *bytes per second* (throughput). Of course, these parameters are not cut in stone even for each particular disk, and the maximum number of requests or bytes greatly depends on the requests' distribution, queuing and concurrency, buffering or caching, disk age, and many other factors. So when performing I/O, a disk must always balance between two inefficiencies—overwhelming the disk with requests and underutilizing it.

Overwhelming the disk should be avoided because when the disk is full of requests it cannot distinguish between the criticality of certain requests over others. Of course, all requests are important, but it makes sense to prioritize latency-sensitive requests. For example, ScyllaDB serves real-time queries that need to be completed in single-digit milliseconds or less and, in parallel, it processes terabytes of data for compaction, streaming, decommission, and so forth. The former have strong latency sensitivity; the latter are less so. Good I/O maintenance that tries to maximize the I/O bandwidth while keeping latency as low as possible for latency-sensitive tasks is complicated enough to become a standalone component called the *I/O Scheduler*.

When evaluating a disk, you would most likely be looking at its four parameters—read/write IOPS and read/write throughput (such as in MB/s). Comparing these numbers to one another is a popular way of claiming one disk is better than the other and estimating the aforementioned "bandwidth capacity" of the drive by applying Little's Law. With that, the I/O Scheduler's job is to provide a certain level of concurrency inside the disk to get maximum bandwidth from it, but not to make this concurrency too high in order to prevent the disk from queueing requests internally for longer than needed.

For instance, Figure 3-6 illustrates how read request latency depends on the intensity of small reads (challenging disk IOPS capacity) vs the intensity of large writes (pursuing the disk bandwidth). The latency value is color-coded, and the "interesting area" is painted in cyan—this is where the latency stays below 1 millisecond. The drive measured is the NVMe disk that comes with the AWS EC2 i3en.3xlarge instance.

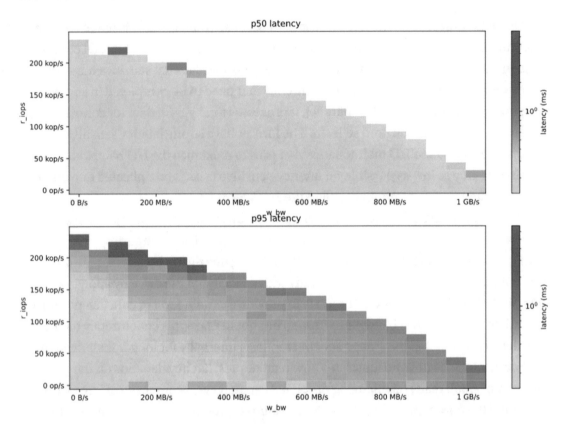

Figure 3-6. *Bandwidth/latency graphs showing how read request latency depends on the intensity of small reads (challenging disk IOPS capacity) vs the intensity of large writes (pursuing the disk bandwidth)*

This drive demonstrates almost perfect half-duplex behavior—increasing the read intensity several times requires roughly the same reduction in write intensity to keep the disk operating at the same speed.

Tip: How to Measure Your Own Disk Behavior Under Load   The better you understand how your own disks perform under load, the better you can tune them to capitalize on their "sweet spot." One way to do this is with Diskplorer,[4] an open-source disk latency/bandwidth exploring toolset. By using Linux fio under the hood

---

[4] You can access Diskplorer at `https://github.com/scylladb/diskplorer`. This project contains instructions on how to generate a graph of your own.

it runs a battery of measurements to discover performance characteristics for a specific hardware configuration, giving you an at-a-glance view of how server storage I/O will behave under load.

For a walkthrough of how to use this tool, see the Linux Foundation video, "Understanding Storage I/O Under Load."[5]

Networking

The conventional networking functionality available in Linux is remarkably full-featured, mature, and performant. Since the database rarely imposes severe per-ping latency requirements, there are very few surprises that come from it when properly configured and used. Nonetheless, some considerations still need to be made.

As explained by David Ahern, "Linux will process a fair amount of packets in the context of whatever is running on the CPU at the moment the IRQ is handled. System accounting will attribute those CPU cycles to any process running at that moment even though that process is not doing any work on its behalf. For example, 'top' can show a process that appears to be using 99+% CPU, but in reality, 60 percent of that time is spent processing packets—meaning the process is really only getting 40 percent of the CPU to make progress on its workload."[6]

However, for truly networking-intensive applications, the Linux stack is constrained:

- **Kernel space implementation:** Separation of the network stack into kernel space means that costly context switches are needed to perform network operations, and that data copies must be performed to transfer data from kernel buffers to user buffers and vice versa.

- **Time sharing:** Linux is a time-sharing system, and so must rely on slow, expensive interrupts to notify the kernel that there are new packets to be processed.

---

[5] Watch the video on YouTube (www.youtube.com/watch?v=Am-nXO6KK58).

[6] For the source and additional detail, see David Ahern's, "The CPU Cost of Networking on a Host" (https://people.kernel.org/dsahern/the-cpu-cost-of-networking-on-a-host).

- **Threaded model:** The Linux kernel is heavily threaded, so all data structures are protected with locks. While a huge effort has made Linux very scalable, this is not without limitations and contention occurs at large core counts. Even without contention, the locking primitives themselves are relatively slow and impact networking performance.

As before, the way to overcome this limitation is to move the packet processing to the userspace. There are plenty of out-of-kernel implementations of the TCP algorithm that are worth considering.

DPDK

One of the generic approaches that's often referred to in the networking area is the poll mode vs interrupt model. When a packet arrives, the system may have two options for how to get informed—set up and interrupt from the hardware (or, in the case of the userspace implementation, from the kernel file descriptor using the *poll* family of system calls) or keep polling the network card on its own from time to time until the packet is noticed.

The famous userspace network toolkit, called *DPDK*, is designed specifically for fast packet processing, usually in fewer than 80 CPU cycles per packet.[7] It integrates seamlessly with Linux in order to take advantage of high-performance hardware.

IRQ Binding

As stated earlier, packet processing may take up to 60 percent of the CPU time, which is way too much. This percentage leaves too few CPU ticks for the database work itself. Even though in this case the backpressure mechanism would most likely keep the external activity off and the system would likely find its balance, the resulting system throughput would likely be unacceptable.

System architects may consider the non-symmetrical CPU approach to mitigate this. If you're letting the Linux kernel process network packets, there are several ways to localize this processing on separate CPUs.

---

[7] For details, see the Linux Foundation's page on DPDK (Data Plane Developers Kit) at www.dpdk.org.

The simplest way is to bind the IRQ processing from the NIC to specific cores or hyper-threads. Linux uses two-step processing of incoming packets called IRQ and soft-IRQ. If the IRQs are properly bound to cores, the soft-IRQ also happens on those cores—thus completely localizing the processing.

For huge-scale nodes running tens to hundred(s) of cores, the number of network-only cores may become literally more than one. In this case, it might make sense to localize processing even further by assigning cores from different NUMA nodes and teaching the NIC to balance the traffic between those using the receive packet steering facility of the Linux kernel.

Summary

This chapter introduced a number of ways that database engineering decisions enable database users to squeeze more power out of modern infrastructure. For CPUs, the chapter talked about taking advantage of multicore servers by limiting resource sharing across cores and using future-promise design to coordinate work across cores. The chapter also provided a specific example of how low-level CPU architecture has direct implications on the database.

Moving on to memory, you read about two related but independent subsystems: memory allocation and cache control. For I/O, the chapter discussed Linux options such as traditional read/write, mmap, Direct I/O (DIO) read/write, and Asynchronous I/O—including the various tradeoffs of each. This was followed by a deep dive into how modern SSDs work and how a database can take advantage of a drive's unique characteristics. Finally, you looked at constraints associated with the Linux networking stack and explored alternatives such as DPDK and IRQ binding. The next chapter shifts the focus from hardware interactions to algorithmic optimizations: pure software challenges.

CHAPTER 4

Database Internals: Algorithmic Optimizations

In the performance world, the hardware is always the unbreakable limiting factor—one cannot squeeze more performing units from a system than the underlying chips may provide. As opposed to that, the software part of the system is often considered the most flexible thing in programming—in the sense that it can be changed at any time given enough developers' brains and hands (and investors' cash).

However, that's not always the case. Sometimes selecting an algorithm should be done as early as the architecting stage in the most careful manner possible because the chosen approach becomes so extremely fundamental that changing it would effectively mean rewriting the whole engine from scratch or requiring users to migrate exabytes of data from one instance to another.

This chapter shares one detailed example of algorithmic optimization—from the perspective of the engineer who led this optimization. Specifically, this chapter looks at how the B-trees family can be used to store data in cache implementations and other accessory and in-memory structures. This look into a representative engineering challenge should help you better understand what tradeoffs or optimizations various databases might be making under the hood—ideally, so you can take better advantage of its very deliberate design decisions.[1]

Note   The goal of this chapter is *not* to convince database users that they need a database with any particular algorithmic optimization—or to educate infrastructure engineers on designing B-trees or the finer points of algorithmic optimization. Rather, it's to help anyone selecting or working with a database understand the

---

[1] This chapter draws from material originally published on the ScyllaDB blog (`www.scylladb.com/blog`). It is used here with permission of ScyllaDB.

© Felipe Cardeneti Mendes, Piotr Sarna, Pavel Emelyanov, Cynthia Dunlop 2023
F. C. Mendes et al., *Database Performance at Scale*, https://doi.org/10.1007/978-1-4842-9711-7_4

level of algorithmic optimization that might impact a database's performance. Hopefully, it piques your curiosity in learning more about the engineering behind the database you're using and/or alternative databases you're considering.

Optimizing Collections

Maintaining large sets of objects in memory deserves the same level of attention as maintaining objects in external memory—say, spinning disks or network-attached storages. For a task as simple as looking up an object by a plain key, the acceptable solution is often a plain hash table (even with great attention to hash function selection) or a binary balanced tree (usually the red-black one due to its implementation simplicity). However, branchy trees like the B-trees family can significantly boost performance. They also have a lot of non-obvious pitfalls.

To B- or Not to B-Tree

An important characteristic of a tree is *cardinality*. This is the maximum number of child nodes that another node may have. In the corner case of cardinality of two, the tree is called a *binary* tree. For other cases, there's a wide class of so-called B-trees. The common belief about binary vs B-trees is that the former ones should be used when the data is stored in the RAM, while the latter trees should live in the disk. The justification for this split is that RAM access speed is much higher than disk. Also, disk I/O is performed in blocks, so it's much better and faster to fetch several "adjacent" keys in one request. RAM, unlike disks, allows random access with almost any granularity, so it's okay to have a dispersed set of keys pointing to each other.

However, there are many reasons that B-trees are often a good choice for in-memory collections. The first reason is cache *locality*. When searching for a key in a binary tree, the algorithm would visit up to *logN* elements that are very likely dispersed in memory. On a B-tree, this search will consist of two *phases*—an intra-node search and descending the tree—executed one after another. And while descending the tree doesn't differ much from the binary tree in the aforementioned sense, intra-node searching will access keys that are located next to each other, thus making much better use of CPU caches. Figure 4-1 exemplifies the process of walking down a binary tree. Compare it along with Figure 4-2, which demonstrates a search in a B-tree set.

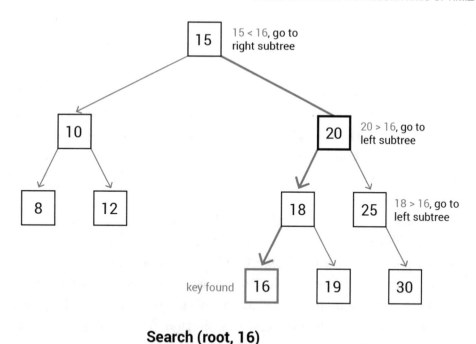

Search (root, 16)

Figure 4-1. *Searching in a binary tree root*

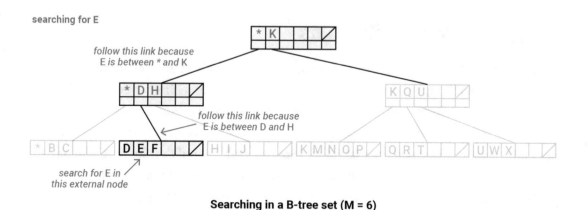

Searching in a B-tree set (M = 6)

Figure 4-2. *Searching in a B-tree set*

The second reason that B-trees are often a good choice for in-memory collections also comes from the dispersed nature of binary trees and from how modern CPUs are designed. It's well known that when executing a stream of instructions, CPU cores split the processing of each instruction into stages (loading instructions, decoding them, preparing arguments, and doing the execution itself) and the stages are run in parallel in a unit called a *conveyor*. When a conditional branching instruction appears in this stream, the conveyor needs to guess which of two potential branches it will have to execute next and start loading it into the conveyor pipeline. If this guess fails, the conveyor is flushed and starts to work from scratch. Such failures are called *branch mispredictions*. They are harmful from a performance point of view[2] and have direct implications on the binary search algorithm. When searching for a key in such a tree, the algorithm jumps left and right depending on the key comparison result without giving the CPU a chance to learn which direction is "preferred." In many cases, the CPU conveyor is flushed.

The two-phased B-tree search can be made better with respect to branch predictions. The trick is in making the intra-node search linear (i.e., walking the array of keys forward key-by-key). In this case, there will be only a "should you move forward" condition that's much more predictable. There's even a nice trick of turning binary search into linear without sacrificing the number of comparisons,[3] but this approach is good for read-mostly collections because insertion into this layout is tricky and has worse complexity than for sorted arrays. This approach has proven itself in ScyllaDB's implementation and is also widely used in the Tarantool in-memory database.[4]

Linear Search on Steroids

That linear search can be improved a bit more. Let's carefully count the number of key comparisons that it may take to find a single key in a tree. For a binary tree, it's well known that it takes log_2N comparisons (on average) where N is the number of elements. We put the logarithm base here for a reason. Next, consider a k-ary tree with k children per node. Does it take fewer comparisons? (Spoiler: no). To find the element, you have to do the same search—get a node, find in which branch it sits, then proceed to it. You have log_kN levels in the tree, so you have to do that many descending steps. However on each step, you need to do the search within k elements, which is, again, log_2k if you're doing a binary search. Multiplying both, you still need at least log_2N comparisons.

---

[2] See Marek Majkowski's blog, "Branch predictor: How many 'if's are too many? Including x86 and M1 benchmarks!" https://blog.cloudflare.com/branch-predictor/.

[3] See the tutorial, "Eytzinger Binary Search" https://algorithmica.org/en/eytzinger.

[4] Both are available as open-source software; see https://github.com/scylladb/scylladb and https://github.com/tarantool/tarantool.

The way to reduce this number is to compare more than one key at a time when doing intra-node searches. In case the keys are small enough, SIMD instructions can compare up to 64 keys in one go. Although a SIMD compare instruction may be slower than a classic cmp one and requires additional instructions to process the comparison mask, linear SIMD-powered search wins on short enough arrays (and B-tree nodes can be short enough). For example, Figure 4-3 shows the times of looking up an integer in a sorted array using three techniques—linear search, binary search, and SIMD-optimized linear search such as the x86 Advanced Vector Extensions (AVX).

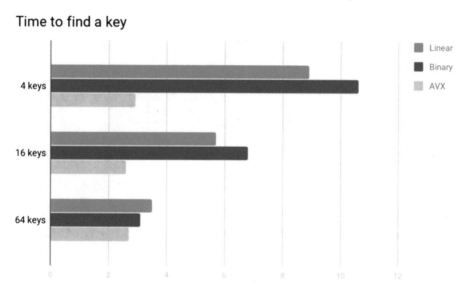

Figure 4-3. *The test used a large amount of randomly generated arrays of values dispersed in memory to eliminate differences in cache usage and a large amount of random search keys to blur branch predictions. These are the average times of finding a key in an array normalized by the array length. Smaller results are faster (better)*

Scanning the Tree

One interesting flavor of B-trees is called a B+-tree. In this tree, there are two kinds of keys—*real* keys and *separation* keys. The real keys live on leaf nodes (i.e., on those that don't have children), while separation keys sit on inner nodes and are used to select which branch to go next when descending the tree. This difference has an obvious consequence that it takes more memory to keep the same amount of keys in a B+-tree as compared to B-tree. But it's not only that.

A great implicit feature of a tree is the ability to iterate over elements in a sorted manner (called a *scan*). To scan a classical B-tree, there are both recursive and state-machine algorithms that process the keys in a very non-uniform manner—the algorithm walks up-and-down the tree while it moves. Despite B-trees being described as cache-friendly, scanning them requires visiting every single node and inner nodes are visited in a cache unfriendly manner. Figure 4-4 illustrates this phenomenon.

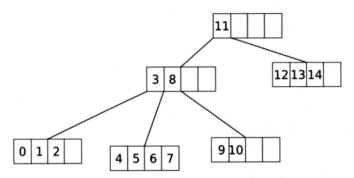

Figure 4-4. *Scanning a classical B-tree involves walking up and down the tree; every node and inner node is visited*

As opposed to this, B+-trees' scan only needs to loop through its leaf nodes, which, with some additional effort, can be implemented as a linear scan over a linked list of arrays, as demonstrated in Figure 4-5.

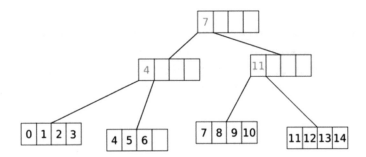

Figure 4-5. *B+ tree scans only need to cover leaf nodes*

When the Tree Size Matters

Talking about memory, B-trees don't provide all these benefits for free (neither do B+-trees). As the tree grows, so does the number of nodes in it and it's useful to consider the overhead needed to store a single key. For a binary tree, the overhead is three pointers—to both left and right children as well as to the parent node. For a B-tree, it will differ for inner and leaf nodes. For both types, the overhead is one parent pointer and k pointers to keys, even if they are not inserted in the tree. For inner nodes there will additionally be $k+1$ pointers to child nodes.

The number of nodes in a B-tree is easy to estimate for a large number of keys. As the number of nodes grows, the per-key overhead blurs as keys "share" parent and children pointers. However, there's a very interesting point at the beginning of a tree's growth. When the number of keys becomes $k+1$ (i.e., the tree overgrows its first leaf node), the number of nodes jumps three times because, in this case, it's needed to allocate one more leaf node and one inner node to link those two.

There is a good and pretty cheap optimization to mitigate this spike, called "linear root." The leaf root node grows on demand, doubling each step like a std::vector in C++, and can overgrow the capacity of k up to some extent. Figure 4-6 shows the per-key overhead for a 4-ary B-tree with 50 percent initial overgrowth. Note the first split spike of a classical algorithm at five keys.

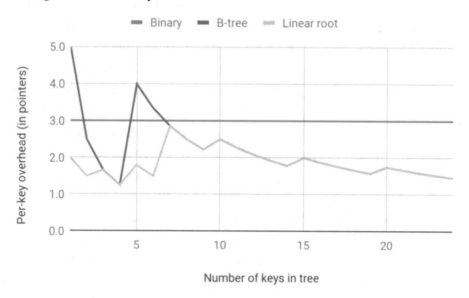

Figure 4-6. *The per-key overhead for a 4-ary B-tree with 50 percent initial overgrowth*

When discussing how B-trees work with small amounts of keys, it's worth mentioning the corner case of one key. In ScyllaDB, a B-tree is used to store sorted rows inside a block of rows called a partition. Since it's possible to have a schema where each partition always has a single row, this corner case is not that "corner" for us. In the case of a binary tree, the single-element tree is equivalent to having a direct pointer from the tree owner to this element (plus the cost of two nil pointers to the left and right children). In case of a B-tree, the cost of keeping the single key is always in having a root node that implies extra pointer fetching to access this key. Even the linear root optimization is helpless here. Fixing this corner case was possible by reusing the pointer to the root node to point directly to the single key.

The Secret Life of Separation Keys

This section dives into technical details of B+-tree implementation.

There are two ways of managing separation keys in a B+-tree. The separation key at any level must be less than or equal to *all* the keys from its right subtree and greater than or equal to all the keys from its left subtree. Mind the "or" condition—the exact value of the separation key *may **or** may not* coincide with the value of some key from the respective branch (it's clear that this *some* will be the rightmost key on the left branch or leftmost on the right). Let's look at these two cases. If the tree balancing maintains the separation key to be independent from other key values, then it's the *light* mode; if it must coincide with some of them, then it will be called the *strict* mode.

In the light separation mode, the insertion and removal operations are a bit faster because they don't need to care about separation keys that much. It's enough if they separate branches, and that's it. A somewhat worse consequence of the light separation is that separation keys are separate values that may appear in the tree by copying existing keys. If the key is simple, (e.g., an integer), this will likely not cause any trouble. However, if keys are strings or, as in ScyllaDB's case, database partition or clustering keys, copying it might be both resource consuming and out-of-memory risky.

On the other hand, the strict separation mode makes it possible to avoid key copying by implementing separation keys as references on real ones. This would involve some complication of insertion and especially removal operations. In particular, upon real key removal, it will be necessary to find and update the relevant separation keys. Another difficulty to care about is that moving a real key value in memory, if it's needed (e.g., in ScyllaDB's case keys are moved in memory as a part of memory defragmentation hygiene), will also need to update the relevant reference from separation keys. However, it's possible to show that each real key will be referenced by at most one separation key.

Speaking about memory consumption, although large B-trees were shown to consume less memory per-key as they get filled, the real overhead would very likely be larger, since the nodes of the tree will typically be underfilled because of the way the balancing algorithm works. For example, Figures 4-7 and 4-8 show how nodes look in a randomly filled 4-ary B-tree.

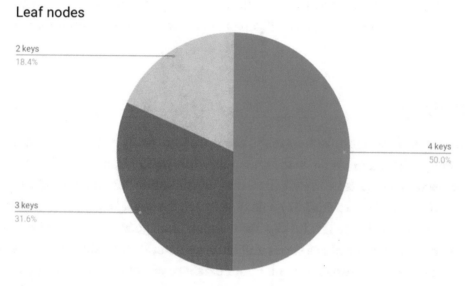

Figure 4-7. *Distribution of number of keys in a node for leaf nodes*

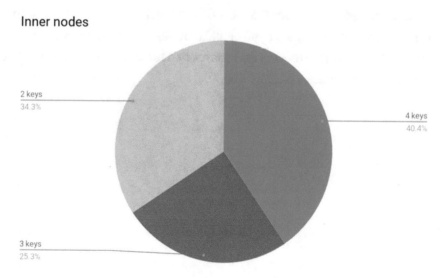

Figure 4-8. *Distribution of number of keys in a node for inner nodes*

It's possible to define a compaction operation for a B-tree that will pick several adjacent nodes and squash them together, but this operation has its limitations. First, a certain amount of underoccupied nodes makes it possible to insert a new element into a tree without the need to rebalance, thus saving CPU cycles. Second, since each node cannot contain less than a half of its capacity, squashing two adjacent nodes is impossible. Even if considering three adjacent nodes, then the amount of really squashable nodes would be less than 5 percent of the leaves and less than 1 percent of the inners.

Summary

As extensive as these optimizations might seem, they are really just the tip of the iceberg for this one particular example. Many finer points that matter from an engineering perspective were skipped for brevity (for example, the subtle difference in odd vs even number of keys on a node). For a database user, the key takeaway here is that an excruciating level of design and experimentation often goes into the software for determining how your database stores and retrieves data. You certainly don't need to be this familiar with every aspect of how your database was engineered. But knowing what algorithmic optimizations your database has focused on will help you understand why it performs in certain ways under different contexts. And you might discover some impressively engineered capabilities that could help you handle more user requests or shave a few precious milliseconds off your P99 latencies. The next chapter takes you into the inner workings of database drivers and shares tips for getting the most out of a driver, particularly from a performance perspective.

CHAPTER 5

Database Drivers

Databases usually expose a specific communication protocol for their users. This protocol is the foundation of communication between clients and servers, so it's often well-documented and has a formal specification. Some databases, like PostgreSQL, implement their own binary format on top of the TCP/IP stack.[1] Others, like Amazon DynamoDB,[2] build theirs on top of HTTP, which is a little more verbose, but also more versatile and compatible with web browsers. It's also not uncommon to see a database exposing a protocol based on gRPC[3] or any other well-established framework.

Regardless of the implementation details, users seldom use the bare protocol themselves because it's usually a fairly low-level API. What's used instead is a *driver*—a programming interface written in a particular language, implementing a higher-level abstraction for communicating with the database. Drivers hide all the nitty-gritty details behind a convenient interface, which saves users from having to manually handle connection management, parsing, validation, handshakes, authentication, timeouts, retries, and so on.

In a distributed environment (which a scalable database cluster usually is), clients, and therefore drivers, are an extremely important part of the ecosystem. The clients are usually the most numerous group of actors in the system, and they are also very heterogeneous in nature, as visualized in Figure 5-1. Some clients are connected via local network interfaces, other ones connect via a questionable Wi-Fi hotspot on another continent and thus have vastly different latency characteristics and error rates. Some might run on microcontrollers with 1MiB of random access memory, while others utilize 128-core bare metal machines from a cloud provider. Due to this diversity, it's

---

[1] See the PostgreSQL documentation (`https://www.postgresql.org/docs/7.3/protocol-protocol.html`).

[2] See the DynamoDB Developer Guide on the DynamoDB API (`https://docs.aws.amazon.com/amazondynamodb/latest/developerguide/HowItWorks.API.html`).

[3] gRPC is "a high performance, open-source universal RPC framework;" see `https://grpc.io` for details.

F. C. Mendes et al., *Database Performance at Scale*, https://doi.org/10.1007/978-1-4842-9711-7_5

very important to take drivers into consideration when thinking about performance, scalability, and resilience to failures. Ultimately it's the drivers that generate traffic and its concurrency, so cooperation between them and database nodes is crucial for the whole system to be healthy and efficient.

Note   As a reminder, *concurrency*, in the context of this book, is the measure of how many operations are performed at the same point in time. It's conceptually similar to parallelism. With concurrency, the operations occur physically at the same time (e.g. on multiple CPU cores or multiple machines). Parallelism does not specify that; the operations might just as well be executed in small steps on a single machine. Nowadays, distributed systems must rely on providing high concurrency in order to remain competitive and catch up with ever-developing technology.

This chapter takes a look at how drivers impact performance—through the eyes of someone who has engineered drivers for performance. It provides insight into various ways that drivers can support efficient client-server interactions and shares tips for getting the most out of a driver, particularly from the performance perspective. Finally, the chapter wraps up with several considerations to keep in mind as you're selecting a driver.

Relationship Between Clients and Servers

Scalability is a measure of how well your system reacts to increased load. This load is usually generated by clients using their drivers, so keeping the relationship between your clients and servers sound is an important matter. The more you know about your workloads, your clients' behavior, and their usage patterns, the better you're prepared to handle both sudden spikes in traffic and sustained, long-term growth in usage.

Each client is different and should be treated as such. The differences come both from clients' characteristics, like their number and volume, and from their requirements. Some clients have strict latency guarantees, even at the cost of higher error rates. Others do not particularly care about the latency of any single database query, but just want a steady pace of progress in their long-standing queries. Some databases target specific types of clients (e.g., analytical databases which expect clients processing large aggregate queries operating on huge volumes of historical data). Other ones strive to be universal, handling all kinds of clients and balancing the load so that everyone is happy (or, more precisely, "happy enough").

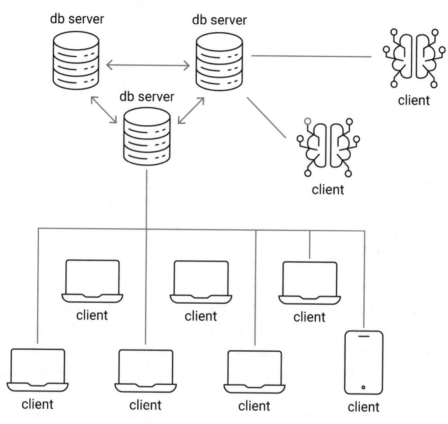

Figure 5-1. *Visualization of clients and servers in a distributed system*

Workload Types

There are multiple ways of classifying database clients. One particularly interesting way is to delineate between clients processing interactive and batch (e.g., analytical) workloads, also known as OLTP (online transaction processing) vs OLAP (online analytical processing)—see Figure 5-2.

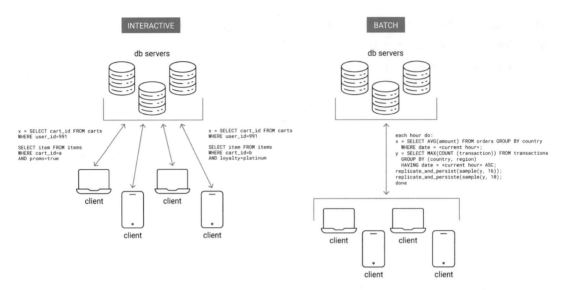

Figure 5-2. *Difference between interactive and batch (analytical) workloads*

Interactive Workloads

A client processing an interactive workload typically wants certain latency guarantees. Receiving a response fast is more important than ensuring that the query succeeded. In other words, it's better to return an error in a timely manner than make the client indefinitely wait for the correct response. Such workloads are often characterized by unbounded concurrency, which means that the number of in-progress operations is hard to predict.

A prime example of an interactive workload is a server handling requests from web browsers. Imagine an online game, where players interact with the system straight from their favorite browsers. High latency for such a player means a poor user experience because people tend to despise waiting for online content for more than a few hundred milliseconds; with multi-second delays, most will just ditch the game as unusable and try something else. It's therefore particularly important to be as interactive as possible and return the results quickly—even if the result happens to be a temporary error. In such a scenario, the concurrency of clients varies and is out of control for the database. Sometimes there might be a large influx of players, and the database might need to refuse some of them to avoid overload.

Batch (Analytical) Workloads

A batch (analytical) workload is the conceptual opposite of an interactive one. With such workloads, it doesn't matter whether any single request is processed in a few milliseconds or hours. The important thing is that the processing makes steady progress with a satisfactory error rate, which is ideally zero. Batch workloads tend to have fixed concurrency, which makes it easier for the database to keep the load under control.

A good example of a batch workload is an Apache Spark[4] job performing analytics on a big dataset (think terabytes). There are only a few connections established to the database, and they continuously send requests in order to fetch data for long computations. Because the concurrency is predictable, the database can easily respond to an increased load by applying backpressure (e.g., by delaying the responses a little bit). The analytical processing will simply slow down, adjusting its speed according to the speed at which the database can consume queries.

Mixed Workloads

Certain workloads cannot be easily qualified as fully interactive or fully batch. The clients are free to intermix their requirements, concurrency, and load however they please—so the databases should also be ready for surprises. For example, a batch workload might suddenly experience a giant temporary spike in concurrency. Databases should, on the one hand, maintain a level of trust in the workload's typical patterns, but on the other hand anticipate that workloads can simply change over time—due to bugs, hardware changes, or simply because the use case has diverged from its original goal.

Throughput vs Goodput

A healthy distributed database cluster is characterized by stable goodput, not throughput. *Goodput* is an interesting portmanteau of good + throughput, and it's a measure of *useful* data being transferred between clients and servers over the network, as opposed to just any data. Goodput disregards errors and other churn-like redundant retries, and is used to judge how effective the communication actually is.

This distinction is important.

---

[4]Apache Spark is "multi-language engine for executing data engineering, data science, and machine learning on single-node machines or clusters." For details, see https://spark.apache.org/.

Imagine an extreme case of an overloaded node that keeps returning errors for each incoming request. Even though stable and sustainable throughput can be observed, this database brings no value to the end-user. Thus, it's essential to track how much useful data can be delivered in an acceptable time. For example, this can be achieved by tracking both the total throughput and throughput spent on sending back error messages and then subtracting one from another to see how much valid data was transferred (see Figure 5-3).

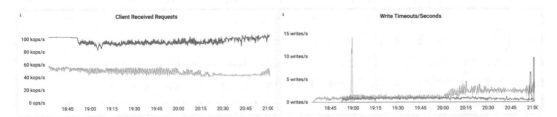

Figure 5-3. *Note how a fraction of the throughput times out, effectively requiring more work from clients to achieve goodput*

Maximizing goodput is a delicate operation and it heavily depends on the infrastructure, workload type, clients' behavior, and many other factors. In some cases, the database shedding load might be beneficial for the entire system. *Shedding* is a rather radical measure of dealing with overload: Requests qualified as "risky" are simply ignored by the server, or immediately terminated with an error. This type of overload protection is especially useful against issues induced by interactive workloads with unbounded concurrency (there's not much a database can do to protect itself except drop some of the incoming requests early).

The database server isn't an oracle; it can't accurately predict whether a request is going to fail due to overload, so it must guess. Fortunately, there are quite a few ways of making that guess educated:

- Shedding load if X requests are already being processed, where X is the estimated maximum a database node can handle.

- Refusing a request if its estimated memory usage is larger than the database could handle at the moment.

- Probabilistically refusing a request if Y requests are already being processed, where Y is a percentage of the maximum a database node can handle, with the probability raising to 100 percent once a certain threshold is reached.

- Refusing a request if its estimated execution time indicates that it's not going to finish in time, and instead it is likely to time out anyway.

While refusing clients' requests is detrimental to user experience, sometimes it's simply the lesser of two evils. If dropping a number of requests allows even more requests to successfully finish in time, it increases the cluster's goodput.

Clients can help the database maximize goodput and keep the latency low by declaring for how long the request is considered valid. For instance, in high frequency trading, a request that takes more than a couple of milliseconds is just as good as a request that failed. By letting the database know that's the case, you can allow it to retire some requests early, leaving valuable resources for other requests which still have a chance to be successful. Proper timeout management is a broad topic and it deserves a separate section.

Timeouts

In a distributed system, there are two fundamental types of timeouts that influence one another: client-side timeouts and server-side timeouts. While both are conceptually similar, they have different characteristics. It's vital to properly configure both of them to prevent problems like data races and consistency issues.

Client-Side Timeouts

This type of timeout is generally configured in the database driver. It signifies how long it takes for a driver to decide that a response from a server is not likely to arrive. In a perfect world built on top of a perfect network, all parties always respond to their requests. However, in practice, there are numerous causes for a response to either be late or lost:

- The recipient died

- The recipient is busy with other tasks

- The network failed, maybe due to hardware malfunction

- The network has a significant delay because packets get stuck in an intermediate router

- A software bug caused the packet to be lost

- And so on

Since in a distributed environment it's usually impossible to guess what happened, the client must sometimes decide that a request is lost. The alternative is to wait indefinitely. That might work for a select set of use cases, but it's often simply unacceptable. If a single failed request holds a resource for an unspecified time, the system is eventually doomed to fail. Hence, client-side timeouts are used as a mechanism to make sure that the system can operate even in the event of communication issues.

A unique characteristic of a client-side timeout is that the decision to give up on a request is made solely by the client, in the absence of any feedback from the server. It's entirely possible that the request in question is still being processed and utilizes the server's resources. And, worst of all, the unaware server can happily return the response to the client after it's done processing, even though nobody's interested in this stale data anymore! That presents another aspect of error handling: Drivers must be ready to handle stray, expired responses correctly.

Server-Side Timeouts

A server-side timeout determines when a database node should start considering a particular request as expired. Once this point in time has passed, there is no reason to continue processing the query. (Doing so would waste resources which could have otherwise been used for serving other queries that still have a chance to succeed.) When the specified time has elapsed, databases often return an error indicating that the request took too long.

Using reasonable values for server-side timeouts helps the database manage its priorities in a more precise way, allocating CPU, memory and other scarce resources on queries likely to succeed in a timely manner. Drivers that receive an error indicating that a server-side timeout has occurred should also act accordingly—perhaps by reducing the pressure on a particular node or retrying on another node that hasn't experienced timeouts lately.

A Cautionary Tale

The CQL protocol, which specifies the communication layer in Apache Cassandra and ScyllaDB, comes with built-in support for concurrency. Namely, each request is assigned a stream ID, unique for each connection. This stream ID is encoded as a 16-bit integer with the first bit being reserved by the protocol, which leaves the drivers 32768 unique values for handling in-flight requests per single connection. This stream ID is later used to match an incoming response with its original request. That's not a particularly large number, given that modern systems are known to handle millions of requests per second. Thus, drivers need to eventually reuse previously assigned stream IDs.

But the CQL driver for Python had a bug.[5] In the event of a client-side timeout, it assumed that the stream ID of an expired request was immediately free to reuse. While the assumption holds true if the server dies, it is incorrect if processing simply takes longer than expected. It was therefore possible that once a response with a given stream ID arrived, another request had already reused the stream ID, and the driver would mistakenly match the response with the new request. If the user was lucky, they would simply receive garbage data that did not pass validation. Unfortunately, data from the mismatched response might appear correct, even though it originates from a totally different request. This is the kind of bug that looks innocent at first glance, but may cause people to log in to other people's bank accounts and wreak havoc on their lives.

A rule of thumb for client-side timeouts is to make sure that a server-side timeout also exists and is strictly shorter than the client-side one. It should take into account clock synchronization between clients and servers (or lack thereof), as well as estimated network latency. Such a procedure minimizes the chances for a late response to arrive at all, and thus removes the root cause of many issues and vulnerabilities.

---

[5] Bug report and applied fixes can be found here:
https://datastax-oss.atlassian.net/browse/PYTHON-1286
https://github.com/scylladb/python-driver/pull/106
https://github.com/datastax/python-driver/pull/1114

Contextual Awareness

At this point it should be clear that both servers and clients can make better, more educated, and mutually beneficial decisions if they know more about each other. Exchanging timeout information is important, but drivers and servers can do even more to keep each other up to date.

Topology and Metadata

Database servers are often combined into intricate topologies where certain nodes are grouped in a single geographical location, others are used only as a fast cache layer, and yet others store seldom accessed cold data in a cheap place, for emergency purposes only.

Not every database exposes its topology to the end-user. For example, DynamoDB takes that burden off of its clients and exposes only a single endpoint, taking care of load balancing, overload prevention, and retry mechanisms on its own. On the other hand, a fair share of popular databases (including ScyllaDB, Cassandra, and ArangoDB) rely on the drivers to connect to each node, decide how many connections to keep, when to speculatively retry, and when to close connections if they are suspected of malfunctioning. In the ScyllaDB case, sharing up-to-date topology information with the drivers helps them make the right decisions. This data can be shared in multiple ways:

- Clients periodically fetching topology information from the servers

- Clients subscribing to events sent by the servers

- Clients taking an active part in one of the information exchange protocols (e.g., gossip[6])

- Any combination of these

Depending on the database model, another valuable piece of information often cached client-side is metadata—a prime example of which is database schema. SQL databases, as well as many NoSQL ones, keep the data at least partially structured. A schema defines the shape of a database row (or column), the kinds of data types stored in different columns, and various other characteristics (e.g., how long a database row is

---

[6] See the documentation on Gossip in ScyllaDB (`https://docs.scylladb.com/stable/kb/gossip.html`).

supposed to live before it's garbage-collected). Based on up-to-date schemas, drivers can perform additional validation, making sure that data sent to the server has a proper type and adheres to any constraints required by the database. On the other hand, when a driver-side cache for schemas gets out of sync, clients can experience their queries failing for no apparent reason.

Synchronizing full schema information can be costly in terms of performance, and finding a good compromise in how often to update highly depends on the use case. A rule of thumb is to update only as often as needed to ensure that the traffic induced by metadata exchange never negatively impacts the user experience. It's also worth noting that in a distributed database, clients are not always up to date with the latest schema information, and the system as a whole should be prepared to handle it and provide tactics for dealing with such inconsistencies.

Current Load

Overload protection and request latency optimization are tedious tasks, but they can be substantially facilitated by exchanging as much context as possible between interested parties.

The following methods can be applied to distribute the load evenly across the distributed system and prevent unwanted spikes:

1. Gathering latency statistics per each database connection in the drivers:

    a. What's the average latency for this connection?

    b. What's the 99th percentile latency?

    c. What's the maximum latency experienced in a recent time frame?

2. Exchanging information about server-side caches:

    a. Is the cache full?

    b. Is the cache warm (i.e., filled with useful data)?

    c. Are certain items experiencing elevated traffic and/or latency?

3. Interpreting server events:

   a. Has the server started replying with "overload errors"?

   b. How often do requests for this server time out?

   c. What is the general rate of errors for this server?

   d. What is the measured goodput from this server?

Based on these indicators, drivers should try to amend the amount of data they send, the concurrency, and the rate of retries as well as speculative execution, which can keep the whole distributed system in a healthy, balanced state. It's ultimately in the driver's interest to ease the pressure on nodes that start showing symptoms of getting overloaded, be it by reducing the concurrency of operations, limiting the frequency and number of retries, temporarily giving up on speculatively sent requests, and so on. Otherwise, if the database servers get overloaded, all clients may experience symptoms like failed requests, timeouts, increased latency, and so on.

Request Caching

Many database management systems, ranging from SQLite, MySQL, and Postgres to NoSQL databases, implement an optimization technique called *prepared statements.* While the language used to communicate with the database is usually human-readable (or at least developer-readable), it is not the most efficient way of transferring data from one computer to another.

Let's take a look at the (simplified) lifecycle of an unprepared statement once it's sent from a ScyllaDB driver to the database and back. This is illustrated in Figure 5-4.

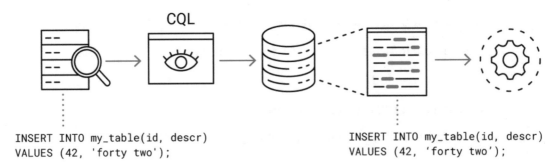

Figure 5-4. Lifecycle of an unprepared statement

1. A query string is created:

    ```
    INSERT INTO my_table(id, descr) VALUES (42,
    'forty two');
    ```

2. The string is packed into a CQL frame by the driver. Each CQL
    frame consists of a header, which describes the purpose of a
    particular frame. Following the header, a specific payload may be
    sent as well. The full protocol specification is available at `https://`
    `github.com/apache/cassandra/blob/trunk/doc/native_`
    `protocol_v4.spec`.

3. The CQL frame is sent over the network.

4. The frame is received by the database.

5. Once the frame is received, the database interprets the frame
    header and then starts parsing the payload. If there's an
    unprepared statement, the payload is represented simply as a
    string, as seen in Step 1.

6. The database parses the string in order to validate its contents and
    interpret what kind of an operation is requested: is it an insertion,
    an update, a deletion, a selection?

7. Once the statement is parsed, the database can continue
    processing it (e.g., by persisting data on disk, fetching whatever's
    necessary, etc.).

Now, imagine that a user wants to perform a hundred million operations on the
database in quick succession because the data is migrated from another system. Even
if parsing the query strings is a relatively fast operation and takes 50 microseconds, the
total time spent on parsing strings will take over an hour of CPU time. Sounds like an
obvious target for optimization.

The key observation is that operations performed on a database are usually similar
to one another and follow a certain pattern. For instance, migrating a table from one
system to another may mean sending lots of requests with the following schema:

```
INSERT INTO my_table(id, descr) VALUES (?, ?)
```

where ? denotes the only part of the string that varies between requests.

This query string with question marks instead of real values is actually also valid CQL! While it can't be executed as is (because some of the values are not known), it can be prepared.

Preparing such a statement means that the database will meticulously analyze the string, parse it, and create an internal representation of the statement in its own memory. Once done, a unique identifier is generated and sent back to the driver. The client can now execute the statement by providing only its identifier (which is a 128-bit UUID[7] in ScyllaDB) and all the values missing from the prepared query string. The process of replacing question marks with actual values is called *binding* and it's the only thing that the database needs to do instead of launching a CQL parser, which offers a significant speedup.

Preparing statements without care can also be detrimental to overall cluster performance though. When a statement gets prepared, the database needs to keep a certain amount of information about it in memory, which is hardly a limitless resource. Caches for prepared statements are usually relatively small, under the assumption that the driver's users (app developers) are kind and only prepare queries that are used frequently. If, on the other hand, a user were to prepare lots of unique statements that aren't going to be reused any time soon, the database cache might invalidate existing entries for frequently used queries. The exact heuristics of how entries are invalidated depends on the algorithm used in the cache, but a naive LRU (least recently used) eviction policy is susceptible to this problem. Therefore, other cache algorithms resilient to such edge cases should be considered when designing a cache without full information about expected usage patterns. Some notable examples include the following:

- **LFU (least frequently used)**

  Aside from keeping track of which item was most recently accessed, LFU also counts how many times it was needed in a given time period, and tries to keep frequently used items in the cache.

- **LRU with two pools**

  One probationary pool for new entries, and another, usually larger, pool for frequently used items. This algorithm avoids cache thrashing when lots of one-time entries are inserted in the cache, because they only evict other items from the probationary pool, while more frequently accessed entries are safe in the main pool.

---

[7] See the memo, "A Universally Unique IDentifier (UUID) URN Namespace," at https://www.ietf.org/rfc/rfc4122.txt.

Finally, regardless of the algorithm used for cache eviction implemented server-side, drivers should take care not to prepare queries too aggressively, especially if it happens automatically, which is often the case in ORMs (object-relational mappings). Making an interface convenient for the user may sound tempting, and developer experience is indeed an important factor when designing a driver, but being too eager with reserving precious database resources may be disadvantageous in the long term.

Query Locality

In distributed systems, any kind of locality is welcome because it reduces the chances of failure, keeps the latency low, and generally prevents many undesirable events. While database clients, and thus also drivers, do not usually share the same machines with the database cluster, it is possible to keep the distance between them short. "Distance" might mean either a physical measure or the number of intermediary devices in the network topology. Either way, for latency's sake, it's good to minimize it between parties that need to communicate with each other frequently.

Many database management systems allow their clients to announce their "location," for example, by declaring which datacenter is their local, default one. Drivers should take that information into account when communicating with the database nodes. As long as all consistency requirements are fulfilled, it's usually better to send data directly to a nearby node, under the assumption that it will spend less time in transit. Short routes also usually imply fewer middlemen, and that in turn translates to fewer potential points of failure.

Drivers can make much more educated choices though. Quite a few NoSQL databases can be described as "distributed hash tables" because they partition their data and spread it across multiple nodes which own a particular set of hashes. If the hashing algorithm is well known and deterministic, drivers can leverage that fact to try to optimize the queries even further—sending data directly to the appropriate node, or even the appropriate CPU core.

ScyllaDB, Cassandra, and other NoSQL databases apply a concept of token[8] awareness (see Figures 5-5, 5-6, and 5-7):

1. A request arrives.

2. The receiving node computes the hash of the given input.

3. Based on the value of this hash, it computes which database nodes are responsible for this particular value.

4. Finally, it forwards the request directly to the owning nodes.

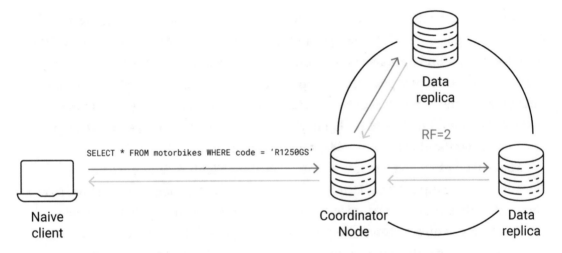

Figure 5-5. *Naive clients route queries to any node (coordinator)*

However, in certain cases, the driver can compute the token locally on its own, and then use the cluster topology information to route the request straight to the owning node. This local node-level routing saves at least one network round-trip as well as the CPU time of some of the nodes.

---

[8] A *token* is how a hash value is named in Cassandra nomenclature.

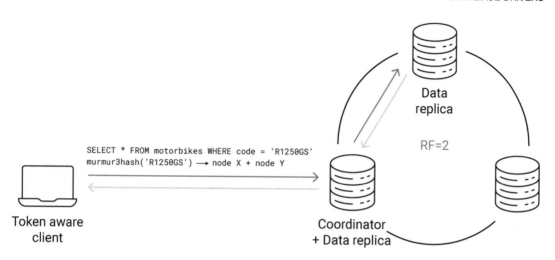

Figure 5-6. *Token-aware clients route queries to the right node(s)*

In the Cassandra/ScyllaDB case, this is possible because each table has a well-defined "partitioner," which simply means a hash function implementation. The default choice—used in Cassandra—is murmur3,[9] which returns a 64-bit hash value, has satisfying distribution, and is relatively cheap to compute. ScyllaDB takes it one step further and allows the drivers to calculate which CPU core of which database node owns a particular datum. When a driver is cooperative and proactively establishes a separate connection per each core of each machine, it can send the data not only to the right node, but also straight to the single CPU core responsible for handling it. This not only saves network bandwidth, but is also very friendly to CPU caches.

---

[9] See the DataStax documentation on Murmur3Partitioner (https://docs.datastax.com/en/cassandra-oss/3.x/cassandra/architecture/archPartitionerM3P.html).

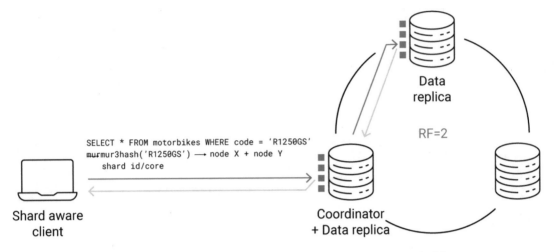

```
SELECT * FROM motorbikes WHERE code = 'R1250GS'
murmur3hash('R1250GS') ──► node X + node Y
          shard id/core
```

Figure 5-7. *Shard-aware clients route queries to the correct node(s) + core*

Retries

In a perfect system, no request ever fails and logic implemented in the drivers can be kept clean and minimal. In the real world, failures happen disturbingly often, so the drivers should also be ready to deal with them. One such mechanism for failure tolerance is a driver's retry policy. A retry policy's job is to decide whether a request should be sent again because it failed (or at least the driver strongly suspects that it did).

Error Categories

Before diving into techniques for retrying requests in a smart way, there's a more fundamental question to consider: does a retry even make sense? The answer is not that obvious and it depends on many internal and external factors. When a request fails, the error can fall into the following categories, presented with a few examples:

1. Timeouts

    a. Read timeouts

    b. Write timeouts

2. Temporary errors

   a. Database node overload

   b. Dead target node

   c. Temporary schema mismatch

3. Permanent errors

   a. Incorrect query syntax

   b. Authentication error

   c. Insufficient permissions

Depending on the category, the retry decision may be vastly different. For instance, it makes absolutely no sense to retry a request that has incorrect syntax. It will not magically start being correct, and such a retry attempt would only waste bandwidth and database resources.

Idempotence

Error categories aside, retry policy must also consider one important trait of the request itself: its *idempotence*. An idempotent request can be safely applied multiple times, and the result will be indistinguishable from applying it just once.

Why does this need to be taken into account at all? For certain classes of errors, the driver cannot be sure whether the request actually succeeded. A prime example of such error is a timeout. The fact that the driver did not manage to get a response in time does not mean that the server did not successfully process the request. It's a similar situation if the network connection goes down: The driver won't know if the database server actually managed to apply the request.

When in doubt, the driver should make an educated guess in order to ensure consistency. Imagine a request that withdraws $100 from somebody's bank account. You certainly don't want to retry the same request again if you're not absolutely sure that it failed; otherwise, the bank customer might become a bit resentful. This is a perfect example of a non-idempotent request: Applying it multiple times changes the ultimate outcome.

Fortunately, there's a large subset of idempotent queries that can be safely retried, even when it's unclear whether they already succeeded:

1. **Read-only requests**

   Since they do not modify any data, they won't have any side effects, no matter how often they're retried.

2. **Certain conditional requests that have compare-and-set characteristics** (e.g., "bump the value by 1 if the previous value is 42")

   Depending on the use case, such a condition may be enough to guarantee idempotence. Once this request is applied, applying it again would have no effect since the previous value would then be 43.

3. **Requests with unique timestamps**

   When each request has a unique timestamp (represented in wall clock time or based on a logical clock[10]), applying it multiple times can be idempotent. A retry attempt will contain a timestamp identical to the original request, so it will only overwrite data identified by this particular timestamp. If newer data arrives in-between with a newer timestamp, it will not be overwritten by a retry attempt with an older timestamp.

In general, it's a good idea for drivers to give users an opportunity to declare their requests' idempotence explicitly. Some queries can be trivially deduced to be idempotent by the driver (e.g., when it's a read-only SELECT statement in the database world), but others may be less obvious. For example, the conditional example from the previous Step 2 is idempotent if the value is never decremented, but not in the general case. Imagine the following counter-example:

1. The current value is 42.

2. A request "bump the value by 1 if the previous value is 42" is sent.

---

[10] See the Logical Clocks lecture by Arvind Krishnamurthy (https://homes.cs.washington.edu/~arvind/cs425/lectureNotes/clocks-2.pdf).

3.   A request "bump the value by 1 if the previous value is 42" is retried.

4.   Another request, "decrement the value by 1," is sent.

5.   The request from Step 2 arrives and is applied—changing the value to 43.

6.   The request from Step 4 arrives and is applied—changing the value to 42.

7.   The retry from Step 3 is applied—changing the value back to 43 and interfering with the effect of the query from Step 4. This wasn't idempotent after all!

Since it's often impossible to guess if a request is idempotent just by analyzing its contents, it's best for drivers to have a `set_idempotent()` function exposed in their API. It allows the users to explicitly mark some queries as idempotent, and then the logic implemented in the driver can assume that it's safe to retry such a request when the need arises.

Retry Policies

Finally, there's enough context to discuss actual retry policies that a database driver could implement. The sole job of a retry policy is to analyze a failed query and return a decision. This decision depends on the database system and its intrinsics, but it's often one of the following (see Figure 5-8):

•   Do not retry

•   Retry on the same database node

•   Retry, but on a different node

•   Retry, but not immediately—apply some delay

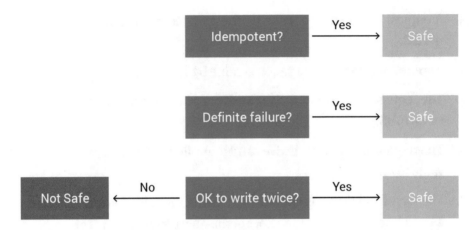

Figure 5-8. *Decision graph for retrying a query*

Deciding not to retry is often a decent choice—it's the only correct one when the driver isn't certain whether an idempotent query really failed or just timed out. It's also the obvious choice for permanent errors; there's no point in retrying a request that was previously refused due to incorrect syntax. And whenever the system is overloaded, the "do not retry" approach might help the entire cluster. Although the immediate effect (preventing a user's request from being driven to completion) is not desirable, it provides a level of overload protection that might pay off in the future. It prevents the overload condition from continuing to escalate. Once a node gets too much traffic, it refuses more requests, which increases the rate of retries, and ends up in a vicious circle.

Retrying on the same database node is generally a good option for timeouts. Assuming that the request is idempotent, the same node can probably resolve potential conflicts faster. Retrying on a different node is a good idea if the previous node showed symptoms of overload, or had an input/output error that indicated a temporary issue.

Finally, in certain cases, it's a good idea to delay the retry instead of firing it off immediately (see Figure 5-9).

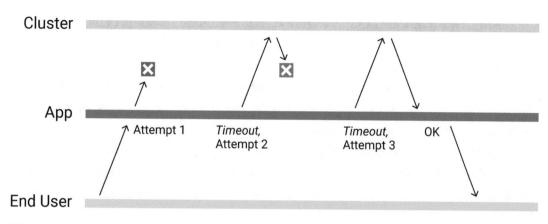

Figure 5-9. *Retry attempts eventually resulting in a successful query*

When the whole cluster shows the symptoms of overload—be it high reported CPU usage or perceived increased latency—retrying immediately after a request failed may only exacerbate the problem. What a driver can do instead is apply a gentle backoff algorithm, giving the database cluster time to recover. Remember that even a failed retry costs resources: networking, CPU, and memory. Therefore, it's better to balance the costs and chances for success in a reasonable manner.

The three most common backoff strategies are constant, linear, and exponential backoff, as visualized in Figure 5-10.

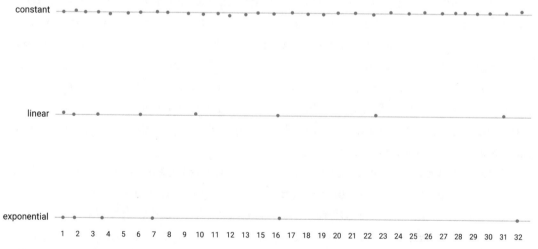

Figure 5-10. *Constant, linear, and exponential backoffs*

The first type (constant) simply waits a certain predefined amount of time before retrying. Linear backoff increases the time between attempts in a linear fashion; it could wait one second before the first attempt, two seconds before the second one, and so forth. Finally, exponential backoff, arguably the most commonly used method, increases the delay by multiplying it by a constant each time. Usually it just doubles it—because both processors and developers love multiplying and dividing by two (the latter ones mostly just to show off their intricate knowledge of the bitwise shift operator). Exponential backoff has especially nice characteristics for overload prevention. The retry rate drops exponentially, and so does the pressure that the driver places on the database cluster.

Paging

Databases usually store amounts of data that are orders of magnitude larger than a single client machine could handle. If you fetch all available records, the result is unlikely to fit into your local disks, not to mention your available RAM. Nonetheless, there are many valid cases for processing large amounts of data, such as analyzing logs or searching for specific documents. It is quite acceptable to ask the database to serve up all the data it has—but you probably want it to deliver that data in smaller bits.

That technique is customarily called *paging*, and it is ubiquitous. It's exactly what you've experienced when browsing through page 17 of Google search results in futile search for an answer to a question that was asked only on an inactive forum seven years ago—or getting all the way to page 24 of eBay listings, hunting for that single perfect offer. Databases and their drivers also implement paging as a mechanism beneficial for both parties. Drivers get their data in smaller chunks, which can be done with lower latency. And databases receive smaller queries, which helps with cache management, workload prioritization, memory usage, and so on.

Different database models may have a different view of exactly what paging involves and how you interface with it. Some systems may offer fine-grained control, which allows you to ask for "page 16" of your data. Others are "forward-only": They reduce the user-facing interface to "here's the current page—you can ask for the next page if you want." Your ability to control the page size also varies. Sometimes it's possible to specify the size in terms of a number of database records or bytes. In other cases, the page size is fixed.

On top of a minimal interface that allows paging to be requested, drivers can offer many interesting features and optimizations related to paging. One of them is *readahead*—which usually means that the driver transparently and speculatively fetches new pages before you actually ask for them to be read. A readahead is a classic example of a double-edged sword. On the one hand, it makes certain read operations faster, especially if the workload consists of large consecutive reads. On the other, it may cause prohibitive overhead, especially if the workload is based on small random reads.

Although most drivers support paging, it's important to check whether the feature is opt-in or opt-out and consciously decide what's best for a specific workload. In particular, pay attention to the following aspects:

1. What's the default behavior (would a read query be paged or unpaged)?

2. What's the default page size and is it configurable? If so, in what units can a size be specified? Bytes? Number of records?

3. Is readahead on by default? Can it be turned on/off?

4. Can readahead be configured further? For example, can you specify how many pages to fetch or when to decide to start fetching (e.g., "When at least three consecutive read requests already occurred")?

Setting up paging properly is important because a single unpaged response can be large enough to be problematic for both the database servers forced to produce it, and for the client trying to receive it. On the other hand, too granular paging can lead to unnecessary overhead (just imagine trying to read a billion records row-by-row, due to the default page size of "1 row"). Finally, readahead can be a fantastic optimization technique—but it can also be entirely redundant, fetching unwanted pages that cost memory, CPU time, and throughput, as well as confuse the metrics and logs. With paging configuration, it's best to be as explicit as possible.

Concurrency

In many cases, the only way to utilize a database to the fullest—and achieve optimal performance—is to also achieve high concurrency. That often requires the drivers to perform many I/O operations at the same time, and that's in turn customarily achieved by issuing asynchronous tasks. That being said, let's take quite a few steps back to explain what that really means and what's involved in achieving that from both a hardware and software perspective.

Note   High concurrency is not a silver bullet. When it's too high, it's easy to overload the system and ruin the quality of service for other users—see Figure 5-11 for its effect on latency. Chapter 1 includes a cautionary tale on what can happen when concurrency gets out of bounds and Chapter 2 also touches on the dangers of unbounded concurrency.

Modern Hardware

Back in the old days, making decisions around I/O concurrency was easy because magnetic storage drives (HDD) had an effective concurrency of 1. There was (usually) only a single actuator arm used to navigate the platters, so only a single sector of data could have been read at once. Then, an SSD revolution happened. Suddenly, disks could read from multiple offsets concurrently. Moreover, it became next to impossible to fully utilize the disk (i.e., to read and write with the speeds advertised in shiny numbers printed on their labels) without actually asking for multiple operations to be performed concurrently. Now, with enterprise-grade NVMe drives and inventions like Intel Optane,[11] concurrency is a major factor when benchmarking input/output devices. See Figure 5-11.

---

[11] High speed persistent memory (sadly discontinued in 2021).

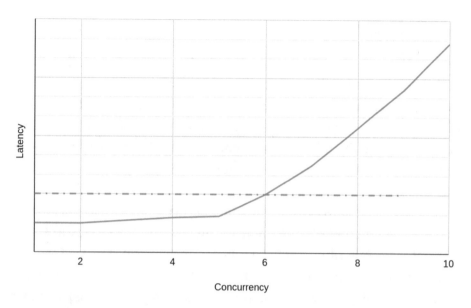

Figure 5-11. *Relationship between the system's concurrency and latency*

Networking technology is not lagging behind either. Modern networking cards have multiple independent queues, which, with the help of receive-side scaling (RSS[12]), enable previously unimaginable levels of performance, with throughput measured in Tbps.[13] With such advanced hardware, achieving high concurrency in software is required to simply utilize the available capabilities.

CPU cores obviously deserve to be mentioned here as well. That's the part of computer infrastructure that's undoubtedly most commonly associated with concurrency. Buying a 64-core consumer-grade processor is just a matter of going to the hardware store next door, and the assortment of professional servers is even more plentiful.

Operating systems focus on facilitating highly concurrent programs too. io_uring[14] by Jens Axboe is a novel addition to the Linux kernel. As noted in Chapter 3, it was developed for asynchronous I/O, which in turn plays a major part in allowing high concurrency in software to become the new standard. Some database drivers already utilize io_uring underneath, and many more put the integration very high in the list of priorities.

---

[12] RSS allows directing traffic from specific queues directly into chosen CPUs.

[13] Terabits per second

[14] See the "Efficient IO with io_uring" article (https://kernel.dk/io_uring.pdf).

Modern Software

How could modern software adapt to the new, highly concurrent era? Historically, a popular model of ensuring that multiple operations can be performed at the same time was to keep a pool of operating system threads, with each thread having its own queue of tasks. That only scales in a limited way though, so now the industry leans toward so-called "green threads," which are conceptually similar to their operating system namesakes, but are instead implemented in userspace, in a much more lightweight manner.

For example, in Seastar (a high-performance asynchronous framework implemented in C++ and based on a future-promise model[15]), there are quite a few ways of expressing a single flow of execution, which could be called a green thread. A fiber of execution can be created by chaining futures, and you can also use the C++ coroutines mechanism to build asynchronous programs in a clean way, with the compiler assisting in making the code async-friendly.

In the Rust language, the asynchronous model is quite unique. There, a future represents the computation, and it's the programmer's responsibility to advance the state of this asynchronous state machine. Other languages, like JavaScript, Go, and Java, also come with well-defined and standardized support for asynchronous programming.

This async programming support is good, because database drivers are prime examples of software that should support asynchronous operations from day one. Drivers are generally responsible for communicating over the network with highly specialized database clusters, capable of performing lots of I/O operations at the same time. We can't emphasize enough that high concurrency is the only way to utilize the database to the fullest. Asynchronous code makes that substantially easier because it allows high levels of concurrency to be achieved without straining the local resources. Green threads are lightweight and there can be thousands of them even on a consumer-grade laptop. Asynchronous I/O is a perfect fit for this use case as well because it allows efficiently sending thousands of requests over the network in parallel, without blocking the CPU and forcing it to wait for any of the operations to complete, which was a known bottleneck in the legacy threadpool model.

---

[15] See the Seastar documentation on futures and promises (`https://seastar.io/futures-promises/`).

Note   The future-promise model and asynchronous I/O are introduced in Chapter 3.

What to Look for When Selecting a Driver

Database drivers are commonly available as open-source software. It's a great model that allows people to contribute and also makes the software easily accessible, ergo popular (precisely what database vendors want). Drivers can be developed either by the vendor, or another company, or simply your next door open-source contributor. This kind of competition is very healthy for the entire system, but it also forces the users to make a choice: which driver to use? For instance, at the time of this writing, the official PostgreSQL documentation lists six drivers for C/C++ alone, with the complete list being much longer.[16]

Choosing a driver should be a very deliberate decision, tailored to your unique situation and preceded by tests, benchmarks, and evaluations. Nevertheless, there are some general rules of thumb that can help guide you:

1. **Clear documentation**

   Clear documentation is often initially underestimated by database drivers' users and developers alike. However, in the long term, it's the most important repository of knowledge for everyone, where implementation details, good practices, and hidden assumptions can be thoroughly explained. Choosing an undocumented driver is a lottery—buying a pig in a poke. Don't get distracted by shiny benchmarks on the front page; the really valuable part is thorough documentation. Note that it does not have to be a voluminous book. On the contrary—concise, straight-to-the-point docs with clear, working examples are even better.

---

[16] See the PostgreSQL Drivers documentation at `https://wiki.postgresql.org/wiki/List_of_drivers`.

2. **Long-term support and active maintainership**

Officially supported drivers are often maintained by their vendors, get released regularly, and have their security vulnerabilities fixed faster. External open-source drivers might look appealing at first, easily winning in their self-presented benchmarks, but it's important to research how often they get released, how often bugs are fixed, and how likely they are to be maintained in the foreseeable future. On the other hand, sometimes the situation is reversed: The most modern, efficient code can be found in an open-source driver, while the official one is hardly maintained at all!

3. **Asynchronous API**

Your code is eventually going to need high concurrency, so it's better to bet on an async-friendly driver, even if you're not ready to take advantage of that quite yet. The decision will likely pay off later. While it's easy to use an asynchronous driver in a synchronous manner, the opposite is not true.

4. **Decent test coverage**

Testing is extremely important not only for the database nodes, but also for the drivers. They are the first proxy between the users and the database cluster, and any error in the driver can quickly propagate to the whole system. If the driver corrupts outgoing data, it may get persisted on the database, eventually making the whole cluster unusable. If the driver incorrectly interprets incoming data, its users will have a false picture of the database state. And if it produces data based on this false picture, it can just as well corrupt the entire database cluster. A driver that cannot properly handle its load balancing and retry policy can inadvertently overload a database node with excess requests, which is detrimental to the whole system. If the driver is at least properly tested, users can assume a higher level of trust in it.

5. **Database-specific optimizations**

   A good driver should cooperate with its database. The more context it gathers from the cluster, the more educated decisions it can make. Remember that clients, and therefore drivers, are often the most ubiquitous group of agents in distributed systems, directly contributing to the cluster-wide concurrency. That makes it especially important for them to be cooperative.

Summary

This chapter provided insights into how the choice of a database driver impacts performance and highlighted considerations to keep in mind when selecting a driver. Drivers are often an overlooked part of a distributed system. That's a shame because drivers are so close to database users, both physically and figuratively! Proximity is an extremely important factor in all networked systems because it directly translates to latency. The next chapter ponders proximity from a subtly different point of view: How to get the data itself closer to the application users.

CHAPTER 6

Getting Data Closer

Location, location, location. Sometimes it's just as important to database performance as it is to real estate. Just as the location of a home influences how quickly it sells, the location of where data "lives" and is processed also matters for response times and latencies.

Pushing more logic into the database can often reduce network latency (and costs, e.g., when your infrastructure provider charges for ingress/egress network traffic) while taking advantage of the database's powerful compute capability. And redistributing database logic from fewer powerful datacenters to more minimalist ones that are closer to users is another move that can yield discernable performance gains under the right conditions.

This chapter explores the opportunities in both of these shifts. First, it looks at databases as compute engines with a focus on user-defined functions and user-defined aggregates. It then goes deeper into WebAssembly, which is now increasingly being used to implement user-defined functions and aggregates (among many other things). Finally, the chapter ventures to the edge—exploring what you stand to gain by moving your database servers quite close to your users, as well as what potential pitfalls you need to negotiate in this scenario.

Databases as Compute Engines

Modern databases offer many more capabilities than just storing and retrieving data. Some of them are nothing short of operating systems, capable of streaming, modifying, encrypting, authorizing, authenticating, and virtually anything else with data they manage.

Data locality is the holy grail of distributed systems. The less you need to move data around, the more time can be spent on performing meaningful operations on it—without excessive bandwidth costs. That's why it makes sense to try to push more logic into the database itself, letting it process as much as possible locally, then return

© Felipe Cardeneti Mendes, Piotr Sarna, Pavel Emelyanov, Cynthia Dunlop 2023
F. C. Mendes et al., *Database Performance at Scale*, https://doi.org/10.1007/978-1-4842-9711-7_6

the results to the users, or some middleware, for further processing. It makes even more sense when you consider that database nodes generally run on powerful hardware, with lots of RAM and fast I/O devices. This usually translates to formidable CPU power. Dedicated large data processing frameworks aside (e.g., Apache Spark, which is out of scope for this book), regular database engines almost always support some level of user-defined computations. These can be classified into two major sections: user-defined functions/procedures and user-defined aggregates.

Note that the definitions vary. Some database vendors use the general name "functions" to mean both aggregate and scalar functions. Others actually mean "scalar functions" when they reference "functions," and use the name "aggregates" for "aggregate functions." That's the convention applied to this chapter.

User-Defined Functions and Procedures

In contrast to native functions, often implemented in database engines (think `lowercase()`, `now()`, `concat()`, type casting, algebraic operations, and friends), user-defined functions are provided by the users of the database (e.g., the developers building applications). A "procedure" is substantially identical to a function in this context, except it does not return any result; instead, it has side effects.

The exact interface of allowing users to define their own functions or procedures varies wildly between database vendors. Still, several core strategies, listed here, are often implemented:

1. A set of hardcoded native functions, not extensible, but at least composable. For example, casting a type to string, concatenating it with a predefined suffix, and then hashing it.

2. A custom scripting language, dedicated and vendor-locked to a specific database, allowing users to write and execute simple programs on the data.

3. Supporting a single general-purpose embeddable language of choice. For example, Lisp, Lua, ChaiScript, Squirrel, or WebAssembly might be used for this purpose. Note: You'll explore WebAssembly in more depth a little later in this chapter.

4. Supporting a variety of pluggable embeddable languages. A good
    example is Apache Cassandra and its support of Java (native
    language) and JavaScript[1] as well as pluggable backend-loaded via
    .jar files.

The first on the list is the least flexible, offers the worst developer experience, and has the lowest security risk. The last has the most flexibility, offers the best developer experience, and also harbors the most potential for being a security risk worthy of its own CVE number.

Scalar functions are usually invoked per each row, at least for row-oriented databases, which is usually the case for SQL. You might wonder if the computations can't simply be performed by end users on their machines. That's a valid point. The main advantage of that approach is fantastic scalability regardless of how many users perform data transformations (if they do it locally on their own machines, then the database cluster does not get overloaded).

There are several great reasons to push the computations closer to where the data is stored:

- Databases have more context to efficiently cache the computed results. Imagine tens of thousands of users asking for the same function to be applied on a certain set of rows. That result can be computed just once and then distributed to all interested parties.

- If the computed results are considerably smaller than their input (think about returning just lengths of text values), it's better to save bandwidth and send over only the final results.

- Certain housekeeping operations (e.g., deleting data older than a week) can be efficiently performed locally, without fetching any information to the clients for validation.

---

[1] It's also a great example of the CVE risk: `https://cve.mitre.org/cgi-bin/cvename.cgi?name=CVE-2021-44521`
`https://jfrog.com/blog/cve-2021-44521-exploiting-apache-cassandra-user-defined-functions-for-remote-code-execution/`

- If the processing is done on database servers, the instruction cache residing on that database's CPU chip is likely to be scorching hot with opcodes responsible for carrying out the computations for each row. And as a rule of thumb, hot cache translates to faster code execution and lower latency.

- Some computations are not trivially distributed to users. If they involve cryptographic private keys stored on the database servers, it might actually be impossible to run the code anywhere but on the server itself.

- If the data on which computations are performed is sensitive (e.g., it falls under infamous, ever-changing European data protection laws such as GDPR), it might be illegal to send raw data to the users. In such cases, running an encryption function server-side can be a way for users to obtain obfuscated, legal data.

Determinism

In distributed environments, idempotence (discussed in Chapter 5) is an important attribute that makes it possible to send requests in a speculative manner, potentially increasing performance. Thus, it is better to make sure that user-defined functions are deterministic. In other words, a user-defined function's value should only depend on the value of its arguments, and not on the value of any external factors like time, date, pseudo-random seed, and so on.

A perfect example of a non-deterministic function is now(). Calling it twice might yield the same value if you're fast enough, but it's generally not guaranteed since its result is time-dependent. If possible, it's a good idea to program the user-defined functions in a deterministic way and mark them as such. For time/date, this might involve computing the results based on a timestamp passed as a parameter rather than using built-in time utilities. For pseudo-random sampling, the seed could also be passed as a parameter, as opposed to relying on sources of entropy provided by the user-defined function runtime.

Latency

Running user-provided code on your database clusters is potentially dangerous in aspects other than security. Most embedded languages are Turing-complete, and customarily allow the developers to use loops, recursion, and other similar techniques in their code. That's risky. An undetected infinite loop may serve as a denial-of-service attack, forcing the database servers to endlessly process a function and block other tasks from used resources. And even if the user-defined function author did not have malicious intentions, some computations simply consume a lot of CPU time and memory.

In a way, a user-defined function should be thought of as a potential "noisy neighbor"[2] and its resources should be as limited as possible. For some use cases, a simple hard limit on memory and CPU time used is enough to ensure that the performance of other database tasks does not suffer from a "noisy" user-defined function. However, sometimes, a more specific solution is required—for example, splitting a user-function definition into smaller time bits, assigning priorities to user-defined functions, and so on.

One interesting metering mechanism was applied by Wasmtime,[3] a WebAssembly runtime. Code running in a WebAssembly instance consumes *fuel,*[4] a synthetic unit used for tracking how fast an instance exhausts system resources. When an instance runs out of fuel, the runtime does one of the preconfigured actions—either "refills" and lets the code execution continue or decides that the task reached its quota and terminates it.

Just-in-Time Compilation (JIT)

Languages used for user-defined functions are often either interpreted (e.g., Lua) or represented in bytecode that runs on a virtual machine (e.g., WebAssembly). Both of these approaches can benefit from just-in-time compilation. It's a broad topic, but the essence of it is that during runtime, the code of user-defined functions can be compiled to another, more efficient representation, and optimized along the way. This may mean translating bytecode to machine code the program runs on (e.g., x86-64 instructions), or compiling the source code represented in an interpreted language to machine code.

---

[2] See the Microsoft Azure documentation on the Noisy Neighbor antipattern (`https://learn.microsoft.com/en-us/azure/architecture/antipatterns/noisy-neighbor/noisy-neighbor`).

[3] See the Bytecode Alliance documentation at `https://wasmtime.dev`.

[4] See the Wasmtime docs (`https://docs.wasmtime.dev/api/wasmtime/struct.Store.html#method.fuel_consumed`).

JIT is a very powerful tool, but it's not a silver bullet—compilation and additional optimization can be an expensive process in terms of resources. A small user-defined function may take less than a millisecond to run, but recompiling it can cause a sudden spike in CPU and memory usage, as well as a multi-millisecond delay in the processing—resulting in high tail latency. It should therefore be a conscious decision to either enable just-in-time compilation for user-defined functions if the language allows it, or disable it altogether.

Examples

Let's take a look at a few examples of user-defined functions. The function serving as the example operates on floating point numbers; given two parameters, it returns the sum of them, inverted. Given 5 and 7, it should return $\frac{1}{5} + \frac{1}{7}$, which is approximately 0.34285714285.

Here's how it could be defined in Apache Cassandra, which allows user-defined function definitions to be provided in Java, its native language, as well as in other languages:

```
CREATE OR REPLACE FUNCTION add_inverse(val1 double, val2 double)
    RETURNS NULL ON NULL INPUT
    RETURNS double LANGUAGE java
    AS '
        return (val1 == 0 || val2 == 0)
            ? Double.NaN
            : (1/val1 + 1/val2);
    ';
```

Let's take a closer look at the definition. The first line is straightforward: it includes the function's name, parameters, and its types. It also specifies that if a function definition with that name already exists, it should be replaced. Next, it explicitly declares what happens if any of the parameters is null, which is a valid value for any type. The function can either return null *without calling the function at all* or allow null and let the source code handle it explicitly (the syntax for that is CALLED ON NULL INPUT). This explicit declaration is required by Apache Cassandra.

That declaration is then followed by the return type and chosen language—from which you can correctly deduce that multiple languages are supported. Then comes the function body. The only non-obvious decision made by the programmer was how to handle 0 as a parameter. Since the type system implemented in Apache Cassandra already handles NaN,[5] it's a decent candidate (next to positive/negative infinity).

The newly created function can be easily tested by creating a table, filling it with a few values, and inspecting the result:

```
CREATE TABLE test(v1 double PRIMARY KEY, v2 double);
INSERT INTO test(v1, v2) VALUES (5, 7);
INSERT INTO test(v1, v2) VALUES (2, 2);
INSERT INTO test(v1) VALUES (9);
INSERT INTO test(v1, v2) VALUES (7, 0);

SELECT v1, v2, add_inverse(v1, v2) FROM test;

cassandra@cqlsh:test> SELECT v1, v2, add_inverse(v1, v2) FROM test;

 v1 | v2   | test.add_inverse(v1, v2)
----+------+--------------------------
  9 | null |                     null
  5 |    7 |                 0.342857
  2 |    2 |                        1
  7 |    0 |                      NaN
```

From the performance perspective, is offloading such a simple function to the database servers worth it? Not likely—the computations are fairly cheap, so users shouldn't have an issue deriving these values themselves, immediately after receiving the data. The database servers, on the other hand, may need to initialize a runtime for user-defined functions, since these functions are often sandboxed for security purposes. That runtime initialization takes time and other resources. Offloading such computations makes much more sense if the data is aggregated server-side, which is discussed in the next section (on user-defined aggregates).

---

[5] Not-a-number

Best Practices

Before you learn about user-defined aggregates, which unleash the true potential of user-defined functions, it's important to sum up a few best practices for setting up user-defined functions in your database management system:

1. Evaluate if you need user-defined functions at all—compare the latency (and general performance) of queries utilizing user-defined functions vs computing everything client-side (assuming that's even possible).

2. Test if offloading computations to the database servers scales. Look at metrics like CPU utilization to assess how well your database system can handle thousands of users requesting additional computations.

3. Recognize that since user-defined functions are likely going to be executed on the "fast path," they need to be optimized and benchmarked as well! Consider the performance best practices for the language you're using for user-defined function implementation.

4. Make sure to properly handle any errors or exceptional cases in your user-defined function to avoid disrupting the operation of the rest of the database system.

5. Consider using built-in functions whenever possible instead of creating a user-defined function. The built-in functions may be more optimized and efficient.

6. Keep your user-defined functions simple and modular, breaking up complex tasks into smaller, more manageable functions that can be easily tested and reused.

7. Properly document your user-defined functions so that other users of the database system can understand how they work and how to use them correctly.

User-Defined Aggregates

The greatest potential for user-defined functions lies in them being building blocks for user-defined aggregates. Aggregate functions operate on multiple rows or columns, sometimes on entire tables or databases.

Moving this kind of operation closer to where the data lies makes perfect sense. Imagine 1TB worth of database rows that need to be aggregated into a single value: the sum of their values. When a thousand users request all these rows in order to perform the aggregation client-side, the following happens:

1. A total of a petabyte of data is sent over the network to each user.

2. Each user performs extensive computations, expensive in terms of RAM and CPU, that lead to exactly the same result as the other users.

If the aggregation is performed by the database servers, it not only avoids a petabyte of traffic; it also saves computing power for the users (which is a considerably greener solution). If the computation is properly cached, it only needs to be performed once. This is a major win in terms of performance, and many use cases can immediately benefit from pushing the aggregate computations closer to the data. This is especially important for analytic workloads that tend to process large volumes of data in order to produce useful statistics and feedback—a process that is its own type of aggregation.

Built-In Aggregates

Databases that allow creating user-defined aggregates usually also provide a few traditional built-in aggregation functions: the (in)famous COUNT(*), but also MAX, MIN, SUM, AVG, and others. Such functions take into account multiple rows or values and return an aggregated result. The result may be a single value. Or, it could also be a set of values if the input is divided into smaller classes. One example of such an operation is SQL's GROUP BY statement, which applies the aggregation to multiple disjoint groups of values.

Built-in aggregates should be preferred over user-defined ones whenever possible— they are likely written in the language native to the database server, already optimized, and secure. Still, the set of predefined aggregate functions is often very basic and doesn't allow users to perform the complex computations that make user-defined aggregates such a powerful tool.

Components

User-defined aggregates are customarily built on top of user-defined scalar functions. The details heavily depend on the database system, but the following components are definitely worth mentioning.

Initial Value

An aggregation needs to start somewhere, and it's up to the user to provide an initial value from which the final result will eventually be computed. In the case of the COUNT function, which returns the number of rows or values in a table, a natural candidate for the initial value is 0. In the case of AVG, which computes the arithmetic mean from all column values, the initial state could consist of two variables: The total number of values, initialized to 0, and the total sum of values, also initialized to 0.

State Transition Function

The core of each user-defined aggregate is its state transition function. This function is called for each new value that needs to be processed, and each time it is called, it returns the new state of the aggregation. Following the COUNT function example, its state transition function simply increments the number of rows by one. The state transition function of the AVG aggregate just adds the current value to the total sum and increments the total number of values by one.

Final Function

The final function is an optional feature for user-defined aggregates. Its sole purpose is to transform the final state of the aggregation to something else. For COUNT, no further transformations are required. The user is simply interested in the final state of the aggregation (the number of values), so the final function doesn't need to be present; it can be assumed to be an identity function. However, in the case of AVG, the final function is what makes the result useful to the user. It transforms the final state—the total number of values and its total sum—and produces the arithmetic mean by simply dividing one by the other, handling the special case of avoiding dividing by zero.

Reduce Function

The reduce function is an interesting optional addition to the user-defined aggregates world, especially for distributed databases. It can be thought of as another state transition function, but one that can combine two partial states into one.

With the help of a reduce function, computations of the user-defined aggregate can be distributed to multiple database nodes, in a map-reduce[6] fashion. This, in turn, can bring massive performance gains, because the computations suddenly become concurrent. Note that this optimization is not always possible—if the state transition function is not commutative, distributing the partial computations may yield an incorrect result.

In order to better imagine what a reduce function can look like, let's go back to the AVG example. A partial state for AVG can be represented as (n, s), where n is the number of values, and s is the sum of them. Reducing two partial states into the new valid state can be performed by simply adding the corresponding values: $(n_1, s_1) + (n_2, s_2) \rightarrow (n_1 + n_2, s_1 + s_2)$. An optional reduce function can be defined (e.g., in ScyllaDB's user-defined aggregate implementation[7]).

The user-defined aggregates support is not standardized among database vendors and each database has its own quirks and implementation details. For instance, in PostgreSQL, you can also implement a "moving" aggregate[8] by providing yet another set of functions and parameters: `msfunc`, `minvfunc`, `mstype`, and `minitcond`. Still, the general idea remains unchanged: Let the users push aggregation logic as close to the data as possible.

Examples

Let's create a custom integer arithmetic mean implementation in PostgreSQL.

That's going to be done by providing a state transition function, called `sfunc` in PostgreSQL nomenclature, `finalfunc` for the final function, initial value (`initcond`), and the state type—`stype`. All of the functions will be implemented in SQL, PostgreSQL's native query language.

---

[6] MapReduce is a framework for processing parallelizable problems across large datasets.

[7] See the ScyllaDB documentation on ScyllaDB CQL Extensions (`https://github.com/scylladb/scylladb/blob/master/docs/cql/cql-extensions.md#reducefunc-for-uda`).

[8] See the PostgreSQL documentation on User-Defined Aggregates (`https://www.postgresql.org/docs/current/xaggr.html#XAGGR-MOVING-AGGREGATES`).

State Transition Function

The state transition function, called accumulate, accepts a new integer value (the second parameter) and applies it to the existing state (the first parameter). As mentioned earlier in this chapter, a simple implementation keeps two variables in the state—the current sum of all values, and their count. Thus, transitioning to the next state simply means that the sum is incremented by the current value, and the total count is increased by one.

```
CREATE OR REPLACE FUNCTION accumulate(integer[], integer) RETURNS integer[]
    AS 'select array[$1[1] + $2, $1[2] + 1];'
    LANGUAGE SQL
    IMMUTABLE
    RETURNS NULL ON NULL INPUT;
```

Final Function

The final function divides the total sum of values by the total count of them, special-casing an average of 0 values, which should be just 0. The final function returns a floating point number because that's how the aggregate function is going to represent an arithmetic mean.

```
CREATE OR REPLACE FUNCTION divide(integer[]) RETURNS float8
    AS 'select case when $1[2]=0 then 0 else $1[1]::float/$1[2] end;'
    LANGUAGE SQL
    IMMUTABLE
    RETURNS NULL ON NULL INPUT;
```

Aggregate Definition

With all the building blocks in place, the user-defined aggregate can now be declared:

```
CREATE OR REPLACE AGGREGATE alternative_avg(integer)
(
    sfunc = accumulate,
    stype = integer[],
    finalfunc = divide,
    initcond = '{0, 0}'
);
```

In addition to declaring the state transition function and the final function, the state type is also declared to be an array of integers (which will always keep two values in the implementation), as well as the initial condition that sets both counters, the total sum and the total number of values, to 0.

That's it! Since the AVG aggregate for integers happens to be built-in, that gives you the perfect opportunity to validate if the implementation is correct:

```
postgres=# CREATE TABLE t(v INTEGER);
postgres=# INSERT INTO t VALUES (3), (5), (9);
postgres=# SELECT * FROM t;
 v
---
 3
 5
 9
(3 rows)

postgres=# SELECT AVG(v), alternative_avg(v) FROM t;
        avg         |   alternative_avg
--------------------+--------------------
 5.6666666666666667 | 5.666666666666667
(1 row)
```

Voilà. Remember that while creating an alternative implementation for AVG is a great academic example of user-defined aggregates, for production use it's almost always better to stick to the built-in aggregates whenever they're available.

Distributed User-Defined Aggregate

For completeness, let's take a look at an almost identical implementation of a custom average function, but one accommodated to be distributed over multiple nodes. This time, ScyllaDB will be used as a reference, since its implementation of user-defined aggregates includes an extension for distributing the computations in a map-reduce manner. Here's the complete source code:

```
CREATE FUNCTION accumulate(acc tuple<bigint, int>, val int)
RETURNS NULL ON NULL INPUT
RETURNS tuple<bigint, int>
```

```
LANGUAGE lua
AS $$
  return { acc[1]+val, acc[2]+1 }
$$;

CREATE FUNCTION reduce(acc tuple<bigint, int>, acc2 tuple<bigint, int>)
RETURNS NULL ON NULL INPUT
RETURNS tuple<bigint, int>
LANGUAGE lua
AS $$
  return { acc[1]+acc2[1], acc[2]+acc2[2] }
$$;

CREATE FUNCTION divide(acc tuple<bigint, int>)
RETURNS NULL ON NULL INPUT
RETURNS double
LANGUAGE lua
AS $$
  return acc[1]/acc[2]
$$;

CREATE AGGREGATE alternative_avg(int)
SFUNC accumulate
STYPE tuple<bigint, int>
REDUCEFUNC reduce
FINALFUNC divide
INITCOND (0, 0);
```

ScyllaDB's native query language, CQL, is extremely similar to SQL, even in its acronym. It's easy to see that most of the source code corresponds to the PostgreSQL implementation from the previous paragraph. ScyllaDB does not allow defining user-defined functions in CQL, but it does support Lua, a popular lightweight embeddable language, as well as WebAssembly. Since this book is expected to be read mostly by human beings (and occasionally ChatGPT once it achieves full consciousness), Lua was chosen for this example due to the fact it's much more concise.

The most notable difference is the reduce function, declared in the aggregate under the REDUCEFUNC keyword. This function accepts two partial states and returns another (composed) state. What ScyllaDB servers can do if this function is present is the following:

1. Divide the domain (e.g., all rows in the database) into multiple pieces and ask multiple servers to partially aggregate them, and then send back the result.

2. Apply the reduce function to combine partial results into the single final result.

3. Return the final result to the user.

Thus, by providing the reduce function, the user also allows ScyllaDB to compute the aggregate concurrently on multiple machines. This can reduce the query execution time by orders of magnitude compared to a large query that only gets executed on a single server.

In this particular case, it might even be preferable to provide a user-defined alternative for a user-defined function in order to increase its concurrency—unless the built-in primitives also come with their reduce functions out of the box. That's the case in ScyllaDB, but not necessarily in other databases that offer similar capabilities.

Best Practices

1. If the computations can be efficiently represented with built-in aggregates, do so—or at least benchmark whether a custom implementation is any faster. User-defined aggregates are very expressive, but usually come with a cost of overhead compared to built-in implementations.

2. Research if user-defined aggregates can be customized in order to better fit specific use cases—for example, if the computations can be distributed to multiple database nodes, or if the database allows configuring its caches to store the intermediate results of user-defined aggregates somewhere.

3. Always test the performance of your user-defined aggregates thoroughly before using them in production. This will help to ensure that they are efficient and can handle the workloads that you expect them to.

4. Measure the cluster-wide effects of using user-defined aggregates in your workloads. Similar to full table scans, aggregates are a costly operation and it's important to ensure that they respect the quality of service of other workloads, not overloading the database nodes beyond what's acceptable in your system.

WebAssembly for User-Defined Functions

WebAssembly, also known as Wasm, is a binary format for representing executable code, designed to be easily embedded into other projects. It turns out that WebAssembly is also a perfect candidate for user-defined functions on the backend, thanks to its ease of integration, performance, and popularity.

There are multiple great books and articles[9] on WebAssembly, and they all agree that first and foremost, it's a misnomer—WebAssembly's usefulness ranges way beyond web applications. It's actually a solid general-purpose language that has already become the default choice for an embedded language around the world. It ticks all the boxes:

☒ It's open-source, with a thriving community

☒ It's portable

☒ It's isolated by default, with everything running in a sandboxed environment

☒ It's fast, comparable to native CPU code in terms of performance

---

[9] For example, "WebAssembly: The Definitive Guide" by Brian Sletten, "Programming WebAssembly with Rust" by Kevin Hoffman, or "ScyllaDB's Take on WebAssembly for User-Defined Functions" by Piotr Sarna.

Runtime

WebAssembly is compiled to bytecode. This bytecode is designed to run on a virtual machine, which is usually part of a larger development environment called a runtime. There are multiple implementations of WebAssembly runtimes, most notably:

- Wasmtime

  `https://wasmtime.dev/`

  A fast and secure runtime for WebAssembly, implemented in Rust, backed by the Bytecode Alliance[10] nonprofit organization.

- Wasmer.io

  `https://wasmer.io/`

  Another open-source initiative implemented in Rust; maintainers of the WAPM[11] project, which is a Wasm package manager.

- WasmEdge:

  `https://wasmedge.org/`

  Runtime implemented in C++, general-purpose, but focused on edge computing.

- V8:

  `https://v8.dev/`

  Google's monolith JavaScript runtime; written in C++, comes with WebAssembly support as well.

Also, since the WebAssembly specification is public, feel free to implement your own! Beware though: The standard is still in heavy development, changing rapidly every day.

---

[10] `https://bytecodealliance.org/`
[11] `https://wapm.io/`

Back to Latency

Each runtime is free to define its own performance characteristics and guarantees. One interesting feature introduced in Wasmtime is the concept of *fuel*, already mentioned in the earlier discussion of user-defined functions. Combined with the fact that Wasmtime provides an optional asynchronous interface for running WebAssembly modules, it gives users an opportunity to fine-tune the runtime to their latency requirements.

When Wasmtime starts executing a given WebAssembly function, this unit of execution is assigned a certain amount of fuel. Each execution step exhausts a small amount of fuel—at the time of writing this paragraph, it simply consumes one unit of fuel on each WebAssembly bytecode instruction, excluding a few flow control instructions like branching. Once the execution unit runs out of fuel, it yields. After that happens, one of the preconfigured actions is taken: either the execution unit is terminated, or its tank gets refilled and it's allowed to get back to whatever it was computing. This mechanism allows the developer to control not only the total amount of CPU time that a single function execution can take, but also how often the execution should yield and hand over the CPU for other tasks. Thus, configuring fuel management the right way prevents function executions from taking over the CPU for too long. That helps maintain low, predictable latency in the whole system.

Another interesting aspect of WebAssembly is its portability. The fact that the code can be distributed to multiple places and it's guaranteed to run properly in multiple environments makes it a great candidate for moving not only data, but also computations, closer to the user.

Pushing the database logic from enormous datacenters to smaller ones, located closer to end users, got its own buzzy name: edge computing.

Edge Computing

Since the Internet of Things (IoT) became a thing, the term *edge computing* needs disambiguation. This paragraph is (unfortunately?) *not* about:

- Utilizing the combined computing power of smart fridges in your area

- Creating a data mesh from your local network of Bluetooth light bulbs

- Integrating your smart watch into a Raft cluster in witness mode

The *edge* described in this paragraph is of a more boring kind. It still means performing computations on servers, but on ones closer to the user (e.g., located in a local Equinix datacenter in Warsaw, rather than Amazon's eu-central-1 in Frankfurt).

Performance

What does edge computing have to do with database performance? It brings the data closer to the user, and closer physical distance translates to lower latency. On the other hand, having your database cluster distributed to multiple locations has its downsides as well. Moving large amounts of data between those regions might be costly, as cloud vendors tend to charge for cross-region traffic. If the latency between database nodes reaches hundreds of milliseconds, which is the customer grade latency between Northern America and Europe (unless you can afford Hibernia Express[12]), they can get out of sync easily. Even a few round-trips—and distributed consensus algorithms alone require at least two—can cause delays that exceed the comfort zone of one second. Failure detection mechanisms are also affected since packet loss occurs much more often when the cluster spans multiple geographical locations.

Database drivers for edge-friendly databases need to be aware of all these limitations mentioned. In particular, they need to be extra careful to pick the closest region whenever possible, minimizing the latency and the chance of failure.

Conflict-Free Replicated Data Types

CRDT (conflict-free replicated data types) is an interesting way of dealing with inconsistencies. It's a family of data structures designed to have the following characteristics:

- Users can update database replicas independently, without coordinating with other database servers.

- There exists an algorithm to automatically resolve conflicts that might occur when the same data is independently written to multiple replicas concurrently.

- Replicas are allowed to be in different states, but they are guaranteed to eventually converge to a common state.

---

[12] A submarine link between Canada, Ireland, and the UK, offering sub-60ms latency.

The concept of CRDT gained traction along with edge computing because the two complement each other. The database is allowed to keep replicas in multiple places and allows them to act without central coordination—but at the same time, users can assume that *eventually* the database state is going to become consistent.

A few interesting data structures that fit the definition of CRDT are discussed next.

G-Counter

Grow-only counter. Usually implemented as an array of counters, keeping a local counter value per each database node. Two array states from different nodes can be merged by taking the maximum of each respective field. The actual value of the G-Counter is simply a sum of all local counters.

PN-Counter

Positive-Negative counter, brilliantly implemented by keeping two G-Counter instances—one for accumulating positive values, the other for negative ones. The final value is obtained by subtracting one from the other.

G-Set

Grow-only set, that is, one that forbids the removal of elements. Converging two G-Sets is a simple set union since values are never removed from a G-Set. One flavor of G-Set is G-Map, where an entry, key, and value associated with the key cannot be removed once added.

LWW-Set

Last-write-wins set (and map, accordingly). This is a combination of two G-Sets, one gathering added elements and the other containing removed ones. Conflict resolution is based on a set union of the "added" G-Set, minus the union of the "removed" G-Set, but timestamps are also taken into account. A value exists if its timestamp in the "added" set is larger than its timestamp in the "removed" set, or if it's not present in the "removed" set at all.

The list is obviously not exhaustive, and countless other CRDTs exist. You're hereby encouraged to do research on the topic if you found it interesting!

CRDTs are not just theoretical structures; they are very much used in practice. Variants of conflict-free replicated data types are common among databases that offer eventual consistency, like Apache Cassandra and ScyllaDB. Their writes have last-write-wins semantics for conflict resolution, and their implementation of counters is based on the idea of a PN-Counter.

Summary

At this point, it should be clear that there are a number of ways to improve performance by using a database a bit unconventionally, as well as understanding (and tapping) specialized capabilities built into the database and its drivers. Let's shift gears and look at the top "do's and don'ts" that we recommend for ensuring that your database is performing at its best. The next chapter begins this discussion by focusing on infrastructure options (CPUs, memory, storage, and networking) and deployment models.

CHAPTER 7

Infrastructure and Deployment Models

As noted in the previous chapter, many modern databases offer capabilities beyond "just" storing and retrieving data. But all databases are ultimately built from the ground up in order to serve I/O in the most efficient way possible. And it's crucial to remember this when selecting your infrastructure and deployment model of choice.

In theory, a database's purpose is fairly simple: You submit a request and expect to receive a response. But as you have seen in the previous chapters, an insane level of engineering effort is spent on continuously enhancing and speeding up this process. Very likely, years and years were dedicated to optimizing algorithms that may give you a processing boost of a few CPU cycles, or minimizing the amount of memory fragmentation, or reducing the amount of storage I/O needed to look up a specific set of data. All these advancements, eventually, converge to create a database suitable for performance at scale.

Regardless of your database selection, you may eventually hit a wall that no engineering effort can break through: the database's physical hardware. It makes very little sense to have a solution engineered for performance when the hardware you throw at it may be suboptimal. Similarly, a less performant database will likely be unable to make efficient use of an abundance of available physical resources.

This chapter looks at critical considerations and tradeoffs when selecting CPUs, memory, storage, and networking for your distributed database infrastructure. It describes how different resources cooperate and how to configure the database to deliver the best performance. Special attention is drawn to storage I/O as the most difficult component to deal with. There's also a close look at optimal cloud-based deployments suitable for highly-performant distributed databases (given that these are the deployment preference of most businesses).

© Felipe Cardeneti Mendes, Piotr Sarna, Pavel Emelyanov, Cynthia Dunlop 2023
F. C. Mendes et al., *Database Performance at Scale*, https://doi.org/10.1007/978-1-4842-9711-7_7

While it is true that a Database-as-a-Service (DBaaS) deployment will shield you from many infrastructure and hardware decisions through your selection process, a fundamental understanding of the generic compute resources required by any database is important for identifying potential bottlenecks that may limit performance. After an introduction to the hardware that's involved in every deployment model—whether you think about it or not—the chapter shifts focus to different deployment options and their impact on performance. It covers the special considerations associated with cloud-hosted deployments, database-as-a-service, serverless, containerization, and container orchestration technologies, such as Kubernetes.

Core Hardware Considerations for Speed at Scale

When you are designing systems to handle large amounts of data and requests at scale, the primary hardware considerations are:

- Storage

- CPU (cores)

- Memory (RAM)

- Network interfaces

Each could be a potential bottleneck for internal database latency: The delay from when a request is received by the database (or a node in the database) and when the database provides a response.

Identifying the Source of Your Performance Bottlenecks

Knowing your database's write and read paths is helpful for identifying potential performance bottlenecks and tracking down the culprit. It's also key to understanding what physical resources your use case may be mostly bound against.

For example, write-optimized databases carry this nomenclature because writes primarily go to memory, rather than being immediately persisted into disk. However, most modern databases need to employ some "crash-recovery" mechanism and avoid data loss caused by unexpected service interruptions. As a result, even write-optimized databases will also resort to disk access to quickly persist your data, just in case. For example, writes to Cassandra clusters will be persisted to a "write ahead log" disk structure called the "commit log" and a memory structure that's named a "memtable." A write is considered successful only after both operations succeed.

On the other side of the spectrum, the database's read path will typically also involve several physical components. Assuming that you're not using an in-memory database, then the read path will start by checking whether the data you are looking for is present within the database cache. But if it's not, the database needs to look up and retrieve the data from disk, de-serialize it, and then answer with the results.

Network also plays a crucial role throughout the entire process. When you write, data needs to be rapidly replicated to other replicas. When you read, the database needs to select the correct replicas (shards) containing the data that the application is after, thus potentially having to communicate with other nodes in the cluster. Moreover, strong consistency use cases always require the response of a majority of members for an operation to be successful—so delayed responses from a replica can dramatically increase the tail latency of a request routed to it.

Achieving Balance

Balance is key to *any* distributed system, including and beyond databases. It makes very little sense to try to achieve 1 million operations per second (OPS) in a system that has the fastest network link available but relies on very few CPUs. Similarly, it's not very efficient to purchase the most expensive and performant infrastructure for your solution if your use case requires only 10K OPS.

Additionally, it's important to recognize that a cluster imbalance can easily drag down performance across your entire distributed system. This happens because a distributed system cannot be faster than your slowest component—a fact that frequently surprises people.

Here's a real-life example. A customer reported elevated latencies affecting their entire 18-node cluster. After collecting system information, we noticed that the majority of their nodes were properly using locally-attached nonvolatile memory express (NVMe) disks—except for one that had a software Redundant Array of Independent Disks (RAID) with a mix of NVMes and network-attached disks. The customer clarified that they were running out of storage space and decided to attach another disk in order to relieve the problem. However, they weren't aware that this introduced a ticking time bomb into their entire cluster. Here's a brief explanation of what happened from a technical perspective:

1. With a slow disk introduced in their RAID array, storage I/O operations in that specific replica took longer to complete.

2. As a result, the remaining replicas took additional time whenever sending or waiting for a response that would require disk I/O.

3. As more and more requests came in, all these delays eventually created a waiting queue on the replicas.

4. As the queue kept growing, this eventually affected the replicas' performance, which ended up affecting the entire cluster's performance.

5. From that point on, the entire cluster speed was impeded by the speed of its slowest node: the one that had the slowest disk.

Setting Realistic Expectations

Even the most powerful hardware cannot ensure impressive *end-to-end (or round-trip)* latency—the entire cycle time from when a client sends a request to the server until it obtains a response. The end-to-end latency could be undermined by factors that might be outside of the database's control. For example:

- Multi-hop routing of packets from your client application to the database server, adding hundreds of milliseconds in latency

- Client driver settings, connecting and sending requests to a remote datacenter

- Consistency levels that require both local and remote datacenter responses

- Poor network performance between clients and database servers

- Protocol overheads

- Client-side performance bottlenecks

Recommendations for Specific Hardware Components

This section takes a deeper look at each of the primary hardware considerations:

- Storage

- CPU (cores)

- Memory (RAM)

- Network interfaces

Storage

One of the fastest ways to undermine all your other performance optimizations is to send every read and write operation through an unsuitable disk. Although recent technology advancements greatly improved the performance of storage devices, disks are (by far) still the slowest component in a computer system.

From a performance standpoint, disk performance is typically measured in two dimensions:

- The bandwidth available for sequential reads and writes

- The IOPS for random reads and writes

Database engineers obsess over optimizing disk access patterns with respect to those two dimensions. People who are selecting, managing, or using a database should focus on two additional disk considerations: the storage technology and the disk size.

Disk Types

Locally-attached NVMe Solid State Drives (SSDs) are the standard when latency is critical. Compared with other bus interfaces, NVMe SSDs connected to a Peripheral Component Interconnect Express (PCIe) interface will generally deliver lower latencies than the Serial AT Attachment (SATA) interface. If your workload isn't super latency sensitive, you could also consider using disks via the SATA interface. But, definitely avoid using network-attached disks if you expect single-digit millisecond latencies. Being network attached, these disks require an additional hop to reach a storage server, and that ends up increasing latency for every database request.

If your focus is on throughput and latency really doesn't matter for your use case (e.g., for moving data into a data warehouse), you *might* be able to get away with a persistent disk—but it's not recommended. By persistent disks, we mean durable network storage devices that your VMs can access like physical disks, but are located independently from your VMs. We're not going to pick on any specific vendors, but a little research should reveal issues like subpar performance and overall instability. If you're forced to work with persistent disks, be prepared to craft a creative solution.[1]

Hard disk drives (HDDs) might fast become a bottleneck. Since SSDs are getting progressively cheaper and cheaper, using HDDs is not recommended. Some workloads may work with HDDs, especially if they play nice and minimize random seeks. An example of an HDD-friendly workload is a write-mostly (98 percent writes) workload with minimal random reads. If you decide to use HDDs, try to allocate a separate disk for the commit log.

ScyllaDB published benchmarking results of several different storage devices—demonstrating how they perform under extreme load simulating typical database access patterns.[2] For example, Figures 7-1 through 7-4 visualize the different performance characteristics from two NVMes—a persistent disk and an HDD.

---

[1] For inspiration, consider Discord's approach—but recognize that this is certainly not a one-size-fits-all solution. It's described in their blog, "How Discord Supercharges Network Disks for Extreme Low Latency" (`https://discord.com/blog/how-discord-supercharges-network-disks-for-extreme-low-latency`).

[2] You can find the results, as well as the tool to reproduce the results, at `https://github.com/scylladb/diskplorer#sample-results`.

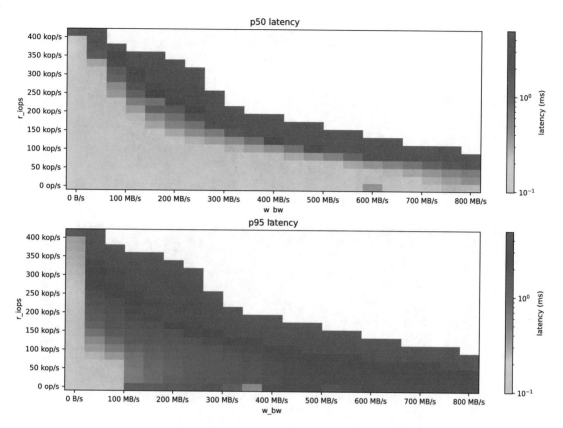

Figure 7-1. *NVMe bandwidth/latency graphs for an AWS i3.2xlarge instance type*

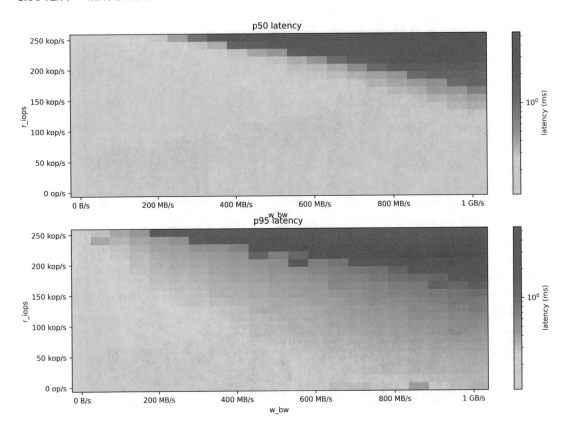

Figure 7-2. *Bandwidth/latency graphs for an AWS Im4gn.4xlarge instance type using AWS Nitro SSDs*

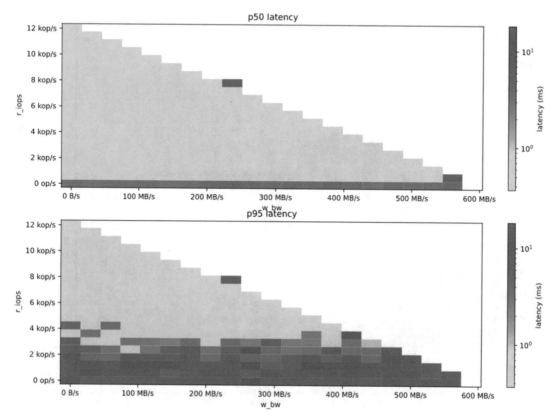

Figure 7-3. *Bandwidth/latency graphs for a Google Cloud n2-standard-8 instance type with a 2TB SSD persistent disk[3]*

---

[3] Strangely, the 95th percentile at low rates is worse than at high rates.

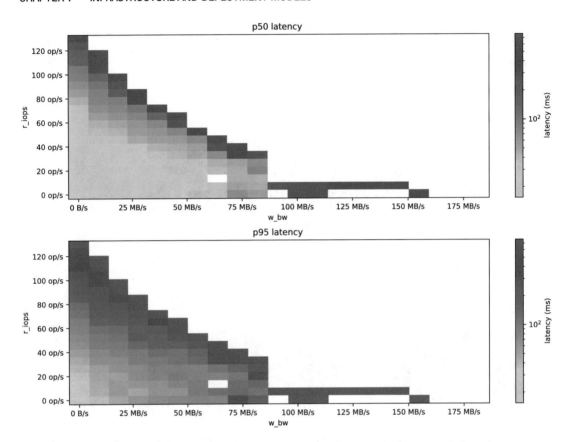

Figure 7-4. *Bandwidth/latency graphs for a Toshiba DT01ACA200 hard disk drive[4]*

Disk Setup

We hear a lot of questions about RAID setups. Hardware RAIDs are commonly used to avoid outages introduced by disk failures. As a result, the RAID-5 (distributed parity) setup is often used.

However, distributed databases typically have their own internal replication mechanism to allow for business continuity and achieve high availability. Therefore, RAID setups employing data mirroring or distributed parity have proven to be very detrimental to disk I/O performance and, fairly often, are used redundantly. On top of that, we have found that some hardware RAID vendors deliver poor performance results

---

[4] Note the throughput and IOPS were allowed to miss by a 15 percent margin rather than the normal 3 percent margin.

depending on your database access mechanisms. One notable example: hardware RAIDs that are unable to perform efficiently via asynchronous I/O or direct I/O calls. If you believe your disk I/O is suboptimal, consider directly exposing the disks from your hardware RAID to your operating system.

Conversely, RAID-0 (striping) setups often provide a boost in disk I/O performance and allow the database to achieve higher IOPS and bandwidth than a single disk can provide. The general recommendation for creating a RAID-0 setup is to use all disks of the same type and capacity to avoid variable performance during your daily workload. While it is true you would lose the entire RAID array in the event of a disk failure, the replication performed by your distributed database should be sufficient to ensure that your data remains available.

A couple of additional considerations related to disk setup:

- **Storage servers often serve several other users and workloads at the same time.** Therefore, even though disks would be dedicated to the database, your access performance can be undermined by factors like the level to which the storage system is serving other users concurrently. Most of the time, the storage medium provided to you will not be optimal for supporting a low-latency database workload. This can often be mitigated by ensuring that the disks are allocated from a high-performing disk pool.

- **It's important to expose your database infrastructure disks directly to the operating system guest from your hypervisor.** We have seen many situations where the I/O capacity of a database was greatly impacted when disks were virtualized. To eliminate any possible bottlenecks in a low-latency environment, give your database direct access to your disks so that they can perform I/O as they were designed to.

Disk Size

When considering how much storage you need, be sure to account for your existing data—replicated—plus your anticipated near-term data growth, and also leave sufficient room for the overhead of internal operations (like compactions [for LSM-tree-based databases], the commit log, backups, etc.).

As Chapter 8 discusses, the most common topology involves three replicas for each dataset. Assume you have 5TB of raw data and use a replication factor of three:

5TB Data X 3 RF = 15TB

But 15TB is just a starting point since there are other sizing criteria:

- What is your dataset's growth rate? (How much do you ingest per hour or day?)

- Will you store everything forever, or will you have an eviction process (for example, based on Time To Live [TTL])?

- Is your growth rate stable (a fixed rate of ingestion per week/day/ hour) or is it stochastic and bursty? The former would make it more predictable; the latter may mean you have to give yourself more leeway to account for unpredictable but probabilistic events.

You can model your data's growth rate based on the number of users or endpoints and how that number is expected to grow over time. Alternately, data models are often enriched over time, resulting in more data per source. Or your sampling rate may increase. For example, your system may begin ingesting data every five seconds rather than every minute. All of these considerations impact your data storage volume.

It's strongly recommended that you select storage that's suitable for where you expect to end up after a certain time span. If you're running your database on a public cloud provider (self-managed or as a fully-managed Database-as-a-Service [DBaaS]), you won't need very much lead time to provision new hardware and expand your cluster. However, for an on-premises hardware purchase, you may need to provision based on your quarterly or annual budgeting process. You could also face delays due to the supply chain disruptions that have become increasingly common.

Also, be sure to leave storage space for internal temporary operations such as compaction, repairs, backups, and commit logs, as well as any other background process that may temporarily introduce a space amplification. On the other hand, if you're using compression, be sure to factor in the amount of space that your selected compression algorithm can save you.

Finally, recognize that every database has an ideal memory-to-storage ratio—for example, a certain amount of TB or GB per node that it can support with optimal performance. If this isn't readily apparent in your database's documentation, press your vendor for their recommendation.

Raw Devices and Custom Drivers

Some database vendors require direct access to storage devices—without needing a filesystem to exist. Such direct access is often referred to as creating a "raw" device, which refers to the fact that the operating system won't know how to manage it, and any I/O is handled directly by the database. Issuing I/O directly to the underlying storage device may provide a performance boost to the database. However, it is important to understand some of this approach's drawbacks, which may not be important for your specific deployment.

1. **Error prone**: Directly issuing I/O to a disk rather than through a filesystem is error prone. While it will provide a performance gain, incorrect handling of the underlying storage could result in data corruption, data loss, or unexpected bugs.

2. **Complex**: Raw devices are not as common as one might expect. In fact, very few databases decided to implement that approach. It's important to note that since raw devices aren't typically mounted as regular filesystems, their manageability will be fully dependent on what your vendor provides.

3. **Lock-in**: Once you are using a raw device, it's extremely difficult to move away from it. You can't mount raw devices or query their storage consumption via typical operating system mechanisms. All of your disks need to be arranged in a certain way, and you can't easily go back to a regular filesystem.

Maintaining Disk Performance Over Time

Databases are very storage I/O intensive, so disks *will* wear out over time. Most disk vendors provide estimates concerning the performance durability of their products. Check on those and compare.

There are multiple tools and programs that can help with SSD performance over time. One example is the `fstrim` program, which is frequently run weekly to discard unused filesystem blocks. `fstrim` is an operating system background process that doesn't require any database action and may improve I/O to a significant extent.

> **Tip** If you have to choose one place to invest—on CPU, storage, memory, or networking—we recommend splurging on storage. Everything else has evolved faster and better than storage. It still remains the slowest component in most systems.

Tiered Storage

Many use cases have different latency requirements for different sets of data. Similarly, industries may see exponential storage utilization growth over time. It is not always desirable, or even possible, to get rid of old data (for example, due to compliance regulations, third-party contracts, or simply because it still carries relevance for the business).

Teams with storage-heavy use cases often seek ways to minimize the costs of storage consumption: by reducing the replication factor of their dataset, using less performant (although cheaper) storage disks, or by employing a manual data rotation process from faster to slower disks.

Tiered storage is a solution implemented by some databases in order to address most of these concerns. It allows users to configure the database to use distinct storage tiers, and to define which criteria the database should use to ensure that the data is correctly replicated to its relevant tier. For example, MongoDB allows you to determine how data is replicated to a specific storage tier by assigning different tier tags to shards, allowing its balancer to migrate data between tiers automatically. On top of that, Atlas Online Archive also allows the database to offload historical datasets to cloud storage.

CPUs (Cores)

Next is the CPU. As of this writing, you are probably looking at modern servers running some reasonably modern Intel, AMD, or ARM chips, which are commonly found across most cloud providers and enterprise hardware vendors. Along with storage, CPUs are another compute resource which—if not correctly sized—may introduce contention to your workload and impact your latencies. Clusters handling hundreds of thousands up to millions of operations per second tend to get very high CPU loads.

More cores will generally mean better performance. This is important for achieving optimal performance from databases that are architected to benefit from multithreading, and it's absolutely essential for databases that are architected with a shard-per-core architecture—running a separate shard on each core in each server. In this case, the more cores the CPU has, the more shards—and the better data distribution—the database will have.

A combination of vendor recommendations and benchmarking (see Chapter 9) can help you determine how much throughput each multicore chip can support. A general recommendation is to avoid running production systems close to the CPU limits and find the sweet spot between supporting your expected performance and leaving room for throughput growth. On top of that, when doing benchmarking, remember to also factor in background database operations that might be detrimental to your performance. For example, Cassandra and Cassandra-compatible databases often need to run repair: a weekly process to ensure data consistency across the cluster. This process requires a lot of coordination and communication across the entire cluster. If your workload is not properly sized to accommodate background database operations and other events (such as node failures), your latency may increase to a level that surprises you.

When using virtual machines, containers, or the public cloud, remember that each virtual CPU is mapped to a single logical core, or thread. In many cloud deployments, nodes are provided on a vCPU basis. The vCPU is typically a single hyperthread from a dual hyperthread x86 physical core for Intel/AMD variants, or a single core for ARM chips.

No matter what your deployment of choice involves, avoid overcommitting CPU resources if performance is a priority. Doing so will prevent other guests from stealing CPU time[5] from your database.

Memory (RAM)

If you're working with an in-memory database, having enough memory to hold your entire dataset is an absolute must. But every database uses in-memory caching to some extent. For example, some databases require enough memory space for indexes to avoid expensive round-trips to storage disks. Others leverage an internal data cache to allow

---

[5] For more on CPU steal time, see "Detecting CPU Steal Time in Guest Virtual Machines" by Jamie Fargen (https://opensource.com/article/20/1/cpu-steal-time).

for lower latencies when retrieving recently used data, Cassandra and Cassandra-like databases implement memtables, and some databases allow you to control which tables are served entirely from memory. The more memory the database has at its disposal, the better you can take advantage of those mechanisms. After all, even the fastest NVMe can't come close to the speed of RAM access.

In general, there is no blanket recommendation for "how much memory is enough" for a database. Different vendors have different requirements and different use cases also require different memory sizes. However, latency-sensitive use cases typically require high memory footprints in order to achieve high cache hit rates and serve low-latency read requests efficiently.

For example, a use case with a higher payload size requires a larger memory footprint than one with a smaller payload size. Another interesting aspect to consider is how frequently the use case in question reads data that may be present in memory (hot data) as opposed to data that was never read (cold data). As mentioned in Chapter 2, the latter can easily undermine your latencies.

Without a sufficient disk-to-memory ratio, you will be hitting your storage far more than you probably want if you intend to keep your latencies low. The ideal ratio varies from database to database since every caching implementation is different, so be sure to ask your vendor for their specific recommendations. For example, ScyllaDB currently recommends that for every 1GB of memory allocated to a node, you can store up to 100GB of data (so if you have 32GB of memory, you can handle around 3TB). The higher your memory-to-storage ratio gets, the less room you have for caching your total dataset. Every database has some sort of hard physical limit. If you don't have enough memory and you have to run a workload on top of a very large dataset, it's either going to be rather slow or increase the risk of the database running out of memory.

Another ratio to keep in mind: memory per CPU core. At ScyllaDB, we recommend at least 8GB of memory per CPU core for production purposes (because, given our shared-nothing architecture, every shard works independently and has its own allocated memory for caching). 8GB per vCPU is the same ratio used by most cloud providers for NoSQL or Big Data-oriented instance types. Again, the recommended ratio will vary across vendors, depending on the database's specific internal cache implementation and other implementation details. For example, in Cassandra and Cassandra-like databases, part of the memory will be allocated for some of its SSTable-components in order to speed up disk lookups when reading cold data. Aerospike will typically store all indexes in RAM. And MongoDB, on average, requires 1GB of RAM per 100K assets.

Distributed databases are notoriously high memory consumers. Regardless of its implementation, the database will always need to store some relevant parts of your dataset in memory in order to avoid wasting time on disk I/O. Insufficient memory can manifest itself as unpredictable, erratic database behavior—even crashes.

Network

Lastly, you have to ensure that network I/O does not become a bottleneck. Networking is often an overlooked component. As with any distributed system, a database involves a lot of traffic between all the cluster members to check for liveness, replicate state and topology changes, and so on. As a result, network delays not only deteriorate your application's latency, but also prevent internode communication from functioning effectively.

At ScyllaDB, we recommend a minimum network bandwidth of 10Gbps because internal database operations such as streaming, repairs, and gossip can become very network intensive. On top of that, you also need to factor in the actual throughput required for the use case in question; the number of operations per second will certainly be the highest bandwidth consumer for your deployment.

As with memory, the required network bandwidth will vary. Be sure to check your vendor recommendations and consider the nature of your use case. A low throughput workload will obviously consume less traffic than a higher throughput one.

Tip: Use CPU pinning to mitigate the impact of hardware interrupts.   Hardware interrupts, which typically stem from (but are not limited to) high network Internet traffic, force the OS kernel to stop everything and respond to the hardware before returning to the job at hand. Too many interrupts (e.g., a high softirq percent) will degrade database performance, as your CPUs may stall during processing for serving network traffic. One way to resolve this is to use CPU pinning. This tells the system that all network interrupts should be handled by specific CPUs that are not being used by the database. With that setup, you can blast the database with network traffic and be reasonably confident that you won't overwhelm it or stall the database processing during normal operations.

For cloud deployments, most IaaS vendors provide a modern network infrastructure with ample bandwidth between your database servers and between the database and the application clients. Be sure to check on your client's network bandwidth consumption if you suspect network problems. A common mistake we see in deployments involves application clients deployed with suboptimal network capacity.

Also, be sure to place your application servers as close as possible to your database. If you are deploying them in a single region, a shorter physical distance between the servers will translate to better network performance (since it will require fewer network hops for communication) and, as a result, lower latencies. If you need to go multi-region and you require strong consistency or replication across these regions, then you need to pay the latency penalty for traversing regions—plus, you also have to pay, quite literally, with respect to cross-region networking transfer fees. For multi-region deployments with cross-region replication, a slow network link may create replication delays that cause the database to apply backpressure on your writes until it manages to replicate the data piled up.

Considerations in the Cloud

The "on-prem vs cloud" decision depends heavily on your organization's security and regulatory requirements as well as its business strategy—and is well beyond the scope of this book. Instead of heading down that path, let's focus on exploring performance considerations that are unique to cloud deployments.

Most cloud providers offer a wide range of instance types that you may choose to host your workload. In our experience, most of the mistakes and performance bottlenecks seen on distributed databases within cloud deployments are due to an incorrect instance or storage type selection during the initial cluster setup. A common misunderstanding (and concern) that many people have is the fact that NVMe-based storage may be more expensive than network-attached storage. The misconception likely stems from the assumption that since NVMes are faster, they would incur elevated costs. However it turns out to be quite the opposite: Since NVMe disks on cloud environments are tied to the lifecycle of an instance, they end up being cheaper than network disks, which require holding up your dataset for a prolonged period of time. We encourage you to compare the costs of NVMe backed-up storage against network-attached disks on your cloud vendor of choice.

Some cloud vendors have different instance types for different distributed database workloads. For example, some workloads may benefit more from compute-heavy instance types, with more compute power than storage capacity. Conversely, storage-dense instance types typically feature a higher storage to memory ratio and are often used by storage-heavy workloads.

To complicate things even more, some cloud providers may offer different CPU generations for the same instance type. If one CPU generation is considerably slower than other nodes, the wrong choice could introduce performance bottlenecks into your cluster.

We have seen some (although rare) scenarios where a noisy neighbor dragged down an entire node performance with no reasonable explanation. The lack of visibility and control in cloud instances makes it harder to diagnose such situations. Often, you need to reach out to your cloud vendor directly to resolve the situation.

As you start configuring your instance, remember that a cloud environment isn't created exclusively for databases. You have access to a wide range of options, but it can be confusing to determine where to start and which options to use. In general, it's best to check with your database vendor on which instance types are recommended for deployment. Even better, go beyond that and compare the results of their benchmarks against those same instance types running your workload.

After you have decided on your instance types and deployment options, it's time to think about instance placement. Most clouds will charge you for both inter-region traffic and inter-zone traffic, which may quite surprisingly increase the overall networking costs. Some companies try to mitigate this cost by placing all instances under a single availability zone (AZ), which also carries the risk of potentially having to face a cluster-wide outage if/when that AZ goes down. Others opt to ignore the cost aspect and deploy their replicas in different AZs to ensure data is properly replicated to an isolated environment. Regardless of your instance's placement of choice, note that some database drivers allow clients in specific AZs to route queries only against database replicas living in the same availability zone in order to reduce costs. Similarly, you will also want to ensure that your application clients are located under the same zones as your database to minimize your networking costs.

Fully Managed Database-as-a-Service

Does the database-as-a-service model help or hurt database performance? It really depends on the following:

- How much attention your database requires to achieve and consistently meet your performance expectations

- Your team's experience working with the specific database you're using

- Your team's time and desire to tinker with that database

- The level of expertise—especially with respect to performance—that your DBaaS provider dedicates to your account

Managed DBaaS solutions can easily speed up your go-to-market and allow you to focus on priorities beyond your database. Most database vendors now provide some sort of managed solution. There are even independent companies in the business of providing this kind of service for a variety of different distributed databases.

We have seen many examples where a managed solution helped users succeed, as well as numerous complaints over the fact that some managed solutions were rather limited. It is not our intention to recommend nor criticize any specific service provider in question. Here is some vendor-agnostic advice on things to consider before selecting a managed solution:

- Does the vendor satisfy your existing security requirements? Does it provide enough evidence of security certifications issued by a known security company?

- What are the options for observability and how do you export the data in question to your monitoring platform of choice?

- What kind of flexibility do you have with your deployment? What are the available tunable options and the support for those within your managed solution?

- Does it allow you to peer traffic from your existing application network(s) to your database in a private and secure way?

- What are the available support options and SLAs?

- Which deployment options are available, what's the flexibility among switching, and what's the cost comparison if you were to deploy and maintain it on your own?

- How easy is it for you to export your data if you need to move your deployment to a different vendor in the future?

- What, if any, migration options are available and what amount of effort do they require?

These are just some of the many questions and concerns that we've frequently heard teams asking (or wishing they asked before they got caught in an undesirable option). Considering a third-party vendor to manage a relatively critical aspect of your infrastructure is very often challenging. However, under the right circumstances and vendor-user fit, it can be a great option for reducing your admin burden and optimizing your performance.

Serverless Deployment Models

Serverless refers to database solutions that offer near-instant scaling up or scaling down of database infrastructure—and charge you for the capacity and storage that you actually consume.

A serverless model could theoretically yield a performance advantage. Before serverless, many organizations faced a tradeoff:

- (Slightly or generously, depending on your risk tolerance) overestimate the capacity they need to guarantee adequate performance.

- Watch performance suffer if their overly-conservative capacity estimates proved inadequate.

Serverless can help in a few different ways and situations.

First, with variable workloads. Since the database can rapidly scale up as your workload increases, you can worry less about performance issues stemming from inadequate capacity. If your traffic ebbs and flows across the day/week/month, you can spend less during the light periods and dedicate those resources to supporting the peak periods. And if your company suddenly experiences "catastrophic success," you don't have to worry about the headaches associated with needing to suddenly scale your infrastructure. If all goes well, the vendor will "automagically" ensure that you're covered, with acceptable performance. You won't need to procure any additional servers, or even contact your cloud provider.

Serverless is also a great option to consider if you're working on a new project and are not sure what capacity you need to meet performance expectations. It gives you the freedom to start fast and scale (or shrink) depending on real-world usage. Database sizing is one less thing to worry about. And you don't need to predict the future.

Finally, serverless also makes it simpler to justify the spend internally. With this model, you can assure your organization that you are never overprovisioned—at least not for long. You're paying for exactly the amount of performance that the database vendor determines you need at all times.

However, a serverless deployment also carries the risk of cost overruns and the uncertainty of unpredictable costs. For example, DynamoDB pricing may not be very attractive for write-heavy workloads. Similarly, serverless database services may charge an arm and a leg (or an eye and a knee) depending on the number of operations per second you plan to sustain over an extended period of time. In some cases, it could become a double-edged sword from a cost perspective if your goal is to sustain a high-throughput performant system at large scale.

Another aspect to consider when thinking about a serverless solution is whether the solution in question is compatible with your existing infrastructure components. For example, you'll want to explore what amount of effort is required to connect your message queueing or analytics tool with that specific serverless solution.

Remember that the overall concept behind serverless is to abstract away the underlying infrastructure in such a way that not all database-configurable options are available to you. As a result, troubleshooting potential performance problems is often more challenging since you might need to rely on your vendor's input and guidance to understand which actions to take. Being serverless also means that you lack visibility into whether the infrastructure you consume is shared with other tenants. Many distributed database vendors may also offer you different pricing tiers for shared and dedicated environments.

Containerization and Kubernetes

Containers and Kubernetes are now ubiquitous, even for stateful systems like databases. Should you use them? Probably—unless you have a good reason not to.

But be aware that there is a performance penalty for the operational convenience of using containers. This is to be expected because of the extra layer of abstraction (the container itself), relaxation of resource isolation, and increased context switches. The good news is that it can certainly be overcome. In our testing using ScyllaDB, we found it is possible to take what was originally a 69 percent reduction in peak throughput down to a 3 percent performance penalty.[6]

Here's the TL;DR on that specific experiment:

> *Containerizing applications is not free. In particular, processes comprising the containers have to be run in Linux cgroups and the container receives a virtualized view of the network. Still, the biggest cost of running a close-to-hardware, thread-per-core application like ScyllaDB inside a Docker container comes from the opportunity cost of having to disable most of the performance optimizations that the database employs in VM and bare-metal environments to enable it to run in potentially shared and overcommitted platforms.*
>
> *The best results with Docker are obtained when resources are statically partitioned and we can bring back bare-metal optimizations like CPU pinning and interrupt isolation. There is only a 10 percent performance penalty in this case as compared to the underlying platform—a penalty that is mostly attributed to the network virtualization. Docker allows users to expose the host network directly for specialized deployments. In cases in which this is possible, we saw that the performance difference compared to the underlying platform falls down to 3 percent.*

Of course, the potential penalty and strategies for mitigating will vary from database to database. But the key takeaway is that there is likely a significant performance penalty—so be sure to hunt it down and research how to mitigate it. Some common mitigation strategies include:

---

[6] See "The Cost of Containerization for Your ScyllaDB" on the ScyllaDB blog (https://www.scylladb.com/2018/08/09/cost-containerization-scylla/).

- Ensure that your containers have direct access to the database's underlying storage.

- Expose the host OS network to the container in order to avoid the performance penalty due to its network virtualization layer.

- Allocate enough resources to the container in question, and ensure these are not overcommitted with other containers or processes running within the underlying host OS.

Kubernetes adds yet another virtualization layer—and thus opens the door to yet another layer of performance issues, as well as different strategies for mitigating them. First off, if you have the choice of multiple options for deploying and managing database clusters on Kubernetes, test them out with an eye on performance. Once you settle on the best fit for your needs, dive into the configuration options that could impact performance. Here are some performance tips that cross databases:

- Consider dedicating specific and independent Kubernetes nodes for your database workloads and use affinities in order to configure their placement.

- Enable hostNetworking and be sure to set up the required kernel parameters as recommended by your vendor (for example, fs. aio-max-nr for increasing the number of events available for asynchronous I/O processing in the Linux kernel).

- Ensure that your database pods have a Guaranteed QoS class[7] to avoid other pods from potentially hurting your main workload.

- Be sure to use an operator[8] in order to orchestrate and control the lifecycle of your existing Kubernetes database cluster. For example, ScyllaDB has its ScyllaDB Operator project.

---

[7] For more detail, see "Create a Pod that Gets Assigned a QoS Class of Guaranteed" in the Kubernetes docs (https://kubernetes.io/docs/tasks/configure-pod-container/quality-service-pod/#create-a-pod-that-gets-assigned-a-qos-class-of-guaranteed).
[8] For more detail, see "Operator Pattern" in the Kubernetes docs https://kubernetes.io/docs/concepts/extend-kubernetes/operator/.

Summary

This chapter kicked off the final part of this book, focused on sharing recommendations for getting better performance out of your database deployment. It looked at infrastructure and deployment model considerations that are important to understand whether you're managing your own deployment or opting for a database-as-a-service (maybe serverless) deployment model. The next chapter looks at performance considerations relevant to the topology itself: replication, geographic distribution, scaling up and/or out, and intermediaries like external caches, load balancers, and abstraction layers.

CHAPTER 8

Topology Considerations

As mentioned in Chapter 5, database servers are often combined into intricate topologies where certain nodes are grouped in a single geographical location; others are used only as a fast cache layer, and yet others store seldom-accessed cold data in a cheap place, for emergency purposes only. That chapter covered how drivers work to understand and interact with that topology to exchange information more efficiently.

This chapter focuses on the topology in and of itself. How is data replicated across geographies and datacenters? What are the risks and alternatives to taking the common NoSQL practice of scaling out to the extreme? And what about intermediaries to your database servers—for example, external caches, load balancers, and abstraction layers? Performance implications of all this and more are all covered here.[1]

Replication Strategy

First, let's look at *replication*, which is how your data will be spread to other replicas across your cluster.

Note If you want a quick introduction to the concept of replication, see Appendix A.

Having more replicas will slow your writes (since every write must be duplicated to replicas), but it could accelerate your reads (since more replicas will be available for serving the same dataset). It will also allow you to maintain operations and avoid data

---

[1] This chapter draws from material originally published on the ScyllaDB blog (`www.scylladb.com/blog/`), ScyllaDB Documentation (`https://docs.scylladb.com/stable/`), the ScyllaDB whitepaper "Why Scaling Up Beats Scaling Out for NoSQL" (`https://lp.scylladb.com/whitepaper-scaling-up-vs-scaling-out-offer.html`), and an article that ScyllaDB co-founder and CEO Dor Laor wrote for *The New Stack*. It is used here with permission of ScyllaDB.

© Felipe Cardeneti Mendes, Piotr Sarna, Pavel Emelyanov, Cynthia Dunlop 2023
F. C. Mendes et al., *Database Performance at Scale*, https://doi.org/10.1007/978-1-4842-9711-7_8

loss in the event of node failures. Additionally, replicating data to get closer to your application and closer to your users will reduce latency, especially if your application has a highly geographically-distributed user base.

A replication factor (RF) of 1 means there is only one copy of a row in a cluster, and there is no way to recover the data if the node is compromised or goes down (other than restoring from a backup). An RF of 2 means that there are two copies of a row in a cluster. An RF of at least three is used in most systems. This allows you to write and read with strong consistency, as a quorum of replicas will be achieved, even if one node is down.

Many databases also let you fine-tune replication settings at the regional level. For example, you could have three replicas in a heavily used region, but only two in a less popular region.

Note that replicating data across multiple regions (as Bigtable recommends as a safeguard against both availability zone failure and regional failure) can be expensive. Before you set this up, understand the cost of replicating data between regions.

If you're working with DynamoDB, you create tables (not clusters), and AWS manages the replication for you as soon as you set a table to be Global. One notable drawback of DynamoDB global tables is that transactions are not supported across regions, which may be a limiting factor for some use cases.

Rack Configuration

If all your nodes are in the same datacenter, how do you configure their placement? The rule of thumb here is to have as many racks as you have replicas. For example, if you have a replication factor of three, run it in three racks. That way, even if an entire rack goes down, you can still continue to satisfy read and write requests to a majority of your replicas. Performance might degrade a bit since you have lost roughly 33 percent of your infrastructure (considering a total zone/rack outage), but overall you'll still be up and running. Conversely, if you have three replicas distributed across two racks, then losing a rack may potentially affect two out of the three natural endpoints for part of your data. That's a showstopper if your use case requires strongly consistent reads/writes.

Multi-Region or Global Replication

By placing your database servers close to your users, you lower the network latency. You can also improve availability and insulate your business from regional outages.

If you do have multiple datacenters, ensure that—unless otherwise required by the business—reads and writes use a consistency level that is confined to replicas within a specific datacenter. This approach avoids introducing a latency hit by instructing the database to only select local replicas (under the same region) for achieving your required consistency level. Also, ensure that each application client knows what datacenter is considered its local one; it should prioritize that local one for connections and requests, although it may also have a fallback strategy just in case that datacenter goes down.

Note that application clients may or may not be aware of the multi-datacenter deployment, and it is up to the application developer to decide on the awareness to fallback across regions. Although different settings and load balancing profiles exist through a variety of database drivers, the general concept for an application to failover to a different region in the event of a local failure may often break application semantics. As a result, its reaction upon a failure must be handled directly by the application developer.

Multi-Availability Zones vs. Multi-Region

To mitigate a possible server or rack failure, cloud vendors offer (and recommend) a multi-zone deployment. Think about it as if you have a datacenter at your fingertips where you can deploy each server instance in its own rack, using its own power, top-of-rack switch, and cooling system. Such a deployment will be bulletproof for any single system or zonal failure, since each rack is self-contained. The availability zones are still located in the same region. However, a specific zone failure won't affect another zone's deployed instances.

For example, on Google Compute Engine, the us-east1-b, us-east1-c, and us-east1-d availability zones are located in the us-east1 region (Moncks Corner, South Carolina, USA). But each availability zone is self-contained. Network latency between AZs in the same region is negligible for the purpose of this discussion.

In short, both multi-zone and multi-region deployments help with business continuity and disaster recovery respectively, but multi-region has the additional benefit of minimizing local application latencies in those local regions. It might come at a cost though: cross-region data replication costs need to be considered for multi-regional topologies.

Note that multi-zonal deployments will similarly charge you for inter-zone replication. Although it is perfectly possible to have a single zone deployment for your database, it is often not a recommended approach because it will effectively be exposed as a single point of failure toward your infrastructure. The choice here is quite simple: Do you want to reduce costs as much as possible and risk potential unavailability, or do you want to guarantee high availability in a single region at the expense of network replication costs?

Scaling Up vs Scaling Out

Is it better to have a larger number of smaller (read, "less powerful") nodes or a smaller number of larger nodes? We recommend aiming for the most powerful nodes and smallest clusters that meet your high availability and resiliency goals—but only if your database can truly take advantage of the power added by the larger nodes.

Let's unravel that a bit. For over a decade, NoSQL's promise has been enabling massive horizontal scalability with relatively inexpensive commodity hardware. This has allowed organizations to deploy architectures that would have been prohibitively expensive and impossible to scale using traditional relational database systems.

Over that same decade, "commodity hardware" has also undergone a transformation. But not all databases take advantage of modern computing resources. Many aren't architected to take advantage of the resources offered by large nodes, such as the added CPU, memory, and solid-state drives (SSDs), nor can they store large amounts of data on disk efficiently. Managed runtimes, like Java, are further constrained by heap size. Multi-threaded code, with its locking and context-switches overhead and lack of attention for Non-Uniform Memory Architecture (NUMA), imposes a significant performance penalty against modern hardware architectures.

If your database is in this group, you might find that scaling up quickly brings you to a point of diminishing returns. But even then, it's best to max out your vertical scaling potential before you shift to horizontal scaling.

A focus on horizontal scaling results in system sprawl, which equates to operational overhead, with a far larger footprint to keep managed and secure. Server sprawl also introduces more network overhead to distributed systems due to the constant replication and health checks done by every single node in your cluster. Although most vendors claim that scaling out will bring you linear performance, some others are more conservative and state that it will bring you "near to linear performance." For example,

Cassandra Production Guidelines[2] do not recommend clusters larger than 50 nodes using the default number of 16 vNodes per instance because it may result in decreased availability.

Moreover, there are quite a few advantages to using large, powerful nodes.

- **Less noisy neighbors**: On cloud platforms, multi-tenancy is the norm. A cloud platform is, by definition, based on shared network bandwidth, I/O, memory, storage, and so on. As a result, a deployment of many small nodes is susceptible to the "noisy neighbor" effect. This effect is experienced when one application or virtual machine consumes more than its fair share of available resources. As nodes increase in size, fewer and fewer resources are shared among tenants. In fact, beyond a certain size, your applications are likely to be the only tenant on the physical machines on which your system is deployed.

- **Fewer failures**: Since large and small nodes fail at roughly the same rate, large nodes deliver a higher mean time between failures (MTBF) than small nodes. Failures in the data layer require operator intervention, and restoring a large node requires the same amount of human effort as a small one. In a cluster of a thousand nodes, you'll likely see failures every day—and this magnifies administrative costs.

- **Datacenter density**: Many organizations with on-premises datacenters are seeking to increase density by consolidating servers into fewer, larger boxes with more computing resources per server. Small clusters of large nodes help this process by efficiently consuming denser resources, in turn decreasing energy and operating costs.

- **Operational simplicity**: Big clusters of small instances demand more attention, and generate more alerts, than small clusters of large instances. All of those small nodes multiply the effort of real-time monitoring and periodic maintenance, such as rolling upgrades.

---

[2] See https://cassandra.apache.org/doc/latest/cassandra/getting_started/production.html.

Some architects are concerned that putting more data on fewer nodes increases the risks associated with outages and data loss. You can think of this as the "big basket" problem. It may seem intuitive that storing all of your data on a few large nodes makes them more vulnerable to outages, like putting all of your eggs in one basket. But this doesn't necessarily hold true. Modern databases use a number of techniques to ensure availability while also accelerating recovery from failures, making big nodes both safer and more economical. For example, consider capabilities that reduce the time required to add and replace nodes and internal load balancing mechanisms to minimize the throughput or latency impact across database restarts.[3]

Workload Isolation

Many teams find themselves in a position where they need to run multiple different workloads against the database. It is often compelling to aggregate different workloads under a single cluster, especially when they need to work on the exact same dataset. Keeping several workloads together under a single cluster can also reduce costs. But, it's essential to avoid resource contention when implementing latency-critical workloads. Failure to do so may introduce hard-to-diagnose performance situations, where one misbehaving workload ends up dragging down the entire cluster's performance.

There are many ways to accomplish workload isolation to minimize the resource contention that could occur when running multiple workloads on a single cluster. Here are a few that work well. Keep in mind that the best approach depends on your existing database's available options, as well as your use case's requirements:

- **Physical isolation**: This setup is often used to entirely isolate one workload from another. It involves essentially extending your deployment to an additional region (which may be physically the same as your existing one, but logically different on the database side). As a result, the workloads are split to replicate data to another

---

[3] ScyllaDB Heat Weighted Load Balancing provides a smarter request redistribution algorithm based on the cache hit ratio of nodes in the cluster. Learn more at `www.scylladb.com/2017/09/21/scylla-heat-weighted-load-balancing/`.

location, but queries are executed only within a particular location—
in such a way that a performance bottleneck in one workload won't
degrade or bottleneck the other. Note that a downside of this solution
is that your infrastructure costs double.

- **Logical isolation**: Some databases or deployment options allow
  you to logically isolate workloads without needing to increase your
  infrastructure resources. For example, ScyllaDB has a workload
  prioritization feature where you can assign different weights for
  specific workloads to help the database understand which workload
  you want it to prioritize in the event of system contention. If your
  database does not offer such a feature, you may still be able to
  run two or more workloads in parallel, but watch out for potential
  contentions in your database.

- **Scheduled isolation**: Many times, you might need to simply run
  batched scheduled jobs at specified intervals in order to support
  other business-related activities, such as extracting analytics
  reports. In those cases, consider running the workload in question
  at low-peak periods (if any exist), and experiment with different
  concurrency settings in order to avoid impairing the latency of the
  primary workload that's running alongside it.

More on Workload Prioritization for Logical Isolation

ScyllaDB users sometimes use workload prioritization to balance OLAP and OLTP
workloads. The goal is to ensure that each defined task has a fair share of system
resources so that no single job monopolizes system resources, starving other jobs of their
needed minimums to continue operations.

In Figure 8-1, note that the latency for both workloads nearly converges. OLTP
processing began at or below 2ms P99 latency up until the OLAP job began at 12:15.
When the OLAP workload kicked in, OLTP P99 latencies shot up to 8ms, then further
degraded, plateauing around 11–12ms until the OLAP job terminated after 12:26.

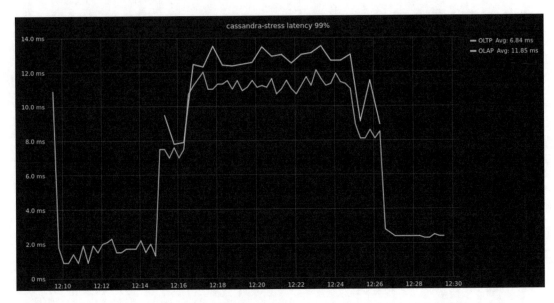

Figure 8-1. *Latency between OLTP and OLAP workloads on the same cluster before enabling workload prioritization*

These latencies are approximately six times greater than when OLTP ran by itself. (OLAP latencies hover between 12–14ms, but, again, OLAP is not latency-sensitive).

Figure 8-2 shows that the throughput on OLTP sinks from around 60,000 OPS to half that—30,000 OPS. You can see the reason why. OLAP, being throughput hungry, is maintaining roughly 260,000 OPS.

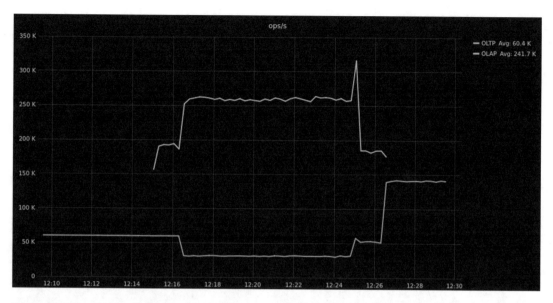

Figure 8-2. *Comparative throughput results for OLTP and OLAP on the same cluster without workload prioritization enabled*

Ultimately, OLTP suffers with respect to both latency and throughput, and users experience slower response times. In many real-world conditions, such OLTP responses would violate a customer's SLA.

Figure 8-3 shows the latencies after workload prioritization is enabled. You can see that the OLTP workload similarly starts out at sub-millisecond to 2ms P99 latencies. Once an OLAP workload is added, OLTP processing performance degrades, but with P99 latencies hovering between 4–7ms (about half of the 11–12ms P99 latencies when workload prioritization was *not* enabled).

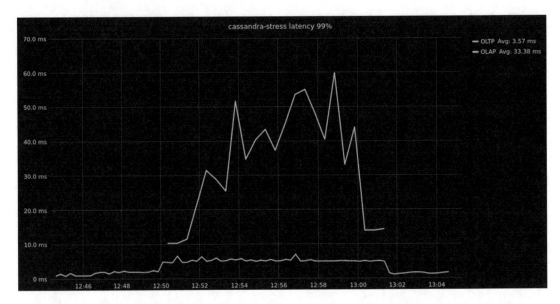

Figure 8-3. *OLTP and OLAP latencies with workload prioritization enabled*

It is important to note that once system contention kicks in, the OLTP latencies are still somewhat impacted—just not to the same extent they were prior to workload prioritization. If your real-time workload requires ultra-constant single-digit millisecond or lower P99 latencies, then we strongly recommend that you avoid introducing *any* form of contention.

The OLAP workload, not being as latency-sensitive, has P99 latencies that hover between 25–65ms. These are much higher latencies than before—the tradeoff for keeping the OLTP latencies lower.

Throughput wise, Figure 8-4 shows that the OLTP traffic is a smooth 60,000 OPS until the OLAP load is also enabled.

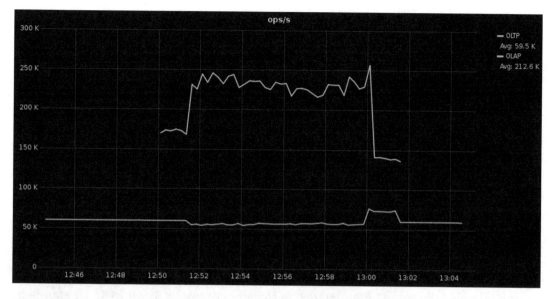

Figure 8-4. *OLTP and OLAP load throughput with workload prioritization enabled*

It does dip in performance at that point, but only slightly, hovering between 54,000 to 58,000 OPS. That is only a 3–10 percent drop in throughput. The OLAP workload, for its part, hovers between 215,000–250,000 OPS. That is a drop of 4–18 percent, which means an OLAP workload would take longer to complete. Both workloads suffer degradation, as would be expected for an overloaded cluster, but neither to a crippling degree.

Abstraction Layers

It's becoming fairly common for teams to write an abstraction layer on top of their databases. Instead of calling the database's APIs directly, the applications connect to this database-agnostic abstraction layer, which then manages the logistics of connecting to the database.

There are usually a few main motives behind this move:

- **Portability**: If the team wants to move to another database, they won't need to modify their applications and queries. However, the team responsible for the abstraction layer will need to modify that code, which could turn out to be more complicated.

167

- **Developer simplicity**: Developers don't need to worry about the inner details of working with any particular database. This can make it easier for people to move around from team to team.

- **Scalability**: An abstraction layer can be easier to containerize. If the API gets overloaded, it's usually easier to scale out more containers in Kubernetes than to spin off more containers of the database itself.

- **Customer-facing APIs**: Exposing the database directly to end-users is typically not a good idea. As a result, many companies expose common endpoints, which are eventually translated into actual database queries. As a result, the abstraction layer can shed requests, limit concurrency across tenants, and perform auditability and accountability over its calls.

But, there's definitely a potential for a performance penalty that is highly dependent on how efficiently the layer was implemented. An abstraction layer that was fastidiously implemented by a team of masterful Rust engineers is likely to have a much more negligible impact than a Java or Python one cobbled together as a quick side project. If you decide to take this route, be sure that the layer is developed with performance in mind, and that you carefully measure its impact via both benchmarking and ongoing monitoring. Remember that every application <> database communication is going to use this layer, so a small inefficiency can quickly snowball into a significant performance problem.

For example, we once saw a customer report an elevated latency situation coming from their Golang abstraction layer. Once we realized that the latency on the database side was within bounds for its use case, the investigation shifted from the database over to the network and client side. Long story short, the application latency spikes were identified as being heavily affected during the garbage collection process, dragging down the client-side performance significantly. The problem was resolved after scaling out the number of clients and by ensuring that they had enough compute resources to properly function.

And another example: When working with a customer through a PostgreSQL to NoSQL migration, we realized that their clients were fairly often opening too many concurrent connections against the database. Although having a high number of sockets opened is typically a good idea for distributed systems, an extremely high number of them can easily overwhelm the client side (which needs to keep track of all open sockets) as well as the database. After we reported our findings to the customer, they discovered that they were opening a new database session for every request they submitted against the cluster. After correcting the malfunctioning code, the overall application throughput was significantly increased because the abstraction layer was then using active sockets opened when it routed requests.[4]

Load Balancing

Should you put a dedicated load balancer in front of your database? In most cases, no. Databases typically have their own way to balance traffic across the cluster, so layering a load balancer on top of that won't help—and it could actually hurt. Consider 1) how many requests the load balancer can serve without becoming a bottleneck and 2) its balancing policy. Also, recognize that it introduces a single point of failure that reduces your database resilience. As a result, you overcomplicate your overall infrastructure topology because you now need to worry about load balancing high availability.

Of course, there are always exceptions. For example, say you were previously using a database API that's unaware of the layout of the cluster and its individual nodes (e.g., DynamoDB, where a client is configured with a single "endpoint address" and all requests are sent to it). Now you're shifting to a distributed leaderless database like ScyllaDB, where clients are node aware and even token aware (aware of which token ranges are natural endpoints for every node in your topology). If you simply configure an application with the IP address of a single ScyllaDB node as its single DynamoDB API endpoint address, the application will work correctly. After all, any node can answer any request by forwarding it to other nodes as necessary. However, this single node will be more loaded than the other nodes because it will be the only node actively serving requests. This node will also become a single point of failure from your application's perspective.

In this special edge case, load balancing is critical—but load balancers are not. Server-side load balancing is fairly complex from an admin perspective. More importantly with respect to performance, server-side solutions add latency. Solutions that involve a TCP or HTTP load balancer require another hop for each

---

[4] Learn about abstraction layer usage at Discord in "How Discord Migrated Trillions of Messages from Cassandra to ScyllaDB "(www.youtube.com/watch?v=S2xmFOAUhsk) and ShareChat in "ShareChat's Path to High-Performance NoSQL with ScyllaDB" (www.youtube.com/watch?v=Y2yHv8iqigA).

request—increasing not just the cost of each request, but also its latency. We recommend client-side load balancing: Modifying the application to send requests to the available nodes versus a single one.

The key takeaway here is that load balancing generally isn't needed—and when it is, server-side load balancers yield a pretty severe performance penalty. If it's absolutely necessary, client-side load balancing is likely a better option.[5]

External Caches

Teams often consider external caches when the existing database cluster cannot meet the required SLA. This is a clear performance-oriented decision. Putting an external cache in front of the database is commonly used to compensate for subpar latency stemming from the various factors discussed throughout this book: inefficient database internals, driver usage, infrastructure choices, traffic spikes, and so on.

Caching may seem like a fast and easy solution because the deployment can be implemented without tremendous hassle and without incurring the significant cost of database scaling, database schema redesign, or even a deeper technology transformation. However, external caches are not as simple as they are often made out to be. In fact, they can be one of the more problematic components of a distributed application architecture.

In some cases, it's a necessary evil—particularly if you have an ultra-latency-sensitive use case such as real-time ad bidding or streaming media, and you've tried all the other means of reducing latency. But in many cases, the performance boost isn't worth it. The following sections outline some key risks and you can decide what makes sense for your use case and SLAs.

An External Cache Adds Latency

A separate cache means another hop on the way. When a cache surrounds the database, the first access occurs at the cache layer. If the data isn't in the cache, then the request is sent to the database. The result is additional latency to an already slow path of uncached data. One may claim that when the entire dataset fits the cache, the additional latency doesn't come into play. However, there is usually more than a single workload/pattern that hits the database and some of it will carry the extra hop cost.

---

[5] For an example of how to implement client-side load balancing, see www.scylladb.com/2021/04/13/load-balancing-in-scylla-alternator/.

An External Cache Is an Additional Cost

Caching means expensive DRAM, which translates to a higher cost per gigabyte than SSDs. Even when RAM can store frequently accessed objects, it is best to use the existing database RAM, and even increase it for internal caching rather than provision entirely separate infrastructure on RAM-oriented instances. Provisioning a cache to be the same size as the entire persistent dataset may be prohibitively expensive. In other cases, the working set size can be too big, often reaching petabytes, making an SSD-friendly implementation the preferred, and cheaper, option.

External Caching Decreases Availability

No cache's high availability solution can match that of the database itself. Modern distributed databases have multiple replicas; they also are topology-aware and speed-aware and can sustain multiple failures without data loss.

For example, a common replication pattern is three local replicas, which generally allows for reads to be balanced across such replicas in order to efficiently use your database's internal caching mechanism. Consider a nine-node cluster with a replication factor of three: Essentially every node will hold roughly 33 percent of your total dataset size. As requests are balanced among different replicas, this grants you more room for caching your data, which could (potentially) completely eliminate the need for an external cache. Conversely, if an external cache happens to invalidate entries right before a surge of cold requests, availability could be impeded for a while since the database won't have that data in its internal cache (more on this in the section entitled "External Caching Ruins the Database Caching" later in this chapter).

Caches often lack high-availability properties and can easily fail or invalidate records depending on their heuristics. Partial failures, which are more common, are even worse in terms of consistency. When the cache inevitably fails, the database will get hit by the unmitigated firehose of queries and likely wreck your SLAs. In addition, even if a cache itself has some high availability features, it can't coordinate handling such failure with the persistent database it is in front of. The bottom line: Rely on the database, rather than making your latency SLAs dependent on a cache.

Application Complexity: Your Application Needs to Handle More Cases

Application and operational complexity are problems for external caches. Once you have an external cache, you need to keep the cache up-to-date with the client and the database. For instance, if your database runs repairs, the cache needs to be synced or invalidated. However, invalidating the cache may introduce a long period of time when you need to wait for it to eventually get warm. Your client retry and timeout policies need to match the properties of the cache but also need to function when the cache is done. Usually, such scenarios are hard to test and implement.

External Caching Ruins the Database Caching

Modern databases have embedded caches and complex policies to manage them. When you place a cache in front of the database, most read requests will reach only the external cache and the database won't keep these objects in its memory. As a result, the database cache is rendered ineffective. When requests eventually reach the database, its cache will be cold and the responses will come primarily from the disk. As a result, the round-trip from the cache to the database and then back to the application is likely to incur additional latency.

External Caching Might Increase Security Risks

An external cache adds a whole new attack surface to your infrastructure. Encryption, isolation, and access control on data placed in the cache are likely to be different from the ones at the database layer itself.

External Caching Ignores the Database Knowledge and Database Resources

Databases are quite complex and built for specialized I/O workloads on the system. Many of the queries access the same data, and some amount of the working set size can be cached in memory in order to save disk accesses. A good database should have sophisticated logic to decide which objects, indexes, and accesses it should cache.

The database also should have various eviction policies (such as the least recently used [LRU] policy as a straightforward example) that determine when new data should replace existing (older) cached objects.

Another example is scan-resistant caching. When scanning a large dataset, say a large range or a full-table scan, a lot of objects are read from the disk. The database can realize this is a scan (not a regular query) and choose to leave these objects outside its internal cache. However, an external cache would treat the result set just like any other and attempt to cache the results. The database automatically synchronizes the content of the cache with the disk according to the incoming request rate, and thus the user and the developer do not need to do anything to make sure that lookups to recently written data are performant. Therefore, if, for some reason, your database doesn't respond fast enough, it means that:

- The cache is misconfigured

- It doesn't have enough RAM for caching

- The working set size and request pattern don't fit the cache

- The database cache implementation is poor

Summary

This chapter shared strong opinions on how to navigate topology decisions. For example, we recommended:

- Using an RF of at least 3 (with geographical fine-tuning if available)

- Having as many racks as replicas

- Isolating reads and writes within a specific datacenter

- Ensuring each client knows and prioritizes the local datacenter

- Considering the (cross-region replication) costs of multi-region deployments as well as their benefits

- Scaling up as much as possible before scaling out

- Considering a few different options to minimize the resource contention that could occur when running multiple workloads on a single cluster

- Carefully considering the caveats associated with external caches, load balancers, and abstraction layers

The next chapter looks at best practices for testing your topology: Benchmarking it to see what it's capable of and how it compares to alternative configurations and solutions.

CHAPTER 9

Benchmarking

We won't sugarcoat it: database benchmarking is hard. There are many moving parts and nuances to consider and manage—and a bit of homework is required to really see what a database is capable of and measure it properly. It's not easy to properly generate system load to reflect your real-life scenarios.[1] It's often not obvious how to correctly measure and analyze the end results. And after extracting benchmarking results, you need to be able to read them, understand potential performance bottlenecks, analyze potential performance improvements, and possibly dive into other issues. You need to make your benchmarking results meaningful, ensure they are easily reproducible, and also be able to clearly explain these results to your team and other interested parties in a way that reflects your business needs. There's also hard mathematics involved: statistics and queueing theory to help with black boxes and measurements, not to mention domain-specific knowledge of the system internals of the servers, platforms, operating systems, and the software running on it.

But when performance is a top priority, careful—and sometimes frequent—benchmarking is essential. And in the long run, it *will* pay off. An effective benchmark can save you from even worse pains, like the high-pressure database migration project that ensues after you realize—too late—that your existing solution can't support the latest phase of company growth with acceptable latencies and/or throughput.

The goal of this chapter is to share strategies that ease the pain slightly and, more importantly, increase the chances that the pain pays off by helping you select options that meet your performance needs. The chapter begins by looking at the two key types of benchmarks and highlighting critical considerations for each objective. Then, it presents a phased approach that should help you expose problems faster and with lower costs. Next, it dives into the do's and don'ts of benchmark planning, execution, and reporting,

---

[1] For an example of realistic benchmarking executed with impressive mastery, see Brian Taylor's talk, "How Optimizely (Safely) Maximizes Database Concurrency," at `www.youtube.com/watch?v=cSiVoX_nq1s`.

with a focus on lessons learned from the best and worst benchmarks we've witnessed over the past several years. Finally, the chapter closes with a look at some less common benchmarking approaches you might want to consider for specialized needs.

Latency or Throughput: Choose Your Focus

When benchmarking, you need to decide upfront whether you want to focus on throughput or latency. Latency is measured in both cases. But here's the difference:

- **Throughput focus**: You measure the maximum throughput by sending a new request as soon as the previous request completes. This helps you understand the highest number of IOPS that the database can sustain. Throughput-focused benchmarks are often the focus for analytics use cases (fraud detection, cybersecurity, etc.)

- **Latency focus**: You assess how many IOPS the database can handle without compromising latency. This is usually the focus for most user-facing and real-time applications.

Throughput tests are quite common, but latency tests are a better choice if you already know the desired throughput (e.g., 1M OPS). This is especially true if your production system must meet a specific latency goal (for example, the 99.99 percentile should have a read latency of less than 10ms).

If you're focused solely on latency, you need to measure and compare latency at the same throughput rates. If you know only that database A can handle 30K OPS with a certain P99 latency and database B can handle 50K OPS with a slightly higher P99 latency, you can't really say which one is "more efficient." For a fair comparison, you would need to measure each database's latencies at either 30K OPS or 50K OPS—or both. Even better, you would track latency across a broader span of intervals (e.g., measuring at 10K OPS increments up until when neither database could achieve the required P99 latency, as demonstrated in Figure 9-1.)

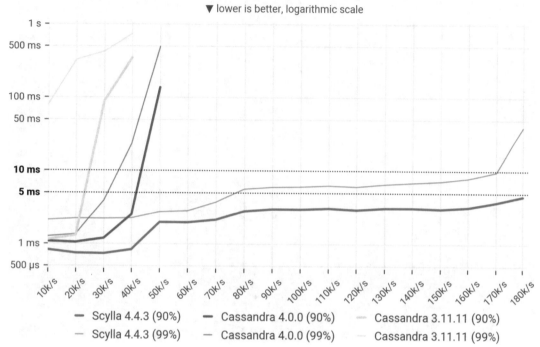

3-node cluster, 100% writes, latencies

▼ lower is better, logarithmic scale

Figure 9-1. *A latency-oriented benchmark*

Not all latency benchmarks need to take that form, however. Consider the example of an AdTech company with a real-time bidding use case. For them, a request that takes longer than 31ms is absolutely useless because it will fall outside of the bidding window. It's considered a timeout. And any request that is 30ms or less is fine; a 2ms response is not any more valuable to them than a 20ms response. They care only about which requests time out and which don't.

Their benchmarking needs are best served by a latency benchmark measuring how many OPS were generating timeouts over time. For example, Figure 9-2 shows that the first database in their benchmark (the top line) resulted in over 100K timeouts a second around 11:30; the other (the horizontal line near the bottom) experienced only around 200 timeouts at that same point in time, and throughout the duration of that test.

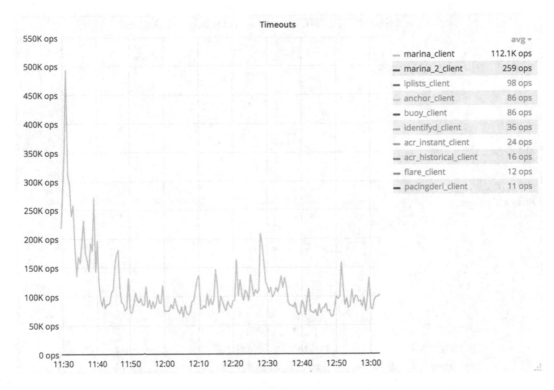

Figure 9-2. *A latency-oriented benchmark measuring how many OPS were generating timeouts over time*

For contrast, Figure 9-3 shows an example of a throughput benchmark.

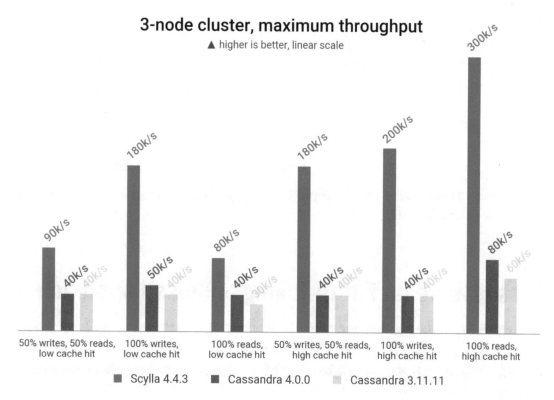

Figure 9-3. *A throughput-oriented benchmark*

With a throughput benchmark, you want to see one of the resources (e.g., the CPU or disk) maxing out in order to understand how much the database can deliver under extreme load conditions. If you don't reach this level, it's a sign that you're not really effectively benchmarking the database's throughput. For example, Figure 9-4 demonstrates the load of two clusters during a benchmark run. Note how one cluster is fully utilized whereas the other is very close to reaching its limits.

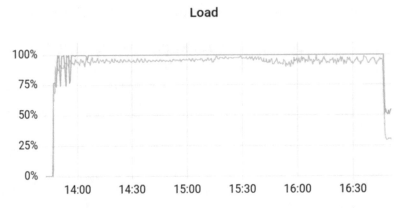

Figure 9-4. *Two clusters' load comparison: one fully maxed out and another very close to reaching its limit*

Less Is More (at First): Taking a Phased Approach

With either focus, the number one rule of benchmarking is to start simple. Always keep a laser focus on the specific questions you want the benchmark to answer (more on that shortly). But, realize that it could take a number of phases—each with a fair amount of trial and error—to get meaningful results.

What could go wrong? A lot. For example:

- Your client might be a bottleneck

- Your database sizing might need adjustment

- Your tests might need tuning

- A sandbox environment could have very different resources than a production one

- Your testing methodology might be too artificial to predict reality

If you start off with too much complexity, it will be a nightmare to discover what's going wrong and pinpoint the source of the problem. For example, assume you want to test if a database can handle 1M OPS of traffic from your client with a P99 latency of 1ms or less. However, you notice the latencies are exceeding the expected threshold. You might spend days adjusting database configurations to no avail, then eventually figure out that the problem stemmed from a bug in client-side concurrency. This would have been much more readily apparent if you started out with just a fraction of that throughput. In addition to avoiding frustration and lost time, you would have saved your team a lot of unnecessary infrastructure costs.

As a general rule of thumb, consider at least two phases of benchmarking: one with a specialized stress tool and one with your real workload (or at least a sampling of it—e.g., sending 30 percent of your queries to a cluster for benchmarking). For each phase, start super small (at around 10 percent of the throughput you ultimately want to test), troubleshoot as needed, then gradually increase the scope until you reach your target loads. Keep optimization in mind throughout. Do you need to add more servers or more clients to achieve a certain throughput? Or are you limited (by budget or infrastructure) to a fixed hardware configuration? Can you achieve your performance goals with less?

The key is to move incrementally. Of course, the exact approach will vary from situation to situation. Consider a leading travel company's approach. Having recently moved from PostgreSQL to Cassandra, they were quite experienced benchmarkers when they decided to evaluate Cassandra alternatives. The goal was to test the new database candidate's raw speed and performance, along with its support for their specific workloads.

First, they stood up a five-node cluster and ran database comparisons with synthetic traffic from cassandra-stress. This gave them confidence that the new database could meet their performance needs with *some* workloads. However, their real workloads are nothing like even customized cassandra-stress workloads. They experience highly variable and unpredictable traffic (for example, massive surges and disruptions stemming from a volcanic eruption). For a more realistic assessment, they started shadowing production traffic. This second phase of benchmarking provided the added confidence they needed to move forward with the migration.

Finally, they used the same shadowed traffic to determine the best deployment option. Moving to a larger 21-node cluster, they tested across cloud provider A and cloud provider B on bare metal. They also experimented with many different options on cloud provider B: various storage options, CPUs, and so on.

The bottom line here: Start simple, confirm, then scale incrementally. It's safer and ultimately faster. Plus, you'll save on costs. As you move through the process, check if you need to tweak your setup during your testing. Once you are eventually satisfied with the results, scale your infrastructure accordingly to meet your defined criteria.

Benchmarking Do's and Don'ts

The specific step-by-step instructions for how to configure and run a benchmark vary across databases and benchmarking tools, so we're not going to get into that. Instead, let's look at some of the more universal "do's and don'ts" based on what we've seen in the field.

Tip   If you haven't done so yet, be sure to review the chapters on drivers, infrastructure, and topology considerations before you begin benchmarking.

Know What's Under the Hood of Your Database (Or Find Someone Who Knows)

Understand and anticipate what parts of the system your chosen workload will affect and how. How will it stress your CPUs? Your memory? Your disks? Your network? Do you know if the database automatically analyzes the system it's running on and prioritizes application requests as opposed to internal tasks? What's going on as far as background operations and how these may skew your results? And why does all this matter if you're just trying to run a benchmark?

Let's take the example of compaction with LSM-tree based databases. As we'll cover in Chapter 11, compactions do have a significant impact on performance. But compactions are unlikely to kick in if you run a benchmark for just a few minutes. Given that compactions have dramatically different performance impacts on different databases, it's essential to know that they will occur and ensure that tests last long enough to measure their impact.

The important thing here is to try to understand the system that you're benchmarking. The better you understand it, the better you can plan tests and interpret the results. If there are vendors and/or user groups behind the database you're benchmarking, try to probe them for a quick overview of how the database works and what you should watch out for. Otherwise, you might overlook something that comes back to haunt you, such as finding out that your projected scale was too optimistic. Or, you might freak out over some KPI that's really a non-issue.

Choose an Environment That Takes Advantage of the Database's Potential

This is really a corollary to the previous tip. With a firm understanding of your database's superpowers, you can design benchmark scenarios that fully reveal its potential. For example, if you want to compare two databases designed for commodity hardware, don't worry about benchmarking them on a broad array of powerful servers. But if you're comparing a database that's architected to take advantage of powerful servers, you'd be remiss to benchmark it only on commodity hardware (or even worse, using a Docker image on a laptop). That would be akin to test driving a race car on the crowded streets of New York City rather than your local equivalent of the Autobahn highway.

Likewise, if you think some aspect of the database or your data modeling will be problematic for your use case, now's the time to push it to the limits and assess its true impact. For example, if you think a subset of your data might have imbalanced access patterns due to user trends, use the benchmark phase to reproduce that and assess the impacts.

Use an Environment That Represents Production

Benchmarking in the wrong environment can easily lead to an order-of-magnitude performance difference. For example, a laptop might achieve 20K OPS where a dedicated server could easily achieve 200K OPS. Unless you intend to have your production system running on a laptop, do not benchmark (or run comparisons) on a laptop.

If you are using shared hardware in a containerized/virtualized environment, be aware that one guest can increase latency in other guests. As a result, you'll typically want to ensure that hardware resources are dedicated to your database and that you avoid resource overcommitment by any means possible.

Also, don't overlook the environment for your load generators. If you underprovision load generators, the load generators themselves will be the bottleneck. Another consideration: Ensure that the database and the data loader are not running under the same nodes. Pushing and pulling data is resource intensive, so the loader will definitely steal resources from the database. This will impact your results with any database.

Don't Overlook Observability

Having observability into KPIs beyond throughput and latency is critical for identifying and troubleshooting issues. For instance, you might not be hitting the cache as much as intended. Or a network interface might be overwhelmed with data to the point that it interferes with latency. Observability is also your primary tool for validating that you're not being overly optimistic—or pessimistic—when reviewing results. You may discover that even read requests served from disk, with a cold cache, are within your latency requirements.

Note   For extensive discussion on this topic, see Chapter 10.

Use Standardized Benchmarking Tools Whenever Feasible

Don't waste resources building—and debugging and maintaining—your own version of a benchmarking tool that has already been solved for. The community has developed an impressive set of tools that can cover a wide range of needs. For example:

- YCSB[2]

- TPC-C[3]

- NdBench[4]

- Nosqlbench[5]

- pgbench[6]

- TLP-stress[7]

- Cassandra-stress[8]

- and more...

---

[2] https://github.com/brianfrankcooper/YCSB

[3] http://tpc.org/tpcc/default5.asp

[4] https://github.com/Netflix/ndbench

[5] https://github.com/nosqlbench/nosqlbench

[6] www.postgresql.org/docs/current/pgbench.html

[7] https://github.com/thelastpickle/tlp-stress

[8] https://github.com/scylladb/scylla-tools-java/tree/master/tools/stress

They are all relatively the same and provide similar configuration parameters. Your task is to understand which one better reflects the workload you are interested in and how to run it properly. When in doubt, consult with your vendor for specific tooling compatible with your database of choice.

Of course, these options won't cover everything. It makes sense to develop your own tools if:

- Your workloads look nothing like the ones offered by standard tools (for example, you rely on multiple operations that are not natively supported by the tools)

- It helps you test against real (or more realistic) workloads in the later phases of your benchmarking strategy

Ideally, the final stages of your benchmarking would involve connecting your application to the database and seeing how it responds to your real workload. But what if, for example, you are comparing two databases that require you to implement the application logic in two totally different ways? In this case, the different application logic implementations could influence your results as much as the difference in databases. Again, we recommend starting small: Testing just the basic functionality of the application against both targets (following each one's best practices) and seeing what the initial results look like.

Use Representative Data Models, Datasets, and Workloads

As you progress past the initial "does this even work" phase of your benchmarking, it soon becomes critical to gravitate to representative data models, datasets, and workloads. The closer you approximate your production environment, the better you can trust that your results accurately represent what you will experience in production.

Data Models

Tools such as cassandra-stress use a default data model that does not completely reflect what most teams use in production. For example, the cassandra-stress default data model has a replication factor set to 1 and uses LOCAL_ONE as a consistency level. Although cassandra-stress is a convenient way to get some initial performance impressions, it is critical to benchmark the same/similar data model that you will use in production. That's why we recommend using a custom data model and tuning your consistency level and queries. cassandra-stress and other benchmarking tools commonly provide ways to specify a user profile, where you can specify your own schema, queries, replication factor, request distribution and sizes, throughput rates, number of clients, and other aspects.

Dataset Size

If you run the benchmark with a dataset that's smaller than your production dataset, you may have misleading or incorrect results due to the reduced number of I/O operations. Eventually, you should configure a test that realistically reflects a fraction of your production dataset size corresponding to your current scale.

Workloads

Run the benchmark using a load that represents, as closely as possible, your anticipated production workload. This includes the queries submitted by the load generator. When you use the right type of queries, they are distributed over the cluster and the ratio between reads and writes remains relatively constant.

The read/write ratio is important. Different combinations will impact your disk in different ways. If you want results representative of production, use a realistic workload mix.

Eventually, you will max out your storage I/O throughput and starve your disk, which causes requests to start queuing on the database. If you continue pushing past that point, latency will increase. When you hit that point of increased latency with unsatisfactory results, stop, reflect on what happened, analyze how you can improve, and iterate through the test again. Rinse and repeat as needed.

Here are some tips on creating realistic workloads for common use cases:

- **Ingestion**: Ingest data as fast as possible for at least a few hours, and do it in a way that doesn't produce timeouts or errors. The goal here is to ensure that you've got a stable system, capable of keeping up with your expected traffic rate for long periods.

- **Real-time bidding**: Use bulk writes coming in after hours or constantly low background loads; the core of the workload is a lot of reads with extremely strict latency requirements (perhaps below a specific threshold).

- **Time series**: Use heavy and constant writes to ever-growing partitions split and bucketed by time windows; reads tend to focus on the latest rows and/or a specific range of time.

- **Metadata store**: Use writes occasionally, but focus on random reads representing users accessing your site. There's usually good cacheability here.

- **Analytics**: Periodically write a lot of information and perform a lot of full table scans (perhaps in parallel with some of the other workloads).

The bottom line is to try to emulate what your workloads look like and run something that's meaningful to you.

Exercise Your Cache Realistically

Unless you can absolutely guarantee that your workload has a high cache hit rate frequency, be pessimistic and exercise it well.

You might be running workloads, getting great results, and seeing cache hits all the way up to 90 percent. That's great. But is this the way you're going to be running in practice all the time? Do you have periods throughout the day when your cache is not going to be that warm, maybe because there's something else running? In real-life situations, you will likely have times when the cache is colder or even super cold (e.g., after an upgrade or after a hardware failure). Consider testing those scenarios in the benchmark as well.

If you want to make sure that all requests are coming from the disk, you can disable the cache altogether. However, be aware that this is typically an extreme situation, as most workloads (one way or another) exercise some caching. Sometimes you can create a cold cache situation by just restarting the nodes or restarting the processes.

Look at Steady State

Most databases behave differently in real life than they do in short transient test situations. They usually run for days or years—so when you test a database for two minutes, you're probably not getting a deep understanding of how it behaves, unless you are working in memory only. Also, when you're working with a database that is built

187

to serve tens or hundreds of terabytes—maybe even petabytes—know that it's going to behave rather differently at various data levels. Requests become more expensive, especially read requests. If you're testing something that only serves a gigabyte, it really isn't the same as testing something that's serving a terabyte.

Figure 9-5 exemplifies the importance of looking at steady state. Can you tell what throughput is being sustained by the database in question?

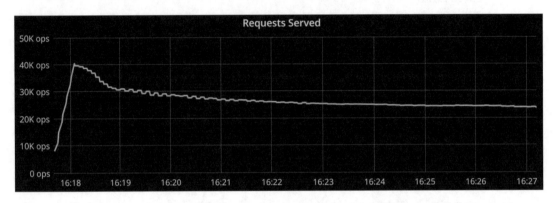

Figure 9-5. *A throughput graph that is not focused on steady state*

Well, if you look just at the first minute, it seems that it's serving 40K OPS. But if you wait for a few minutes, the throughput decreases.

Whenever you want to make a statement about the maximum throughput that your database can handle, do that from a steady state. Make sure that you're inserting an amount of data that is meaningful, not just a couple of gigabytes, and make sure that it runs for enough time so it's a realistic scenario. After you are satisfied with how many requests can be sustained over a prolonged period of time, consider adding noise, such as scaling clients, and introducing failure situations.

Watch Out for Client-Side Bottlenecks

One of the most common mistakes with benchmarks is overlooking the fact that the bottleneck could be coming from the application side. You might have to tune your application clients to allow for a higher concurrency. You may also be running many application pods on the same tenant—with all instances contending for the same hardware resources. Make sure your application is running in a proper environment, as is your database.

Also Watch Out for Networking Issues

Networking issues could also muddle the results of your benchmarking. If the database is consuming too much softirq from processing, this will degrade your performance. You can detect this by analyzing CPU interrupt shares, for example. And you can typically resolve it by using CPU pinning, which tells the system that all network interrupts should be handled by specific CPUs that are not being used by the database.

Similarly, running your application through a slow link, such as routing traffic via the Internet rather than via a private link, can easily introduce a networking bottleneck.

Document Meticulously to Ensure Repeatability

It's difficult to anticipate when or why you might want to repeat a benchmark. Maybe you want to assess the impact of optimizations you made after getting some great tips at the vendor's user conference. Maybe you just learned that your company was acquired and you should prepare to support ten times your current throughput—or much stricter latency SLAs. Perhaps you learned about a cool new database that's API-compatible with your current one, and you're curious how the performance stacks up. Or maybe you have a new boss with a strong preference for another database and you suddenly need to re-justify your decision with a head-to-head comparison.

Whatever the reason you're repeating a benchmark scenario, one thing is certain: You will be immensely appreciative of the time that you previously spent documenting exactly what you did and why.

Reporting Do's and Don'ts

So you've completed your benchmark and you've gathered all sorts of data—what's the best way to report it? Don't skimp on this final, yet critical step. Clear and compelling reporting is critical for convincing others to support your recommended course of action—be it embarking on a database migration, changing your configuration or data modeling, or simply sticking with what's working well for you.

Here are some reporting-focused do's and don'ts.

Be Careful with Aggregations

When it comes to aggregations, proceed with extreme caution. You could report the result of a benchmark by saying something like "I ran this benchmark for three days, and this is my throughput." However, this overlooks a lot of critical information. For example, consider the two graphs presented in Figures 9-6 and 9-7.

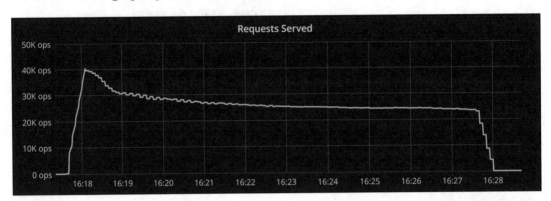

Figure 9-6. *Lower baseline throughput that's almost constant and predictable throughout a ten-minute period*

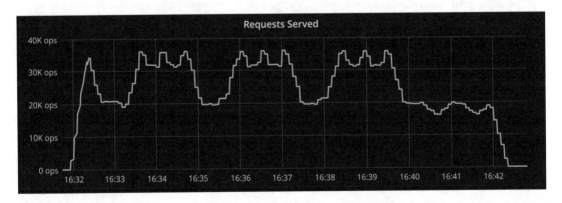

Figure 9-7. *A bumpier path to a similar throughput at the end*

Both of these loads have roughly the same throughput at the end. Figure 9-6 shows lower baseline throughput—but it's constant and very predictable throughout the period. The OPS in Figure 9-7 dip much lower than the first baseline, but it also spikes to a much higher value. The behavior shown in Figure 9-6 is obviously more desirable. But if you aggregate your results, it would be really hard to notice a difference.

Another aggregation mistake is aggregating tail latencies: taking the average of P99 latencies from multiple load generators. The correct way to determine the percentiles over multiple load generators is to merge the latency distribution of each load generator and then determine the percentiles. If that isn't an option, then the next best alternative is to take the maximum (the P99, for example) of each of the load generators. The actual P99 will be equal to or smaller than the maximum P99.

For example, assume you have the following clients:

- Client1: 100 total requests: 98 of them took 1ms, 2 took 3ms

- Client2: 100 total requests: 99 of them took 30ms, 1 took 31ms

The 99th percentile in the first example is 3 milliseconds. The 99th percentile for the second client is 30 milliseconds. Average that out, and you get 16.5 milliseconds. However, the true 99th percentile is acquired by putting those two arrays together and taking the 99th percentile from there. The actual 99th percentile was 30 milliseconds. That 16.5 millisecond "average" is meaningless—it doesn't correlate to anything in reality.

Also, do not blindly trust only your application latencies. In general, when evaluating benchmarking results, be sure to consult your database-reported latencies to rule out bottlenecks related to the database itself. Situations where the database latencies are within your specific thresholds, but the client-side results deviate from your expected numbers are fairly common—and may indicate a problem on either the network or at the client side.

Don't Assume People Will Believe You

Assume that any claim you make will be met with a healthy dose of skepticism. One of the best ways to combat this is to share fine granularity details about your setup. Just reporting something like "Our cluster has a P99 which is lower than 1ms" is not sufficient.

A better statement is: "We set up three cluster nodes with 3x i3.4xlarge (16vCPU, 122GiB RAM, up to 10Gbps network, 2x1.9TB NVMe). For loaders, we used 3x c5n.9xlarge (36vCPU, 96GiB RAM, up to 50Gbps network). Here's the graph of our P99 over time. Here's the benchmarking profile used to stress the given workload."

Also, provide enough detail so that the benchmark can be repeated. For example, for a Cassandra benchmark, consider including details such as:

- JVM settings

- Any non-default settings used in `cassandra.yaml`

- Cassandra-stress parameters (driver version, replication factor, compaction strategy, etc.)

- Exactly how you inserted data, warmed up the cache, and so on

Finally, keep in mind that the richer your reports, the easier it is for someone to support your recommendation that option A is preferable to option B. For example, if you're looking into how two different databases compare on the same hardware, you might share details in Table 9-1 in addition to the standard throughput and latency graphs.

Table 9-1. *Communicating the Results of Comparing Two Different Databases on the Same Hardware*

Test	Database A	Database B	Difference	Better Is:
Time to populate	5h 21m 29s	4h 27m 19s	20%	Lower
Time to compact	7h 32m	21m	21x	Lower
Total quiesce time (populate and compact)	12h 43m	4h 48m	2.68x	Lower
Read throughput (small dataset)	51,267 reads/second	124,958 reads/second	2.43x	Higher
Read throughput (medium dataset)	7,363 reads/second	6,958 reads/second	-5%	Higher
Read throughput (large dataset)	5,089 reads/second	5,592 reads/second	9.8%	Higher
Reads during writes	547 reads/second	920 reads/second	68%	Higher
99.9th latency (at 5,000 writes/second)	130.3 milliseconds	11.9 milliseconds	10.9x	Lower
99.9th latency (at 10,000 writes/second)	153.3 milliseconds	16.9 milliseconds	9.0x	Lower

Take Coordinated Omission Into Account

A common problem when measuring latencies is the *coordinated omission* problem, which causes the worst latencies to be omitted from the measurements and, as a consequence, renders the higher percentiles useless.

Gil Tene coined this term to describe what happens when a measuring system inadvertently coordinates with the system being measured in a way that avoids measuring outliers and misses sending requests.[9]

Here's a great analogy by Ivan Prisyazhynyy:[10]

"Let's imagine a coffee-fueled office. Each hour a worker has to make a coffee run to the local coffee shop. But what if there's a road closure in the middle of the day? You have to wait a few hours to go on that run. Not only is that hour's particular coffee runner late, but all the other coffee runs get backed up for hours behind that. Sure, it takes the same amount of time to get the coffee once the road finally opens, but if you don't measure that gap caused by the road closure, you're missing measuring the total delay in getting your team their coffee. And, of course, in the meanwhile you will be woefully undercaffeinated."

Prisyazhynyy notes that most standard benchmarking tools now account for coordinated omission (e.g., cassandra-stress and YCSB do; TLP-stress did not at the time of writing). However, by default, they do not *respect* coordinated omissions, so anyone using these tools still needs to be vigilant about spotting and combatting coordinated omission. We strongly recommend reading his complete article. But, for brevity's sake, here's his conclusion:

"We found that the best implementation involves a static schedule with queueing and latency correction, and we showed how those approaches can be combined together to effectively solve coordinated omission issues: queueing with correction or simulation, or queueless with simulation.

---

[9] See Tene's talk, *"How NOT to Measure Latency"* (https://www.youtube.com/watch?v=lJ8ydIuPFeU)

[10] See Prisyazhynyy's blog, "On Coordinated Omission" (https://www.scylladb.com/2021/04/22/on-coordinated-omission/)

To mitigate coordinated omission effects, you must:

- Explicitly set the throughput target, the number of worker threads, the total number of requests to send, or the total test duration

- Explicitly set the mode of latency measurement

  - Correct for queueing implementations

  - Simulate non-queuing implementations

For example, for YCSB the correct flags are:

```
-target 120000 -threads 840 -p recordcount=1000000000 -p
measurement.interval=both
```

For cassandra-stress, they are:

```
duration=3600s -rate fixed=100000/s threads=840"
```

Beyond these tips, there are even more parameters that impact coordinated omissions. We strongly recommend that you seek recommendations from your vendor, Stack Overflow, or other community resources.

Special Considerations for Various Benchmarking Goals

Many database benchmarks are performed primarily so the team can check a "due diligence" box in the selection process. Since you're now pretty deep into a book focused on database performance, we assume that's not *your* team. You have some lofty performance goals and you know that benchmarking is key to achieving them. So what exactly are you hoping to achieve with your latest and greatest benchmark? Here are some common reasons and use cases, as well as tips and caveats for each.

Preparing for Growth

You just learned that your application is expected to handle increased traffic—perhaps as a result of a merger/acquisition, from some unexpected publicity or market movement, or just the slow and steady accumulation of more users over time. Is your database up to the task? You may want to test how your database scales under pressure. How long does it take to add more resources? What about scaling it up?

Comparing Different Databases

Maybe you have the luxury of architecting an application with "the best" database from the ground up. Maybe you've hit the wall with your existing database and need to justify a potentially painful and costly migration. Or maybe you're curious if it's worth it to move across your existing database vendor's various offerings. It's critical to know how each database is built and understand both how to test its strengths as well as how to assess the true impact of its constraints.

Comparing the Same Database on Different Infrastructure

Your preferred cloud vendor just released a shiny new series of instances with the potential for great power. But will you see any impact given your database and your workloads? Could vertical scaling reduce the size of your clusters (and the scope of your maintenance headaches)?

Pay attention to any configuration changes that might be needed (and sometimes unintended!) between both infrastructure settings. Recognize that some level of tuning will inevitably be required to ensure you get the maximum out of each.

Also keep in mind that some databases have limits as to how far they can scale. Some databases will be more efficient if you horizontally scale using smaller nodes. Others will excel when they're run on larger capacity nodes.

Finally, consider the application latency. In some cases, you can "bring" a testing application with you to the same cloud environment and reproduce it as if it were a local datacenter in order to reduce network RTT. In other cases, you might need to account for network latency on top of the results you received. If the application is in a separate environment, that can contribute to additional latency toward the database.

Assessing the Impact of a Data Modeling or Database Configuration Change

Say you just started reworking your data model and want to "unit test" it to check if you're going down the right path. Your team is debating among different options and wants an objective assessment of how much they will optimize—or undermine—your performance.

In this case, you have to consider a multitude of aspects. For instance, while assessing the impact of encryption-in-transit on your workload, you might collect the initial tests while the database was running with a hot cache. Then, after applying the necessary changes, you restart your database and get higher latencies as a result. You might think, "Oh no! The encryption setting is really hurting my latency!" But, you forgot that restarting the cluster to apply the change also cleared the cache—and upon restarting your tests, you're basically reading from disk. In the end, after warming up the cache, you notice the encryption option barely impacted your latency. Whew!

Beyond the Usual Benchmark

Considering that you're now many chapters deep into this book, you're clearly quite obsessed. Perhaps you want to put your database to some less common or more extreme tests? Here are a few options.

Benchmarking Admin Operations

Even if you don't anticipate expanding capacity often or dramatically, checking how long it takes to add a new node or increase your cluster capacity certainly falls under the realm of "due diligence." And if you do expect sudden and significant increases, it's a good idea to test something more extreme—like how rapidly you can double capacity.

Keep in mind that databases must stream data into new nodes, and that this will consume some CPU time, along with disk I/O and networking bandwidth—so it's important to assess this in a safe and controlled environment.

Other admin operations you might want to benchmark include the time required to replace nodes as well as the latency impacts of compaction and other background operations. For example, in Cassandra or ScyllaDB, you might look into how repair operations running in the background impact the live workload. If you notice that the operation causes latency increases, you might be able to schedule a time window to run repairs weekly or run them with a lower intensity.

Testing Disaster Recovery

You need to test your ability to sustain regular life events. Nodes will crash. Disks will become corrupt. And network cables will be disconnected. That will happen for sure—and it could very well be during the worst possible time (e.g., Black Friday or during the big game you're streaming to millions). You need to account for potential disasters and test capacity planning with reduced nodes, a network partition, or other undesired events. This has the added benefit of teaching you about the true capabilities of the system's resiliency.

Also, test the time and effort required to restore from a backup. Yes, this requires spending a fair bit of time and money on what's essentially a fire drill. But knowing what to expect in a time of crisis is quite valuable—and avoiding databases with unacceptable recovery times can be priceless.

If you're running on the cloud, you might think you're safe from disaster. "I'll just spin up another cluster and move forward. Right?" Wrong! Apart from the data migration itself, there are a ton of other things that can go wrong. You'll need to reconnect all network VPCs, redo all the networking configuration between the application and database, and so on. You may also run out of instances of the desired type in a given region or availability zone. Did you ever go to the supermarket to buy a basic item, say toilet paper, and find empty shelves because everybody suddenly started filling their carts with it (e.g., due to a disaster)? This can happen to anything, even virtual instances. It's best to test disaster scenarios to gain a better understanding of what issues you could experience—and practice how you'll react.

Benchmarking at Extreme Scale

Benchmarks performed at petabyte scale can help you understand how a particular database handles extremely large workloads that your company expects (or at least hopes) to encounter. However, such benchmarks can be challenging to design and execute.

The ScyllaDB engineering team recently decided to perform a petabyte-scale benchmark on a rather short timeline. We constructed a 20-node ScyllaDB cluster and loaded it with 1PB (replicated) of user data and 1TB of application data. The user workload was ~5 million TPS, and we measured two variants of it: one read-only and another with 80 percent reads and 20 percent writes. Since this workload simulated online analytics, high throughput was critical. At the same time, we ran a smaller 200,000 TPS application workload with 50 percent reads and 50 percent writes. Since this workload represented online transaction processing, low latency was prioritized over high throughput.

To give you an idea of what this involved from a setup perspective, we provisioned 20 x i3en.metal AWS instances for the ScyllaDB cluster. Each instance had:

- 96 vCPUs

- 768 GiB RAM

- 60 TB NVMe disk space

- 100 Gbps network bandwidth

For the load generators, we used 50 x c5n.9xlarge AWS instances. Each instance had:

- 36 vCPUs

- 96 GiB RAM

- 50 Gbps network bandwidth

If you're thinking about performing your own extreme-scale benchmark, here are some lessons learned that you might want to consider:

- **Provisioning**: It took a few days to find an availability zone in AWS that had sufficient instance types for a petabyte-scale benchmark. If you plan to deploy such a large cluster, make sure to provision your resources well ahead.

- **Hardware tuning/interrupt handling**: At the time, our default assignment of cores to I/O queue handling wasn't optimized for this extreme scenario. Interrupt handling CPUs had to be manually assigned to maximize throughput.

- **Hardware tuning/CPU power governor**: We needed to set the CPU power governor on each node to "performance" to maximize the performance of the system.

- **cassandra-stress**: cassandra-stress was not designed for this scale (the default population distribution is too small). Be prepared to experiment with non-default settings if you're aiming to create and iterate through a petabyte dataset.

Summary

Benchmarking is tedious and painstaking, so make sure that you have clear goals and effective reporting to ensure the work pays off. Some of the top tips we shared include:

- Start small so you don't end up wasting time and money.

- Understand your database in order to craft tests that showcase its strengths and assess whether you can live with its weaknesses.

- Rely on standard tools to start, but be sure to work up to representative data models, datasets, and workloads.

- Get your monitoring stack in shape prior to benchmarking, and use it to benchmark strategically (e.g., to exercise your cache realistically).

- Plan to dedicate a good amount of time to crafting convincing reports and beware of challenges such as coordinated omission.

The next chapter dives into best practices for the ongoing monitoring that is critical to interpreting many benchmarking results, as well as preventing and troubleshooting performance issues in production.

CHAPTER 10

Monitoring

Databases require ongoing care and attention, especially when performance is a priority and the data being stored is growing rapidly and/or changing frequently. Adverse events that could place the business at risk—for example, node failures or a misbehaving client—will inevitably occur. Given the complexity of both databases and data-intensive applications, it's not a matter of *if* some combination of factors ends up degrading performance, but *when*.

Enter observability and monitoring. A proactive approach is the key to understanding and optimizing your baseline performance, catching emerging issues before your end-users feel the pain, and reacting fast when they do. This chapter helps you determine where to focus your monitoring efforts—with examples from different use cases—offers tips for exploring issues as they emerge, and details how you might proceed when your key performance indicators (KPIs) are trending in the wrong direction.

Taking a Proactive Approach

Monitoring often doesn't become a priority until something goes wrong. Users start complaining about slowness, the system runs out of space, or your application simply stops responding.

At that point, monitoring is a vital tool for digging into the problem, understanding the root cause, and hopefully verifying that your mitigation attempts were successful. Having insightful monitoring and knowing what to look for is invaluable at this point. But what's even more helpful is the knowledge gained by monitoring performance over time, even when everything was humming along nicely.

If you have a good grasp of how your database generally behaves when it works well, it's much easier to spot the problem when it's unhealthy. For example, if you see a spike in request concurrency but you know that your system always properly applies a

© Felipe Cardeneti Mendes, Piotr Sarna, Pavel Emelyanov, Cynthia Dunlop 2023
F. C. Mendes et al., *Database Performance at Scale*, https://doi.org/10.1007/978-1-4842-9711-7_10

concurrency limiter, then you might focus your investigation on background operations that may be slowing down your database. Or, maybe your application got scaled out to handle more traffic, therefore breaking your previous client-side assumptions.

Monitoring trends over time can also help you predict and plan for peaks. For instance, assume you're a streaming media company. If you know that last year's version of a big sporting event drew over 25M active users when you had 250M subscribers, you can use that data to make some predictions as to how much traffic you might need to support this year—now that you have almost twice as many subscribers. It's a similar case for retail, fraud detection, or any other industry that experiences "Black Friday" surges. One of the best ways to prepare for the next peak is to understand what happened during the previous one.

Making monitoring a regular routine rather than an emergency response can also help you spot potential issues as they emerge—and avoid them causing a crisis. For example, one of the most common database mistakes is failing to carefully watch disk utilization. By the time you realize that the system is running out of storage space, it might be too late to respond.

As a nice side effect, monitoring can also provide a window into how your data and application usage are evolving. For example, if you note a steady increase in data volume and/or IOPs, you might consider benchmarking your database against what's feasible in the next year. Maybe you're already built for that scale, or maybe you need to think about your options for increasing capacity. Additionally, assessing what's required to achieve the expected latencies at the likely new scale also helps you predict and plan for the associated cost increase.

Note: Do You Need to Monitor a DBaaS?   You selected a DBaaS because you didn't want to worry about your database, right? So does that mean you don't have to worry about monitoring? Yes ... and no.

You *should* rest assured that your vendor of choice is carefully watching over your instance with a great deal of automation as well as expertise. If you're not confident that this is the case, you might want to consider rethinking your DBaaS vendor. But even if you *are* confident, it's still advisable to keep a close eye on database performance. To earn and retain your trust, your DBaaS vendor should offer full transparency into what they're monitoring. At a minimum, you should understand:

- Which KPIs are correlated to your team's greatest performance concerns

- What triggers them to review KPIs, take action internally, and notify you of an issue

- What level of effort they make in order to guarantee these KPIs

It's probably overkill to keep a DBaaS monitoring dashboard open on one of your monitors 24/7. But at least know enough for a basic level of confidence that your database—and your DBaaS vendor—are both doing their job.

Tracking Core Database KPIs

Less is more when you're tracking database KPIs. We recommend zeroing in on a small set of KPIs in each area (cluster, infrastructure, application) that really matter to your business. Then, showcase those core KPIs prominently in a dashboard and set alerts to trigger when they reach levels that you believe warrant an immediate response. Be brutally honest here. It's much better to have one custom alert you'll really act on than 30 you'll ignore. If you won't address it immediately, it's "noise" that will desensitize the team to even the most critical issues.

What about all other KPIs? They'll be key when it's time to a) optimize your baseline performance, b) see what's needed to maintain that performance at a greater scale, or c) diagnose an emerging performance issue.

Rather than try to cover every KPI for every popular high-performance database, let's take a critical look at what we've found are the most common and critical ones for meeting throughput and latency expectations.

Database Cluster KPIs

These are metrics that provide insight into a database cluster's health. This bucket might cover things like I/O queues, task groups, internal errors, reads/writes, timeouts and errors, replicas, cache, and change data capture.

The ultimate goal of monitoring a cluster is to ensure a steady state "healthy system." Before looking at specific KPIs, consider what an ideal cluster state looks like for your database. For example, with a wide column database like ScyllaDB or Cassandra, your target might be:

- All nodes are up and running

- There are no alerts indicating that a KPI you care about has exceeded the acceptable threshold

- Clients are driving traffic to all nodes and shards in a balanced manner

    - Connections are balanced (your driver might balance them automatically)

    - The amount of traffic to the various shards is roughly the same

    - The queries are spread out across the shards

- Requests for a partition/row are balanced (e.g., you don't have a "hot partition" with 50 percent of read requests going to a single partition)

- Partitions are balanced (e.g., you don't have an average partition size of .5 MB and a few partitions that are 10GB)

- The cache hit rate (rows read from the cache) follows a specific distribution pattern

- Disk utilization has enough room to accommodate growth and other background operations, such as compactions

Here are some specific KPIs to look into regarding your cluster health:

- **Node availability**: Indicates if a node is online and responding through liveness checks. This can be used to assess whether the node is available on the network and to the rest of the cluster. If the cluster has one or more nodes that are unavailable, this means that the cluster has fewer resources to process its workload, which could result in increased latencies. Note that just because a node is available does not necessarily mean it is healthy.

- **Average read/write latencies**: Tells you the average latencies per operation type. This is a good way of knowing how your cluster delivers part of the requests, but there is more than meets the eye when you inspect it closely (for example, P99 latencies).

- **P99 read/write latencies**: Provides insight into the latency of the 99th percentile of requests in your cluster. Most performance-sensitive use cases aim at keeping P99 latencies (and sometimes P999 latencies) within acceptable ranges for the business case.

- **Requests per second**: Specifies how many operations per second your database is processing. This KPI, along with latency, is crucial to assess how the cluster processes the intended workloads. A sudden drop in throughput might indicate a network failure, misbehaving clients, or simply when a given high throughput workload processing finished.

- **Timeouts**: Reveals if any timeouts have recently occurred on the cluster. A timeout is not a bad sign per se. But the team might want to consider how to tackle them from the application side and how to stop timeouts from becoming common on a busy system. A cluster's timeout rates will usually spike when it is malfunctioning.

- **Caching**: This can vary from how much data your cache contains to how much data is being read from the cache (as opposed to the disk). The latter measurement will help you assess how the database is using its caching system and if any tuning is required for it. It could also explain some latency spikes, which would be correlated to reads primarily hitting the disk.

- **Connections**: It is crucial to understand how your database is being accessed over the network. Knowing how many connections are currently active on the database can help you gauge application connectivity issues and understand if connections are balanced throughout the cluster (to catch whether a node is malfunctioning or overloaded).

- **Garbage Collector (GC) pauses**: If you're using a database that requires GC pauses to purge unused memory objects, pay close attention to how GC pauses may be affecting your latencies and throughput. In general, a GC pause is a small fraction of time when a database is unavailable to process its work. That means that long GC pauses may be wasting resources and hurting your workload.

What to Look for at Different Levels (Datacenter, Node, CPU/Shard)

Monitoring solutions will typically provide different views of your distributed topology. For example, a global view of your P99 latencies within a multi-regional active-active deployment will quickly help you identify whether your entire infrastructure is stable and operational. However, when things go wrong, you may need a different level of granularity in order to identify the culprit.

The higher the level of detail you choose, the more data points and information you will have. However, it is not always a good idea to navigate through your monitoring solution with a high level of detail until you identify possible suspects.

When investigating an unknown problem, we recommend that you initiate your research with the datacenter-level view if you have a multi-regional topology. This allows you to isolate whether a problem is specifically confined to a single region or whether the problem in question affects all regions.

Once you have isolated the impacted location, the next step is to look into the data points on a per-node level. This will reveal whether any specific replica may be misbehaving, receiving more requests, experiencing an imbalance, or suffering from higher latencies than the others.

For most databases, a per-node view is the lowest possible level. However, databases with a shard-per-core architecture offer an additional granularity: the CPU level. Switching your observability to the CPU level makes sense once you have identified the main suspects of your performance problem. Otherwise, it will simply show you too many data points that might look unintelligible at first glance. However, when used properly, a per-CPU level view can greatly empower your observability and troubleshooting skills.

Three Industry-Specific Examples

Here are a few examples of how cluster monitoring approaches vary across industries and use cases:

- **AdTech**: AdTech is one of the most recognizable use cases that relies heavily on sub-millisecond latencies. For example, in real-time bidding, a single millisecond spike might be all it takes to miss a targeted ad opportunity. As a result, these use cases often monitor P99, P999, and even P9999 latencies and set up very aggressive custom alerting thresholds so that spikes can be identified and addressed immediately.

- **Streaming media**: Streaming media use cases typically serve several distinct media types across several tenants, often through different regions. At a region, data balancing is critical since a single bottlenecked shard can introduce a widespread impact.

- **Blockchain**: Blockchain solutions are typically required to store, compute, and analyze large amounts of data. As the blockchain in question grows, tracking the history of transactions at fast speeds may become very challenging. This specific use case focuses on two main drivers: storage growth and disk I/O performance.

Application KPIs

Your distributed database is the single most important stateful component in your infrastructure. It is therefore no surprise that many database vendors invest a lot of time and effort into improving and bundling observability capabilities within their products. However, monitoring a database alone can only do so much. There will always be an application (or an entire infrastructure) behind it which, if not observed properly, may cause important business impacts. Application KPIs are the key to exposing things like query issues, poor data models, and unexpected driver behavior.

Here are some important KPIs to look into regarding your application (client side):

- **Latency**: High P99 latency on your client side does not necessarily mean that there's a problem with your database latency. Client-side latencies will typically be slightly higher than your database latencies due to the natural network round-trip delays involved when communicating to and from your database. However, this metric alone does not help you identify the actual culprit. Look at whether your application is behaving erratically or whether it is simply bottlenecked (in which case, you can scale it out as necessary).

- **CPU consumption**: High CPU consumption could stem from several causes. Maybe your client is simply overwhelmed, unable to keep up with the pace of incoming requests. Maybe your request balancing is not appropriate. Maybe a "noisy neighbor" is stealing your CPU capacity, among other things. In general, if you suspect that the root cause of the high CPU consumption is due to an inefficiency in your code, you could collect tracepoints on your code or use advanced Heat Map profiling tools, such as perf.[1] Otherwise, simply scaling out your application deployments or moving the application to another host might be enough to resolve the problem.

- **Network IRQs**: Applications that need to achieve a high throughput with low latencies can be rather network intensive. As a result, a high network IRQ consumption may prevent your application from fully maximizing the intended rate of requests you initially projected. Use low-level CPU observability tools to check your softirq consumption, such as the top and htop commands available in most Linux platforms. Another mechanism employed to stop IRQs from undermining your performance involves CPU-pinning or simply scaling out your application to run on different host machines.

- **Readiness/liveness**: Any application is prone to bugs and infrastructure failures. Readiness and liveness probes will help you identify when a specific set of your distributed application may start to misbehave and—in many situations—will automatically redeploy or restart the faulty client. Readiness and liveness probes are standard for Kubernetes stateless applications. Whenever your application pods start to misbehave, your Kubernetes controller will typically take action to move it back into a healthy state. Applications

---

[1] See www.brendangregg.com/blog/2014-07-01/perf-heat-maps.html.

that frequently restart due to readiness or liveness problems may indicate problematic logic, a memory leak, or other issues. Check your application or Kubernetes logs for more details on the actual cause of such events.

- **GC pauses**: Many applications are developed in programming languages that experience garbage collection pauses while freeing up memory. Depending on its aggressiveness, it can cause CPU spikes (preventing your application from keeping up with its incoming rate) or introduce severe latency spikes. It indicates either a problematic memory management algorithm, or an inefficiency with your garbage collector overall. Consider spreading out your application to run with more independent clients and see if that improves the situation.

Infrastructure/Hardware KPIs

Keeping an eye on the database and application sounds reasonable, but what about the underlying hardware and infrastructure? Keeping it all healthy and humming is the top priority of infrastructure teams. After all, what good does tuning and monitoring a database do if the server that powers it goes offline due to a weeks-long malfunction that went unnoticed?

Here are the top infrastructure/hardware KPIs that are relevant from a database perspective:

- **Disk space utilization**: A database, being a stateful application, certainly has disk space utilization as a top priority KPI. It's extremely dangerous to have disks reaching full capacity because the database has no option other than to shed requests. A database might even shut itself down to avoid unintentional data loss. Keeping disk utilization well under control is crucial to a healthy, performant database.

- **Disk bandwidth utilization**: Apart from the disk space utilization, monitor how disks are being actively used and performing. In a world of multi-gigabyte RAM, disk bandwidth cannot fall behind; otherwise, you might risk increased latencies or even a complete failure due to disks being unable to attend to requests within acceptable timeframes.

- **CPU utilization**: This is the one and only metric that counts…or is it? CPU utilization can be looked at from different perspectives. On the one hand, the OS might say that a CPU is 100 percent busy and therefore it has certainly reached its limit and cannot possibly accept more work. Right? Wrong! A busy CPU does not always mean that the system has reached its limits. Databases such as ScyllaDB have internal mechanisms to prioritize user workloads over background internal processes such as compactions and repairs. In such a system, it is actually expected to see CPU utilization at 100 percent most of the time—and it does not mean that the system has reached its limits!

- **Memory utilization**: No one wants to see a database swapping to disk since it can become very detrimental to performance. Heavy memory pressure can trigger your database to crash (or get its process killed) if the underlying operating system runs out of memory. In general, database nodes should be the only memory-hungry resource running on a given server and the system must be configured to avoid swapping unless strictly necessary.

- **Network availability**: A distributed database heavily relies on networking in order to communicate with other nodes to replicate your data, liveness information, and—at the same time—serve your application queries. Network failures may introduce a split-brain situation, or make node(s) completely inaccessible momentarily, whereas hitting network bandwidth limits may result in additional latency to your workloads.

Creating Effective Custom Alerts

Most tools you use to monitor databases provide built-in alerting systems with predefined rules that should meet most users' needs. But what if you'd sleep better with more specialized monitoring rules and alerts in place?

First, start by understanding what you want to monitor, then see how that can be achieved using existing metrics (or a combination of them). After selecting the metric(s) that will drive the custom alert, think about the frequency of checks and set a threshold for the possible values. For instance, maybe you think that a workload crossing its expected peak for one minute is acceptable, three minutes should trigger warnings, and five minutes indicates something is definitely wrong. Set your monitoring system accordingly and bind the appropriate alerting channels for each type of alert.

Also, make good use of alerting channels! Be sure to tag and appropriately direct each level of alert to its own set of target channels. You don't want the alerting system automation to silently drop a message on a random Slack channel in the middle of the night if the production system is down.

Walking Through Sample Scenarios

To help you see how these principles translate into practice, here are two sample scenarios.

One Replica Is Lagging in Acknowledging Requests

Assume that you're looking at the dashboard in Figure 10-1 and notice that one replica is taking much longer than all the others to acknowledge requests. Since the application's incoming request rate is constant (you're not throttling requests), the other replicas will also start suffering after some time.

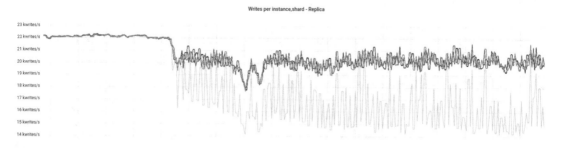

Figure 10-1. *One replica taking much longer than all the others to acknowledge requests*

To see what's going on here, let's look at the foreground and background write queues. But first: what's a foreground and background queue? Foreground queues are requests that the application directed to the specified node, but were not yet acknowledged back to the client. That is, the requests were received, but are waiting to be processed because the database is currently busy serving other requests. Background queues are application requests that were already acknowledged back to the application, but still require additional work in the database before they can be considered done. Delays replicating data across nodes are typically the reason for high background queues. High foreground and background queues both correlate with high latencies.

So what's the true problem here? Figure 10-2 indicates that the application is overloading the system. It's sending more requests than the database can handle. And since the running time of a single task in a distributed system is governed by the slowest node, the entire system will throttle down to the speed of that slow node.

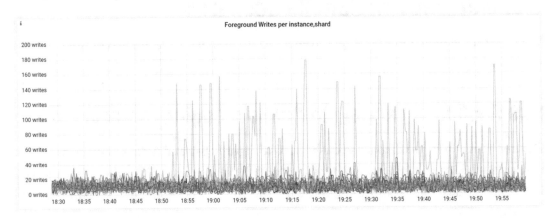

Figure 10-2. *Foreground writes per shard*

Figure 10-3 shows that the background queues in other nodes start climbing right after one node gets overwhelmed with requests it can't handle. This makes sense, because the busy node is clearly taking longer to acknowledge requests sent to it.

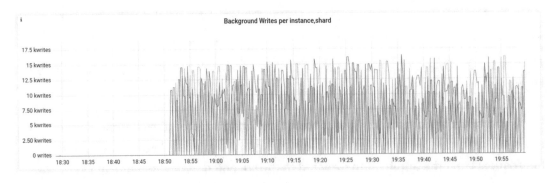

Figure 10-3. *Background writes per shard*

There are a couple of options for resolving this. First, consider modifying the application to throttle requests. If you can't do that, then scale out the cluster to give it more capacity.

Disappointing P99 Read Latencies

Assume that you're looking at the dashboard shown in Figure 10-4 and notice that the read latencies seem disappointing. The P99 read latency is 40ms most of the time, with a spike above 100ms under some circumstances. What's going on here?

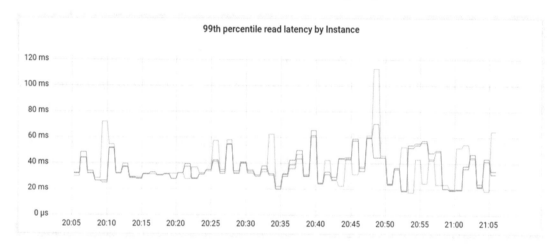

Figure 10-4. *Disappointing P99 read latencies*

To analyze this, let's look at the internal cache metrics. The Reads with Misses graph in Figure 10-5 shows that the reads aren't hitting the cache—they're all going to disk instead. Fetching information from the disk is an order of magnitude slower than doing so from memory. At this point, you know something weird is going on.

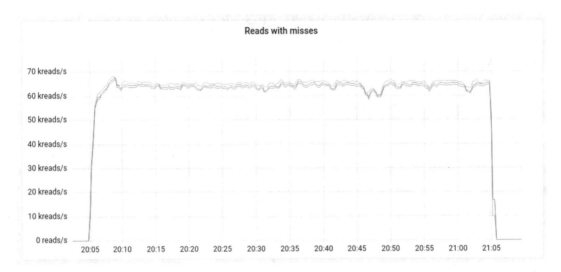

Figure 10-5. *Database reads with cache misses; reads are going to disk instead of cache*

Similarly, Figure 10-6 shows the cache hits. You can see that almost no requests are being served by the cache. This is a likely indication that the workload in question heavily relies on reading cold (uncached) data.

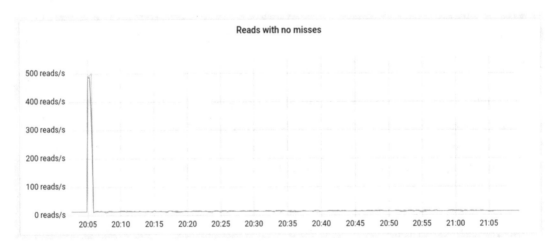

Figure 10-6. *Database reads with cache hits*

To investigate further, look at the Active SSTable Reads graph in Figure 10-7. Here, you can see that the amount of active read requests going to the disk is quite high.

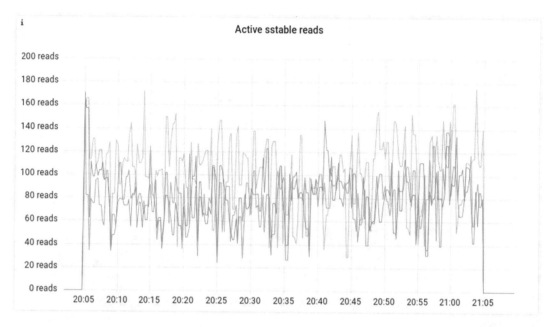

Figure 10-7. *Active SSTable Reads graph showing that the amount of active read requests going to the disk is quite high*

On the Queued Reads graph in Figure 10-8, you can see there's a bit of queuing. This queuing means that the underlying storage system can't keep up with the request rate. Requests need to wait longer before being served—and latency increases.

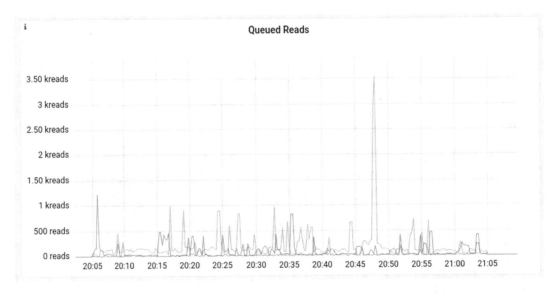

Figure 10-8. *Queued Reads graph demonstrates that several requests are getting queued*

How do you resolve this? Review your queries and access patterns to use the cache more efficiently. This is where query analysis is helpful. For example, with CQL, you could look at the distribution of inserts, reads, deletes, and updates, the number of connections per node or shard, and how many rows you're currently reading. If available, also check whether your queries are following the relevant best practices (for CQL, this could be using prepared statements, token-aware queries, paged queries, and so on).

Also, watch out for queries that require nodes across datacenters to participate before requests are considered successful. Cross-datacenter traffic is usually more expensive in terms of latencies and actual cost. Figure 10-9 shows an example of how to identify queries traversing to remote regions.

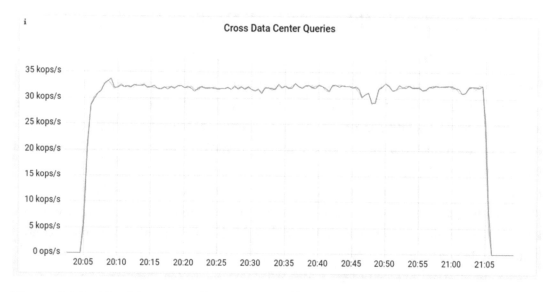

Figure 10-9. *Tracking cross-datacenter traffic, which is usually more expensive in terms of latencies and cost*

Monitoring Options

Once you have a good grasp of what you're looking for, how do you find it? There are a number of tools and technologies available; here's a quick rundown of the pros and cons of common options.

The Database Vendor's Monitoring Stack

Under most circumstances, your database's bundled monitoring solution should be sufficient for gaining insight into how the database is performing. It is typically the recommended solution for a number of reasons. Since it was engineered by your vendor, it likely contains many of the details you should care about the most. Moreover, if you turn to your vendor with a performance problem that you're unable to diagnose on your own, the vendor is likely to request visibility through their provided solution. For that reason, we recommend that you always deploy your vendor's monitoring stack—even if you plan to use another solution you prefer.

Build Your Own Dashboards and Alerting (Grafana, Grafana Loki)

What if the vendor-provided monitoring stack doesn't allow you customization options and the ability to create additional monitors that could yield additional insight into your use case, application, or database? In this case, it's great to have the flexibility of going open-source to build your own monitoring stack by stitching together every monitor and chart that you need.

Just keep in mind that a vendor's monitoring system is usually tuned to provide valuable metrics that are commonly used during troubleshooting. It's still important to keep that foundation operational alongside the additional monitoring options you and your team decide to use.

Third-Party Database Monitoring Tools

Some teams might already be using a database monitoring tool that's built and maintained by someone other than their database vendor. If it's a tool you're already familiar with, you get the benefit of working with a familiar solution that's probably already integrated into your existing monitoring framework. However, you might need to manually build and track all the relevant dashboards you want, which can be tedious and time-consuming. Other potential drawbacks of implementing a third-party monitoring tool can be the lack of vendor support and the risk of your dashboards becoming obsolete whenever your vendor implements a new metric or changes the meaning of a metric.

Full Stack Application Performance Monitoring (APM) Tool

A full-stack APM system collects remote metrics and aggregates them in a central solution that provides insight across different types of services and products. An organization might use an APM tool for a global view of all assets, services, and nodes across a portfolio. It is the preferred way for larger companies to manage infrastructure, and it certainly has its benefits. It's usually serverless and only a client is required to push information to the centralized service.

However, a centralized solution requires a subscription and constant internet access. You might also be charged per device and have less flexibility on how to customize metrics collection, create panels and alerts, and so on. APM platforms usually offer a wide range of plugins that can be tailor-made to monitor products. But not all of them are created the same, so your mileage may vary.

Teams often ask if their favorite observability solution can impact their performance. Yes, it can. We have learned from experience that some observability or monitoring solutions, especially those that require an agent to be installed on top of your database nodes, may introduce performance problems. In one extreme example, we saw an agent totally hanging the database process, introducing a real business outage. Whenever installing third-party solutions that could directly interact with your database process, ensure that you first consult with your vendor about its compatibility and support.

Summary

This chapter began by recommending that you make monitoring a regular habit so that you're well-prepared to spot emerging issues and effectively diagnose the problem when something goes wrong. It outlined a number of KPIs that have proven helpful for tracking business-critical enterprise deployments. For each KPI, it explained what to look for and offered some tips for how to react when the trends indicate a problem. The chapter offered some high-level guidelines for creating custom alerts. Finally, we walked through two sample monitoring scenarios and shared our take on the pros and cons of different monitoring platform options. The next (and final) chapter looks at the performance impacts of common admin operations and offers some tips on how you might mitigate them.

CHAPTER 11

Administration

A database's automated admin operations work to keep things tight and tidy behind the scenes, but a level of supervision is required. Databases don't know your business and could very naively decide to execute resource-intensive admin operations at what's actually a performance-critical time. This final chapter details how common admin operations tend to impact performance. It covers the nature and severity of representative impacts and offers some tips on how you might mitigate them.

Admin Operations and Performance

You might see promises of "zero impact" admin operations, but remember that the laws of physics mean that's not possible. Performing any operation consumes resources. And when you're operating at extreme speed and scale, these operations may introduce exacerbated impacts. Given use cases that need to operate at sub-millisecond or single-digit millisecond P99 latency, it doesn't take much for background tasks to have a noticeable impact. With a latency-sensitive use case, there can be absolutely no system contention during its execution. Even admin operations that will ultimately improve your database performance could inevitably hurt performance to some extent as they are executing. The better you understand the extent of their impact on your specific workload, the more effectively you can strategize to minimize disruption.

Low-level details about what admin operations are required will vary from database to database and also change over time; that's well beyond the scope of this book. This chapter focuses on how admin operations could end up undermining the other work you've done to optimize database performance—and how to avoid that scenario. It starts by presenting a quick rule of thumb to prioritize your focus. Then, examples of backups and compaction will showcase the potentially significant—and also highly variable—impact of admin operations on performance.

© Felipe Cardeneti Mendes, Piotr Sarna, Pavel Emelyanov, Cynthia Dunlop 2023
F. C. Mendes et al., *Database Performance at Scale*, https://doi.org/10.1007/978-1-4842-9711-7_11

Looking at Admin Operations Through the Lens of Performance

Every admin operation, from backups to data migrations to adding and reducing capacity, consumes resources that *might* otherwise be spent on your workload. The impact of an admin operation will vary across databases and workloads. What's more, an impact that results in lost revenue for one company might be completely acceptable for another.

What admin operations should you focus on from the performance perspective? As shown in Figure 11-1, work through three key considerations for every admin operation that's being performed.

1. What's the impact on your specific workload at your current or projected scale?

2. How much does that impact matter to your business?

3. To what extent can you control it?

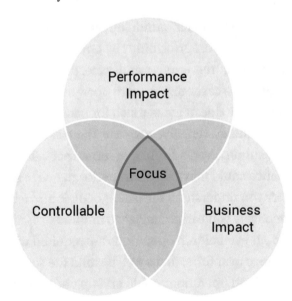

Figure 11-1. *A quick rule of thumb for where to focus your admin-related performance optimizations*

If there is no discernible performance impact for your scenario, then the second and third questions don't really matter. If there's a significant and business-critical impact but you can't control it, you're in the tough position of deciding whether to accept it or consider moving to an alternative database. If the stars align and you *can* control something that's both impactful and business-critical, that's a great place to focus.

For example, consider PostgreSQL's autovacuum function. As of this writing, autovacuum is triggered when a specified scale factor/threshold is exceeded. This is likely to coincide with heavy activity on the table—which is probably *not* when you want background admin tasks to kick in. Starving some tables while repeatedly vacuuming others is common, and users trying to compel autovacuum to hit starved tables can easily end up pushing the system beyond its limit. What's the likely impact on the business? Probably fairly high for any performance-sensitive use case. And to what extent can you control it? Quite well. For example, you can tune autovacuum settings at both the global and table level, as well as apply strategies like supplementing autovacuum with additional scheduled vacuum jobs. The bottom line here is that this is a great performance optimization opportunity.

On the other hand, if you are using a managed DBaaS such as DynamoDB, admin operations such as data cleanup might be largely beyond your scope of visibility and control. It certainly doesn't hurt to ask your vendor what they're willing to divulge about what, when, and how admin operations are performed. Even if you discover that an admin operation undermines performance in a way that matters for you, you might not be able to control it—but at least you can better prepare for it and diagnose the performance hit when it occurs.

Among admin operations that could negatively impact performance, some of the most common suspects are:

- **Node recovery**: This involves existing replicas streaming data in order to recover the missing replica. Existing replicas need to read through all the data required by the recovered replica and transfer its results via the network.

- **Ramping up/down capacity**: This often requires an entire cluster or region to rebalance data. Ramping up capacity means that data will be streamed from other replicas to the new one, while ramping down means that the node being removed will stream data out to existing replicas.

- **Data migration**: Migration often affects latency on the source cluster. Since a data migration typically involves no downtime, a balance between speed and service stability is needed in order to avoid impacting existing production workloads.

- **Database upgrades**: Although the outcome of an upgrade is likely to improve performance, remember that restarting a database instance results in a cold cache. This may affect read latencies if the use case in question is cache heavy.

- **Logging and tracing**: When you're trying to understand a specific pattern or impact, logging and tracing will be important. Databases provide several verbosity levels for many logging components, as well as the ability to enable tracepoints toward your query plans. However, enabling both logging and tracing should be done with caution because they can potentially be resource-intensive operations.

- **Data synchronization**: Eventually consistent databases don't guarantee that all the data you're looking for will be immediately available across all natural replicas. As a result, a background process is often needed to get data in sync. This typically involves each replica reading through its existing data, comparing it with its peers, and applying any relevant changes.

Two of the most common operations that impact performance across a variety of databases are backups and compaction. Let's take a deeper look at both.

Backups

Backups—a common maintenance procedure for any database—can be surprisingly resource intensive. For example, consider a backup strategy where data deduplication is required. As data in the database frequently gets written or overwritten, backups may consume several CPU cycles and disk I/O on reads in order to compare whether the data to be backed up has already been saved. Then, as it finds newer data that must be retained, it eventually uploads the data (which also involves issuing underlying I/O reads) to a safe location. As the process is repeated across multiple nodes, its parallelism often ends up hurting latencies, especially for use cases that heavily rely on disk I/O to fetch information.

Impacts

Factors that influence a backup's performance impact include:

- **Dataset size and replication factor**: The more data you're backing up, the more time it takes to run a backup. Depending on the number of files stored on disk, backing up may use a lot of read I/O to scan through all the required database blobs.

- **Scope**: Are you backing up all on-disk data files all the time (full backup)? A specific cluster? A system-wide snapshot? An incremental backup? A properly defined backup strategy and scope will help you mitigate the impact.

- **Frequency**: Frequent small backups will result in a more constant low-level pain; less frequent, but larger backups will cause a sharper pain, but that pain will be inflicted less frequently.

- **Bandwidth throttling**: The option to compress or spread out the backup pain helps teams who want to get backups completed as fast as possible during low peak periods (if any exist) or to run them as unobtrusively as possible during steady workloads.

- **Scheduling options**: The ability to control precisely when backups occur allows teams with spiky workloads to avoid backups during likely peak periods.

- **Data compression**: Greater compression will save on storage, but it comes at the cost of increased CPU usage as the backup runs.

- **Parallelism**: The more nodes you back up in parallel, the faster it completes—but at the risk of starving disk I/O capacity along with your ongoing workload.

- **Storage medium**: Reads from local SSDs are noticeably faster than regular disks. As a result, if your database relies on slow-access storage devices, it is much easier for backups to deplete your available read capacity.

Optimization

Before you start adjusting any options, consider these two critical questions:

- What's your business' tolerance for data loss?

- What type of backup makes the most sense given your workloads?

For example, if you're working on a food delivery app, a large backup that kicks off in the middle of the Friday lunch surge could result in lost business. The pain could be alleviated by running regular backups during predictable downtimes (e.g., very early in the morning), when there are resources to spare.

But other businesses don't have a predictable downtime. For another example, consider an application that provides location tracking services for ambulances—a use case where a catastrophic event could bring a dramatic surge at any time without warning. In that case, many small and frequent backups might be the best strategy. This way, backups are unlikely to significantly impact database performance, no matter when the unpredictable demand happens to rise.

Work with your team to understand the backup coverage that you need and what type of backup pain you're willing to accept, then adjust your options accordingly.

Note   Repairs are a totally different process, but they have a similar impact. Eventually consistent databases need to ensure that replicas (eventually) all have the appropriate updates. In Cassandra and Cassandra-like databases, this process is referred to as *repairs*. When repair runs, it could cause latency to spike. The key to minimizing its performance impact varies according to your workload. If there's a time when your database is predictably idle, run repair then—with high parallelism and intensity. If your use case can withstand minor latency spikes, you can try to limit the repair's intensity and parallelism. But, if you can't afford *any* latency spikes (e.g., a real-time bidding use case that must provide sub-millisecond P9999 latencies around the clock), your best bet is to limit the operation to run as slowly as possible.

Compaction

As mentioned in Chapter 2 and covered more in Appendix A, LSM-based databases use *compaction*—a process of rewriting tables to remove deleted entries and reorganize data to enable faster, more efficient reads and writes. Compaction operations are expensive in terms of CPU, memory, and disk I/O.[1]

The degree to which you can control compaction varies dramatically from database to database. For example, with Bigtable, it's all done automatically. However, databases such as Couchbase, HBase, Cassandra, and ScyllaDB let you choose from a variety of compaction strategies, many of which have additional options you can use to fine-tune how compaction is performed, as well as other settings that influence compaction performance (for example, rate-limiting it).

Impacts

The performance impact of compaction also varies dramatically from database to database. One fundamental factor that influences compaction speed is whether the database is performing the major compactions on each shard/CPU concurrently, or the compaction is bound to a single thread. As shown in Figure 11-2, benchmarks found that there can reflect a nearly 60X difference in the time required to run a major compaction of 1TB of data at RF=1 on i3.4xlarge machines.

---

[1] For an interesting perspective on compaction, see Avi Kivity's real-time visualization in "How a Database Looks from a Disk's Perspective" (`www.p99conf.io/session/how-a-database-looks-from-a-disks-perspective/`).

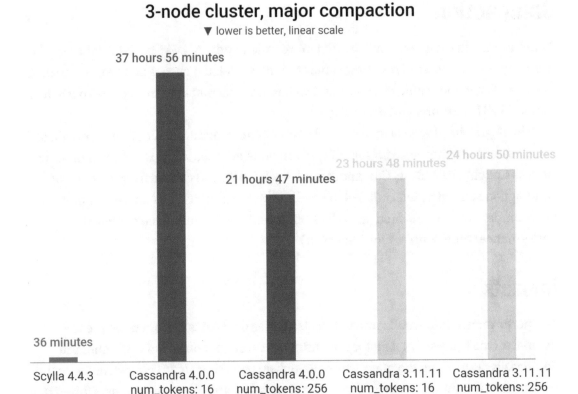

Figure 11-2. *The wide range of time required to perform compaction on similar databases—from 36 minutes to 37 hours and 56 minutes*

Additional factors that influence the impact of compaction include:

- **Compaction backlog**: Since compacting data is a process that is always running in the background, the amount of data to compact is expressed by its growing backlog. If compaction falls behind, it will eventually try to catch up in an attempt to keep the database from running out of resources and to minimize read amplification. A growing compaction backlog indicates that the cluster is not sized appropriately, the use case in question is using an inappropriate compaction strategy, or the process is being throttled too aggressively in the database settings.

- **Inefficient compaction strategy selection**: Write-mostly workloads are different from read-mostly workloads, which are different from update-heavy and delete-heavy workloads. Understanding the concepts behind every compaction strategy and how it impacts your workload is important to avoid read amplification, write amplification, or space amplification.

- **Compaction throughput**: In situations where your use case relies heavily on reading from cold data, having overly aggressive compaction throughput would end up stealing some important IOPS and bandwidth needed for your workload. Play with different rate-limiting values and keep an eye on your compaction backlog until you find your sweet spot.

An inefficient compaction strategy may affect workloads differently, depending on what level of inefficiency it is. For example, a write-heavy workload will typically want to prevent compactions from running too aggressively; otherwise, it may exhaust the existing disk bandwidth capacity and eventually throttle down the database write path. On the other hand, a read-heavy workload will likely want compaction to run *more* aggressively, given that compactions may actually improve read latencies by requiring the database to issue fewer underlying storage disk I/O operations. Time-series use cases will typically prefer data to be separated into buckets so that eventual eviction can be done efficiently. And so on, and so on.

Optimization

When selecting a compaction strategy, keep in mind that the ultimate goal should be low amplification. You want to avoid:

- Read amplification (read requests needing many files to look up relevant data)
- Excessive temporary disk space that requires the disk to be larger than a perfectly-compacted representation of the data (space amplification)
- Compacting the same data over and over again (write amplification)
- Overwritten/deleted/expired data remaining on disk, slowing down your read path

Since not everyone is using a database that performs compaction, this chapter doesn't go deep into the weeds of the pros and cons of specific strategies. Table 11-1 provides an overview of which compaction strategy *generally* works best for different workloads (your results may vary).

Table 11-1. *Comparing Compaction Strategies*

	Size-Tiered	Leveled	Incremental	Time Window	Comments
Write-only	✓	✗	✓	✗	When using size-tiered with write-only workloads, it will use approximately 2x peak space. With incremental, the size amplification is much less. When using leveled compaction with write-only workloads, you will experience high write amplification.
Overwrite	✓	✗	✓	✗	When using size-tired or incremental with overwrite workloads, size amplification occurs. When using leveled compaction with overwrite workloads, write amplification occurs.
Read-mostly, with few updates	✗	✓	✗	✗	When using size-tiered with read-mostly workloads with few updates, size amplification and read amplification occur.
Read-mostly, with many updates	✓	✗	✓	✗	When using leveled with read-mostly workloads with many updates, write amplification occurs in excess.
Time series	✗	✗	✗	✓	When using size-tiered or incremental with time series workloads, size amplification, read amplification, and write amplification all occur. When using leveled with time series workloads, size amplification and write amplification occur.

Two key takeaways should be that 1) one size never fits all, so it's nice to have a choice in admin matters, and 2) tradeoffs are inevitable—know what pain you can tolerate best so pick your poison.

To drive the point home, here's a real-world story. Once upon a time, a new ScyllaDB user reported high read latencies. The use case was a TTL'd time series to support live media streaming. Time series use cases heavily rely on fetching data in specific timeframes and expect that such lookups are fast enough to be served by the database. As a result, time series use cases often rely on a Time-Bucketed compaction strategy, which ensures that the data in question is compacted together under the same time window to avoid the database having to potentially scan through multiple files across distinct windows just to retrieve the data. However, if configured incorrectly, the strategy may backfire and introduce severe performance headaches.

In this particular situation, we discovered that their time buckets were too small for the amount of data they were frequently retrieving as part of a single query. For example, if you decide to time-bucket your data every ten minutes, but always want to retrieve ten hours' worth of data, that will require the database to scan through 60 (6 buckets/hour * 10 hours) of buckets! With the right amount of concurrency, every query scanning through these large chunks of data could starve the underlying disk I/O capacity. Therefore, the resolution was to update the compaction configuration to reflect a more realistic data grouping as required by the use case.

One final note on adjusting your compaction strategy for performance: Remember that when you adjust your compaction strategy, your database will need to rewrite all your table data. This will incur a significant performance penalty and should be carefully planned to occur at a time that works best for your business.

Summary

Admin operations like repair, compactions, and backups are an unavoidable part of running a healthy, well-performing database. There's no such thing as a "zero impact" admin operation; performing any operation consumes resources, and these operations can have exacerbated impacts if you're operating at extreme scale. This chapter used the examples of backups and compaction to showcase the potentially significant—and also highly variable—impact of admin operations on performance.

This is the final official chapter of this book—the end of these highly opinionated recommendations for improving database performance based on what we've seen working with a broad range of database users and databases. It's hardly the end of options for optimizing database performance though. Some potential next steps:

- Flag the considerations/recommendations that seem to offer potential for your specific workloads and use case, then discuss with your team.

- Take another look at your database's specific options (e.g., for monitoring, drivers, admin, etc.) and see if it's time to rethink any of your previous decisions.

- Tap your database vendor and/or community to learn about performance-related engineering decisions and optimizations that might offer untapped opportunities (or be responsible for some of your current constraints).

- Consider whether your data modeling might need a tune-up or overhaul (monitoring can help you assess this). If so, we recommend *NoSQL Distilled* by Pramod J. Sadalge and Martin Fowler—assuming you're using NoSQL. If not, browse the wealth of resources on RDBMS data modeling.

- Continue learning more about the fundamental database design decisions made when building any distributed database: replication and sharding strategies, consensus algorithms, data structures (B-tree vs LSM tree), and so on. You can get a performance-focused introduction to these topics, as well as recommendations for learning more from the masters, in Appendix A.

A Brief Look at Fundamental Database Design Decisions

This appendix briefly touches on a number of fundamental database design decisions that impact database performance. Why "briefly?" First, because we suspect that many readers are already familiar with them. But, more importantly, because other resources have covered them quite extensively, and extremely well. Honestly, there's not much to add. So, we'll offer a short take on some of the most pressing decisions that any distributed database must make, then share our top picks for learning more on each topic.

Sharding and Replication

Modern databases can rarely afford to be a single-node instance. The most obvious reason for being distributed is the need to avoid data loss in the case of a crash of any kind. Keeping data distributed across several nodes in a cluster inevitably means that the data needs to be split up (sharded) and copied between those nodes (replicated). The result is a distributed system in which users can quickly access data according to their queries.

F. C. Mendes et al., *Database Performance at Scale*, https://doi.org/10.1007/978-1-4842-9711-7

Sharding

The point of sharding is to ensure that data is well-balanced across your cluster for reading and writing. You're going to get the best performance by having all available nodes reading and writing data—not by overloading some nodes while others are idle or highly underutilized.

With most databases, sharding is built into its architecture. If that's the case, it's important to get the data modeling correct (e.g., high cardinality partition keys) to help the database's automated sharding approach achieve an efficient balance across nodes. However, if the database requires you to define the sharding strategy, you're going to have to bear the burden of more decisions that can impact balancing and, ultimately, performance. If you see that certain shards are receiving or handling more requests than others, it's time to reconsider your strategy.

Also, all automated sharding is not the same. The two most common approaches used in the class of databases we've been covering in this book are:

- **Range-based sharding**: Dividing data into contiguous ranges determined by the shard key values. This offers the best performance for range lookups, but is otherwise prone to hotspots. (Bigtable and HBase use this approach.)

- **Hash-based sharding**: Dividing data evenly and randomly across shards as determined by a sharding algorithm. This offers the best performance for most scenarios. (Cassandra, ScyllaDB, DynamoDB, and Redis use this approach.)

The level at which the sharding is performed also matters. The most common approach is to shard per node: Distribute data into separate database server nodes. Another option is to shard per each core in your server, across all the servers in the cluster. This divides a server's resources into shared-nothing units of CPU core, RAM, persistent storage, and network I/O. The advantage of this approach is that it maximizes utilization of all the available cores of multi-CPU hardware architectures. If paired with shard-aware drivers, each client writing or requesting data can send queries directly to the CPU core responsible for that shard of data. This minimizes hot shards and removes extra hops—improving performance. However, if you're not running on powerful servers, you're less likely to take full advantage of the potential performance gains here.

Replication

Being synchronous, replication affects the performance of the database at runtime. Poorly designed or inappropriately selected replication can cause performance bottlenecks.

There are many possible approaches to the design and implementation of database replication. Database replication can either happen on an explicit command or be an ongoing background process. Either approach should be well-accommodated by the infrastructure that the database is running on.

For data replication, the database engineer needs to select a replication strategy: The process for selecting the nodes to which each portion of data will be copied. Some replication strategies don't just copy data to a set of nodes; they also apply prioritization. One or more nodes are called *primary replicas* for this portion of data, while the other nodes are called *secondary replicas.*

Think about the number of nodes in the replica sets. To begin with, each piece of data can be replicated to a single node, as shown in Figure A-1.

Data Sharding

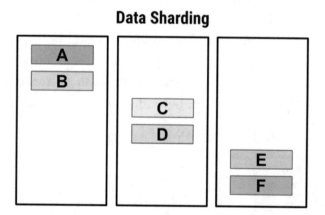

Figure A-1. *Replicating data to a single node*

Here, data is sharded across the different nodes for load balancing, but it doesn't provide high availability because none of the shards is replicated.

In more complex cases (shown in Figure A-2), there's one primary replica and one or more secondary replica nodes.

Data Replication (Primary/Replica)

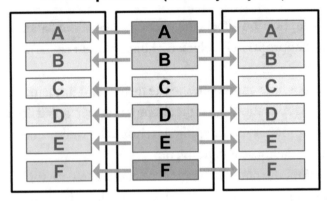

Figure A-2. *Replicating data to several nodes, with a single primary and multiple secondary replicas*

Here, one node writes data, which then can be propagated to other read-only nodes. This approach provides some level of high availability since a replica can take over the cluster if the primary goes offline. However, it does not properly balance your workload. All writes must be handled by the primary—which means that the primary becomes a bottleneck. As a result, this method of data replication may be impractical for write-intensive workloads. Spreading out the primary replicas for different portions of data across different nodes in the cluster is one potential way to address this.

In a more extreme form, there are no secondary replicas (like in Figure A-3).

Data Replication (Active-Active)

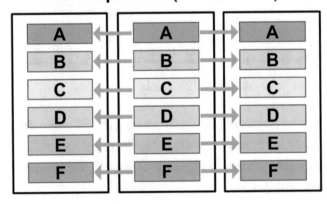

Figure A-3. *Full active-active-style replication*

Here, all data is replicated in an active-active leaderless topology. Every node can accept read and write operations, so all are peers in managing the workload. When this strategy is applied, any loss to part of the cluster will not result in lost data.

This active-active leaderless topology leads to what is called *eventual consistency*: The guarantee that when an update is made in a distributed database, that update will *eventually* be reflected in all nodes that store the data—resulting in the same response every time the data is queried. In an eventually consistent system, the replication strategy defines a number called the "replication factor" (RF), which is the number of nodes on which the portion of data can be found. Writing the data to (and reading the data from) such a system also conforms to different consistency requirements, which is referred to as *consistency level* (CL).

The most restrictive consistency level is often called "all." Writing in this mode means that the data must be written on disk on all replica nodes in the cluster. Reading returns the data after all replicas have responded, and the read operation fails if at least one replica does not respond.

Some less restrictive, but more performant, consistency levels may specify the exact number of nodes that must confirm the operation. Usually, this number is selected in the range of one through three, depending on how many replicas the cluster operator expects to crash.

"Quorum" consistency level provides much stronger consistency for the data. Writing or reading the data at this level means that the majority of nodes from the replica set should confirm the operation. In multi-datacenter setups, quorum consistency often has sub-levels depending on which datacenters the nodes from the replica set belong to.

Note that read and write consistency levels are independent of each other. Even if data was written with one consistency level (e.g. quorum), reading can use a different consistency level depending on the intention. For example, a CL of ONE can be used for data that doesn't need to be consistent, QUORUM CL can be used for a regular (or "unsure") case, and the most restrictive level of ALL can be used to effectively force full data repair.

Learning More

Designing Data-Intensive Applications, by Martin Kleppman (Chapters 5 and 6)

Database Internals: A Deep Dive Into How Distributed Data Systems Work, by Alex Petrov (Chapters 11, 12, and 13)

NoSQL Distilled: A Brief Guide to the Emerging World of Polyglot Persistence, by Pramod J. Sadalage and Martin Fowler (Chapters 4 and 5)

Consensus Algorithms

Even though quorum consistency level works extremely well and provides data persistence, data consistency, and low latency access, it still does not guarantee the linearizability, isolation, and atomicity required by transactions: queries that heavily rely on ACID properties. One of the simplest and most obvious examples of a transaction can be any CAS (compare-and-set) operation (e.g., increment a counter provided its value is below 42). When transactions come into play, simple eventually consistent models stop working and call for stronger means. One option can be a consensus algorithm on a distributed system.

Consensus algorithms provide strong consistency guarantees about the underlying data and allow a set of replicas to work together as a coherent unit. Provided the nodes conform to the protocol, algorithms tolerate failures of less than half of replicas even in the presence of message loss and reordering. They guarantee the following properties:

- **Validity**: If a decision is made, it must have been proposed by at least one of the replicas.

- **Agreement**: If a decision is made at some point, nodes shouldn't decide differently.

- **Stability**: If a decision is made at some point, it remains such forever.

- **Termination**: If a decision is made, it eventually gets spread to all correct replicas.

Consensus algorithms fall into two large classes—those that need a leader to make a decision and those that don't. The latter are called leaderless. Algorithms from the former class can suffer from periods of silence if the leader fails, so the new leader election process is started and the cluster cannot service requests while it's happening.

Raft

Raft is an example of a consensus algorithm with a leader. Raft was invented to be simple. It replicates a log of commands from a leader to follower nodes; that log of commands is called a "replicated state machine." And, of course, it has the leader-election algorithm on board too.

Each replica participating in Raft replication can be in one of three states: follower, candidate, or leader (see Figure A-4). Any attempt to make a decision over the cluster must be described in terms of a state change in the replicated state machine. Since the client may not know who the leader is, it sends its decision requests to whatever node it selects first. Thus, if the decision request is not sent to the leader, followers would re-route it to one, and then the leader would replicate the decision across its followers. In the case of leader failure, the followers turn into candidates. The election process ultimately converts one of those candidates into a leader after it obtains votes from a majority of replicas.

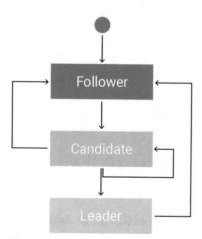

Figure A-4. *Each replica participating in Raft replication can be a follower, leader, or candidate; upon leader failure, followers can turn into candidates, and a candidate is elected leader*

Paxos

Paxos appeared earlier than Raft. It's an example of a leaderless algorithm, and it was one of the first algorithms that proved the quorum-based way of making distributed decisions.

According to the algorithm, each replica can play one or more of three roles—the proposer, the acceptor, and the learner (see Figure A-5). The decision is made through a two-step process in which the roles are involved, but from a practical perspective, nodes usually combine those roles. The first step, or, as it's usually called—the phase—is in proposing some value. In order to be proposed, the value must be accompanied with the sequence number. After the proposal is confirmed by the majority of acceptors, the proposer may proceed to the confirmation phase. After the confirmation phase is confirmed (again) by the majority of acceptors, the decision is made.

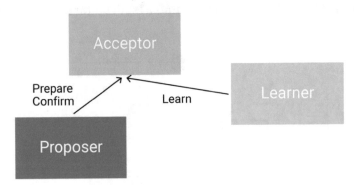

Figure A-5. *Each replica participating in Paxos can be the proposer, accepter, or learner*

Once the decision is made, none of the participants may fall back to the first phase. If the next decision should be made, a new run of the algorithm should be taken. Due to this, Paxos is never used alone. It's always part of a larger algorithm that implements all the necessary "paperwork" needed to instantiate, execute, and wrap up algorithm runs for individual decisions. One example of such a larger algorithm might be "distributed log replication."

Note   It's worth mentioning that Paxos was one of the first consensus algorithms that appeared and its goal was to prove how the distributed consensus is made. It's not used in its pure form; it's commonly extended with something else. One such extension was Raft, which (pretty successfully) tried to reduce Paxos' complexity at the cost of a potential imbalance in nodes' roles.

Comparing Leaderless and "Leader-Based" Classes

Although both leaderless and leader-based algorithm classes solve similar problems, the approach that involves a leader in the decision is considered to be simpler to implement and maintain. It also requires less time to converge upon a decision.

Even though "new leader selection" is just as complex as leaderless algorithms, it happens rarely and is considered to be a necessary evil. On the other hand, the single-leader approach often becomes a limitation to scaling consensus on large clusters—then, leader-less algorithms come to the rescue. Another option to overcome the leadership bottleneck is to apply some sharding on the decisions themselves. However, even when this is feasible, the added complexity might not be worth it.

Learning More

Designing Data-Intensive Applications, by Martin Kleppman (Chapter 9)

Database Internals: A Deep Dive Into How Distributed Data Systems Work, by Alex Petrov (Chapter 14)

NoSQL Distilled: A Brief Guide to the Emerging World of Polyglot Persistence, by Pramod J. Sadalage and Martin Fowler (Chapter 4)

B-Tree vs LSM Tree

As mentioned when talking about read-write ratios back in Chapter 2, LSM trees, illustrated in Figure A-6, are optimized for heavy write workloads and B-trees are optimized for heavy read workloads. LSM-based databases are append-only. They never update values; they just add new ones. This means that when the database is servicing reads, it might have to search quite a while to find the appropriate value. However, compaction can help to avoid this read amplification. Choosing an effective compaction strategy for your workload, as well as optimizing when compactions are performed, can significantly impact the read penalty sometimes associated with LSM trees. Also, mechanisms like built-in caching can enable an LSM-based database to achieve fast reads as well as writes.

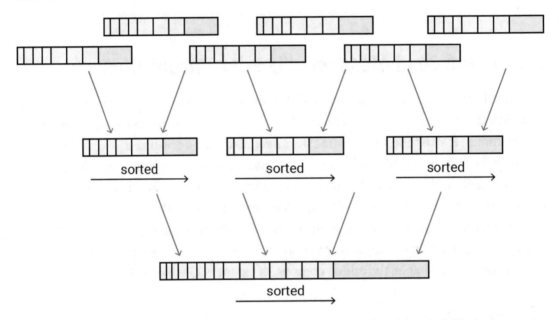

Figure A-6. *With LSM trees, compaction creates fewer (and larger) files*

On the other hand, B-tree based databases (as in Figure A-7) are optimized for reads. B-trees offer fast reads since their structure—and lack of duplication—makes them much more efficient to search than LSM trees. Traversing the tree is a straightforward path down a tree (as opposed to searching through potentially many files, as is the case with LSM trees).

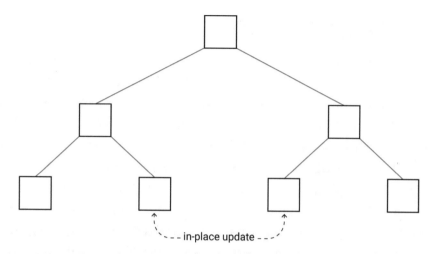

Figure A-7. *B-trees are updated in place (vs LSM trees, which are append only*

The B-tree write path is not optimized for speed, though. Each time there's a write, the database must traverse the tree to find the appropriate location. If a value already exists there, it's updated. If not, a new leaf is added. This is quite disk-intensive, even for small records. In some cases, moving to faster disks can improve performance.

The database creates a snapshot of the tree each time, which enables you to perform rollback (including point-in-time restore). B-trees are also well suited to transactions. When you are going to perform a transaction, you typically want to read the data and then start snapshotting everything. If the conflict resolution doesn't go as planned, you can simply roll it all back. B-trees make this feasible.

Learning More

Designing Data-Intensive Applications, by Martin Kleppman (Chapter 3)

Database Internals: A Deep Dive Into How Distributed Data Systems Work, by Alex Petrov (Chapters 2, 4, 6, and 7)

The B-Tree, LSM-Tree, and the Bw-Tree in Between, by PhotonDB

Record Storage Approach

One of the fundamental properties of the database is the way to store the data records in persistent storage. A wrong choice at this stage may force end-users into one of two alternatives—exabytes of data migrations vs extremely inefficient disk usage on user queries. To explore the impact, let's look at two fundamentally different approaches— row-oriented and column-oriented, each of which is suitable for different use cases.

Data stored on a hard disk is always split into blocks of a fixed size, which is the smallest I/O unit the application can use (see Figure A-8). Databases looking for the data will need to load all the information from the blocks that contain it. Respectively, the fewer blocks the target data is stored in, the faster the database operates. For spinning disks, this requirement always comes next to the data locality one—it's better for the blocks the database reads to get data that's adjacent rather than dispersed across the disk.

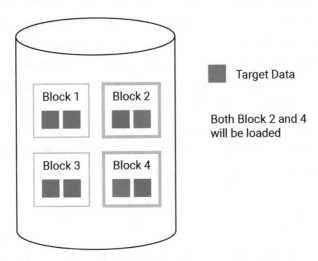

Figure A-8. *Data is split into blocks of a fixed size; adjacent data is preferred over data dispersed across the disk*

There are many algorithms to group data in a logical way, each trying to improve search efficiency (for example, partition and clustering).

When data is organized in the form of a table, the cells can be stored in at least two ways: row-oriented (e.g., wide column) and column-oriented. It's not feasible to shift from one approach to the other because of the amount of I/O required to convert data between versions. At the same time, this decision has a major impact on the database's performance. The choice between row-oriented or column-oriented usually aligns with different access patterns (i.e. whether it's optimized for analytical or transactional workloads).

Row-Oriented Databases

Let's look at a sample table for a better understanding of how different storage approaches work. Figure A-9 shows a table containing information about a person in each row (the person's name, age, address, etc.).

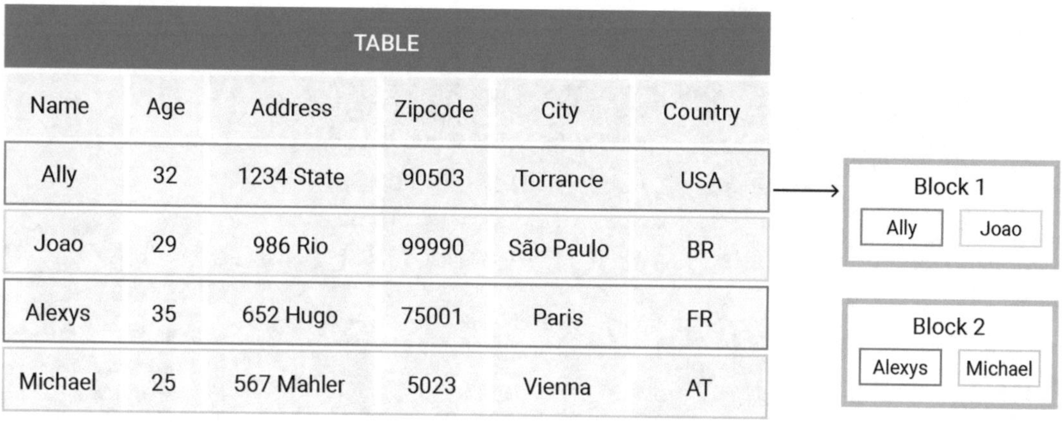

Figure A-9. *Row-based storage*

With row-oriented storage, data is put on disk row-by-row, and each chunk of data from a block consists of the cells from one table row. This design is perfect for so-called OLTP (Online Transaction Processing) applications, since such workloads can often modify the data by adding—or deleting—entities in the table. Writing a new row is optimal because it involves just appending an entire row to the existing blocks or putting it into new blocks. Another reason that row-oriented storage is good for OLTP workloads is because these workloads are typically loaded with requests retrieving every attribute from a single entity. Some examples of row-oriented databases are Cassandra, ScyllaDB, Postgres, and MySQL.

In other words, row-oriented storage is beneficial when all or most of the record needs to be accessed in the same query or transaction. In this case, it's better to have narrow tables. The more columns there are in a given table, the less likely it is that your query will need all of them. In the extreme case when the query requires only a few

245

columns (or even a single column), the row-store becomes too expensive. It needs to read the whole block, but the whole block will likely contain redundant data that would just be thrown away after being read.

Column-Oriented Databases

On the other hand, column-oriented databases store data on disk column-by-column. Let's take the same table, but consider each data chunk to be its column, not the row. As shown in Figure A-10, the "names" will be grouped together on the disk, the "ages" will be grouped together on the disk, the "addresses" will be grouped together on the disk, and so on and so forth.

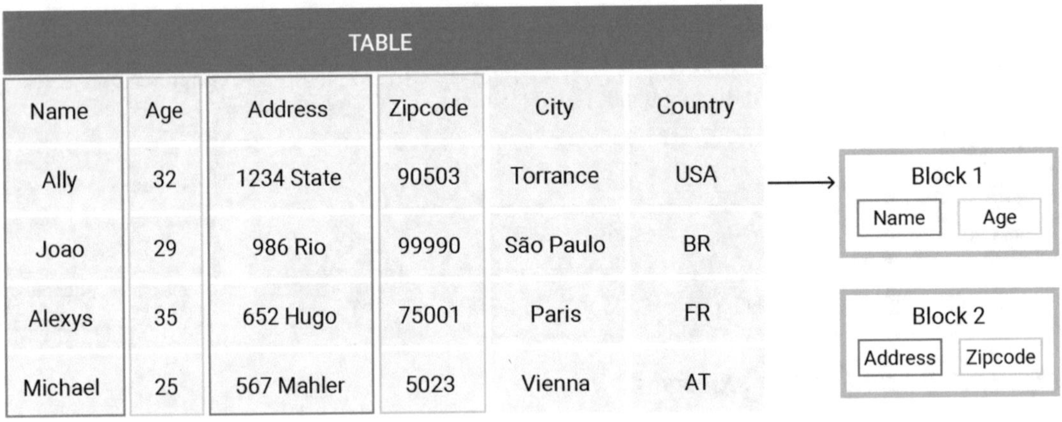

Figure A-10. *Column-based storage*

   This approach is a good choice for OLAP (Online Analytical Processing) workloads because those workloads generally aggregate specific data over a very large number of records. OLAP queries are mainly interested in a small subset of columns; for example, calculating the average age of the people from the table. Also, these workloads rarely modify data, and even when they do, the modification is appending new records. Some examples of column-oriented databases are Google BigQuery and Amazon Redshift.

   It's also worth mentioning that the compression rate is often much higher in column-store rather than in row-store. That's because in column-store, all cells from the column have the same data type, and that makes it quite compression-friendly.

Table A-1 breaks down the impact of these different approaches to storing records on the disk.

Table A-1. *Row-Oriented and Column-Oriented Approaches at a Glance*

	Pros	Cons
Row-oriented databases	• Good for OLTP applications • Inserting, updating, and deleting data is easy	• The compression rate is often not very high, so the data takes up more space • Queries might result in reading unnecessary data
Column-oriented databases	• Perfect for OLAP applications • The compression rate can be made very high even with simple methods like RLE (Run Length Encoding) because the compression algorithms usually work better on values having the same data type • The query may skip scanning unnecessary columns, which is extremely useful for aggregation queries	• Reading and writing a full record is significantly slower • Modifying data is only efficient when appending

These are just two representative examples. Data can also be stored using document, graph, and other models. See the following resources for a comprehensive discussion of how the various models store data, and the best and worst use cases for each.

Learning More

Designing Data-Intensive Applications, by Martin Kleppman (Chapter 3)

Database Internals: A Deep Dive Into How Distributed Data Systems Work, by Alex Petrov (Chapter 1)

NoSQL Distilled: A Brief Guide to the Emerging World of Polyglot Persistence, by Pramod J. Sadalage and Martin Fowler (Chapters 8-11)

Index

A

Active-active leaderless topology, 237
Administration
  backups
    definition, 224
    impacts, 225
    optimization, 226
  compaction
    impacts, 227–229
    optimization, 229, 231
    strategies, 230
  operation/performance, 221–224, 232
AdTech use case, 40, 207
Advanced Vector Extensions (AVX), 69
Algorithmic optimization
  B-trees, 66, 67
  cache implementations, 65
  database, 74
  linear search, steroids, 68, 69
  optimizing collections, 66
  scanning tree, 69, 70
  separation key, 72, 73
  tree size, 71
Amazon DynamoDB, 16, 24, 36, 77, 86,
    158, 223
Apache Cassandra-compatible database, 20,
    21, 25, 36, 85, 111, 114, 115, 129, 145
Asynchronous Direct I/O (AIO/DIO), 53, 54
Atomic, consistent, isolated, and durable
    (ACID), 1, 34–36, 238

B

B+-tree, 69, 70, 72
B-tree *vs.* LSM Tree, 241–243
Batch (analytical) workload, 79–81
Benchmarking
  admin operations, 196
  cache, 187
  client side mistakes, 188
  database's superpowers, 183
  data models, 185
  dataset size, 186
  domain-specific knowledge, 175
  extreme scale, 197, 198
  goals, 194–196
  latency/throughput, 176–178, 180
  networking issues, 189
  observability, 184
  phased approach, 180, 181
  production, 183
  repeatability, 189
  reporting, 189–193
  results, 199
  steady state, 187, 188
  testing disaster
    recovery, 197
  tools, 184, 185
  workloads, 186
Binary tree, 66–68, 71, 72
Blockchain, 207
Branch mispredictions, 68

© Felipe Cardeneti Mendes, Piotr Sarna, Pavel Emelyanov, Cynthia Dunlop 2023
F. C. Mendes et al., *Database Performance at Scale*, https://doi.org/10.1007/978-1-4842-9711-7

W, X, Y, Z

Printed in the United States
by Baker & Taylor Publisher Services